THE NEW TESTAMENT IN THE CHRISTIAN CHURCH

THE NEW TESTAMENT

IN THE

CHRISTIAN CHURCH

𝔈𝔦𝔤𝔥𝔱 𝔏𝔢𝔠𝔱𝔲𝔯𝔢𝔰

BY

EDWARD CALDWELL MOORE

PROFESSOR OF THEOLOGY IN HARVARD UNIVERSITY

WIPF & STOCK · Eugene, Oregon

Wipf and Stock Publishers
199 W 8th Ave, Suite 3
Eugene, OR 97401

The New Testament in the Christian Church
Eight Lectures
By Moore, Edward Caldwell
Softcover ISBN-13: 978-1-6667-6447-5
Hardcover ISBN-13: 978-1-6667-6448-2
eBook ISBN-13: 978-1-6667-6449-9
Publication date 11/10/2022
Previously published by The Macmillan Company, 1904

This edition is a scanned facsimile of
the original edition published in 1904.

TO MY WIFE

*WITHOUT WHOSE ENCOURAGEMENT THE STUDIES
WHICH HAVE ISSUED IN THIS BOOK WOULD
NEVER HAVE BEEN KEPT UP*

PREFACE

THESE Lectures were delivered in Boston in March and April, 1903, before the Lowell Institute. The material has been somewhat increased, but the Lectures are published substantially as they were delivered. Even the form of personal address has not been changed.

It is not claimed that the Lectures make contribution of great magnitude to this discussion. But the problem has been thought through. Material has been taken with freedom from such works as those of Zahn upon the history of the New Testament Canon, of Harnack and Krüger upon the history of the early Christian literature, of Holtzmann and Jülicher upon Introduction to the New Testament, and of Caspari and Kattenbusch upon the Apostles' Creed. The debt to Jülicher is especially great. In the Sixth and Seventh Lectures the direct endeavor has been to present, for purposes of our comparison, what is substantially Harnack's interpretation of the beginnings of Christian doctrine and Sohm's theory of the origin of church government.

There is no book in English which presents the results of the labors of scholars during the last fifteen years in the study of the growth of the New Testament Canon and in that of the attribution to the early Christian writings of a scriptural authority. Nor is there a book in any language in which these three things, the Canon of the New Testament, the Organization of the Church for Government, and the Rule of Faith, are compared in their development, and treated with the purpose of making each, in its evolution, throw light upon the others, and all together illustrate the nature of that authority which was ascribed to them all. It was the freshness of the topic, when taken in this way, which led the author to choose this subject for the Lowell Lectures. It is the lack of literature in English in which, in any wider way, the materials of the discussion are brought together which has led him to feel that the publication of the Lectures might be of use.

Judgments may differ as to the best possible selection from the mass of material at hand. The difficulty of the task is to keep the thing in bold outline, and yet not to convey a false notion through suppression of details. No undue zeal is felt on behalf of opinions which are here candidly expressed or everywhere plainly implied concerning some disputed matters. It is hoped only to furnish the reader with material for the formation, criticism, or confirmation of his own opinions.

The hold of the Scripture over a man's mind is a very different thing from the theory which a man holds concerning the Scripture. Nevertheless, the Scripture cannot long maintain its hold over the minds, at least of cultivated people, if they hold a theory of Scripture which is at variance with the other elements of their cultivation. The power of the Scripture is, fortunately, not the same thing with the explanation which men from age to age have given of that power. But what we wish to know is this: What are the facts concerning the Scripture of which we, in common with so many other men of all ages, have felt the power? It is only upon the basis of these facts that a theory of Scripture can be framed.

Thanks are due to the Trustee of the Lowell Institute for his kind invitation and for consideration shown in the postponement of the delivery of the course for a year, and to Professor George F. Moore for valuable aid in the revision of the sheets.

CAMBRIDGE, MASSACHUSETTS,
September 8, 1903.

CONTENTS

LECTURE I
THE AUTHORITIES OF THE EARLY CHRISTIANS . . 1

LECTURE II
THE WITNESS OF THE EARLIEST CHRISTIAN LITERATURE TO THE NEW TESTAMENT 39

LECTURE III
THE NEW TESTAMENT AT THE END OF THE SECOND CENTURY 79

LECTURE IV
THE CLOSING OF THE CANON IN THE WEST . . 121

LECTURE V
THE CLOSING OF THE CANON IN THE EAST. THE RENAISSANCE AND THE REFORMATION . . 165

LECTURE VI
THE CANONIZATION AND THE ORIGIN OF CHURCH GOVERNMENT 211

LECTURE VII

The Canonization and the Beginnings of the History of Doctrine 259

LECTURE VIII

The Idea of Authority in the Christian Church 309

Index 361

LECTURE I

THE AUTHORITIES OF THE EARLY CHRISTIANS

LECTURE I

THE AUTHORITIES OF THE EARLY CHRISTIANS

CHRISTIANS hold in reverence a small collection of writings which together bear the somewhat noteworthy title, The New Testament. The writings are twenty-seven in number. They would seem to have had at least ten different authors. They are of varied sort, and some of them bear plain traces of the occasions to which they severally owe their origin.

There are letters. Thirteen of these purport to be letters of one man, a missionary, to churches in which he was interested or to individuals whom he knew. There is a book of poetical and prophetical material, of a style familiar in the Judaism of the period. There are four biographical sketches. Three of these are closely related the one to the other, and present in simple fashion teachings of Jesus of Nazareth and facts concerning his life. One of them is full also of profound reflection upon that life and teaching. There is a brief history of the progress of the new faith from the capital of the Jewish religion to the centre of the Gentile world.

No one of these writings is from the hand of the Founder of the Christian religion. Nor does the substance of any one of them claim to have been literally taken down by a hearer, as the revelations of Mohammed are said to have been taken down from his lips and afterward put together to form the Koran. They were none of them, not even the Fourth Gospel, written directly to elucidate the system of the Master, in the manner in which Plato is deemed to have written certain dialogues to elucidate the system of his master, Socrates.

The production of by far the larger part, at all events, of the New Testament writings covers a period of considerably less than two generations. In this respect the collection presents a marked contrast to the Old Testament. Here the interval between the composition of the first books and of the last is probably seven centuries. If we should reckon from the supposed date of the earliest document embedded in the Hexateuch to the Book of Daniel or the last Psalm, we should have, of course, an interval much greater. The more easy was it for men, in later time, because of this relative shortness of the historic perspective of the New Testament collection, to lose the historical sense about these New Testament writings, and to come to view all that which they portrayed as a flat picture, and not rather as a deep vista. Something of this sort had already taken place in the minds of many in the synagogue regarding the Hebrew Scriptures, despite the far greater length of the period which that revelation had involved.

It must never be forgotten that the Christian church, even the Gentile part of it, inherited the Jewish Scriptures of the Old Testament, so to say, ready made. It then proceeded, by a most interesting and wonderful process, covering an interval of more than two hundred years, to make certain of its own earliest documents into a New Testament, and to place that beside the Hebrew sacred book. It is the process of the making of these new Scriptures, or rather, more accurately, it is the process of the investing of certain perfectly natural and incidental and occasional writings of the earliest Christianity with the character of Scripture, which it is the main purpose of these lectures to set forth.

The Old Testament writings were also the literature which had been incidental to the progress of a great religious movement, viewed by the men of later ages in the light of that divine inspiration of a book for the guidance of the life of the race, which is implied in the use of the word Scripture. But beyond pointing out this parallel, we have nothing to do with those writings. As regards the New Testament books we may say, that to give an account of the making of each individual work, to discuss in detail its authorship, its time, place, circumstance, that also would be a task different from that which we propose. Some knowledge of these facts is assumed in all that we have to say. It is the making of these twenty-seven little writings of the earliest Christianity to be Scripture, it is the process of their being gathered together into a collection and of their coming to be viewed as inspired and sacred writings, which is our main theme.

The peculiar rabbinical way of conceiving the inspiration of the Old Testament, the earliest Christians brought along with them from the synagogue. They impressed that mode of thought concerning the Old Testament even upon Gentile Christians who had had little or nothing to do with the synagogue. The mode of thought itself was not altogether foreign to the Gentile mind. The Gentiles also were familiar, in a general way, with the notion of books of oracles, words of God for the guidance of man. They also were familiar with the thought of an inspiration which took the place, less or more, of a man's own intellectual initiative, which suspended the working of a man's faculties and left him but the instrument of utterance of the god.

But this way of regarding the Old Testament, when it came, at the end of the second century, to be applied to the books which now constitute the New Testament, gave to these books also a sacredness different from that sacredness which for Christians they had always had through dealing with the person and teachings of Jesus. It gave them an authority which was, to say the least, of a different sort from that authority which they had always possessed through treating of the origins of Christianity. And this sacredness as Scripture, this authority as Canon, once it was achieved, would perhaps effectually have prevented any man from the middle, say, of the sixth to the middle of the fourteenth centuries, from ever raising a question as to how these books came to be a Canon and to have a scriptural authority. And perhaps we should add that during that period the state of historical knowledge would have prevented the answering of the question, even if it had been raised.

Under the influence of the revival of learning and in the fresh impulse of the Reformation, men like Luther and Calvin saw the thing more nearly in its true light. But the men of the second, and still more of the third, generations of Protestantism, in their effort to ground an external authority of the Bible which should offset the infallible authority of the church, underwent a great reaction. In their emphasis upon the divine side of the Scripture they lost sight almost wholly of the facts pertaining to the human origin and history of the Book. And the notion, not always clearly thought through, was yet widely prevalent until after the beginning of the nineteenth century, that the church had always had, since the Apostles' day, a New Testament Canon placed, perhaps by the Apostles themselves, side by side with the Old Testament, and possessed of an authority equal to that of the Old Testament and, implicitly, even greater than that of the Old Testament.

To many thoughtful readers, even now, it may never have occurred that the literature which we know collectively as the New Testament cannot have borne to the men of the first, or even of the greater part of the second, centuries the semblance which it bears to us. To them it was really a literature, a more or less fugitive literature, which was produced merely as one of the incidents of a religious movement. This fact lies right on the face of the works themselves. So truly are the letters of Paul but the substitute for the personal presence of the Apostle himself that one gathers the impression that, had the Apostle been able to be everywhere present, we should have had no letters. Had the concrete situation in a given community, at the moment, been other than it was, the letter would be different from what it is. So palpably are the written Gospels the deposit from an oral tradition, and but the substitute for the personal testimony of apostolic men to that which they had seen with their eyes and their hands had handled of the Word of Life, that we are prepared to find that written Gospels then first begin to appear when the ranks of these men are being thinned.

The Christian movement is great and infinitely significant as we look back upon it. It had even in its own time a certain sublime self-consciousness and moral forecast. But its adherents assuredly did not live and make literature in that kind of prevision of the long course of history, which has sometimes been supposed. If there was one opinion which was widely current among them, it was that the course of history was not going to be long. The sporadic literature of this movement was at first nowhere collected, nor does there seem to have been, at first, any disposition thus to collect it. We have to think of the letters as remaining, for a time at least, the private property of the churches to which they were addressed. The earliest Gospels seem to have taken shape, and in some cases even to have drawn their names, from the tradition as it was current in different local communities. The literature which we know as the canonical was only slowly sifted out from other literature not wholly unlike itself. The sifting was, as we shall see, a purely historical and somewhat uncertain process. The principle of the sifting was not always clearly apprehended, nor even always correctly applied. The books, meantime, had, indeed, the authority of the Lord whose word and spirit they enshrined, and of the Apostles whose testimony they embodied. But they had not yet the authority of Scripture as such. That is to say, the books, as books, were not yet regarded as on the same level with the Old Testament. They had inspiration; but their central inspiration was the Christ himself. In them spoke the Holy Spirit; but in the sense that in their authors dwelt a holy spirit which prompted all the other things which the men did. It was the living Christ who stood beside and above the Old Testament Scriptures as the early Christian man's authority. It was one hundred and fifty years after Jesus' death before writings concerning him were clearly apprehended as new Scriptures, and fully took that place.

Here comes out clearly our definition of Scripture. By Scripture we mean such writings as have obtained in religious communities the repute of a divine authorship, direct or indirect, absolute, or concurrent in some way with the human authorship, and have enjoyed unique esteem and exercised authority in consequence of this repute. We have used the word Canon many times. We may attempt to define that term also. The word Canon means, primarily a reed, a measuring rule, then a standard. As the root first occurs in Christian writers, it is always in verbal and participial forms. It seems to imply nothing more than that the works referred to as "canonized" constituted a class, the class, namely, of works widely in sacred use among the Christians, acknowledged by the Christians. Precisely in this way, the Alexandrine critics of classic literature had used the phrase to describe works acknowledged as representing the standard of taste. Later, the word Canon came to signify a ruling by ecclestiastical authority. Specifically, it meant the decision that such and such books, and those only, should form the accredited body of New Testament literature. And finally, the word came to be used of the body of literature which was thus exclusively accredited.

It has been common to assume that the Bible made the church. If what we have been saying is true, it is clear, on the contrary, that the church made the Bible. The religious community was before its documents. It received the impulse which made it a community from persons. Only later did it seek to embalm something of that personal influence in documents, and then, still later, came to shape its life by those documents, which it now apprehended as its law. The church made the Bible. And just how the Christian church made its part of the Bible, how it came to take certain literature identified with its earlier stages and its most significant personages and to invest that literature with the character of Bible — this, as we said, is the precise question the understanding of which it is earnestly hoped that these lectures may further.

The moment we have put it in this way it becomes evident that we are to deal with a fact, or rather with a long and complex series of facts, and with a subtle historical process, most interesting in itself, and concerning which we must own that few have had greater influence upon the whole life of the world.

Students of comparative religion are familiar with the fact that religions other than Judaism and Christianity have shown a tendency, at some time in their history, to canonize their earlier literature. These early writings may have come into existence in the simplest and most natural manner imaginable. They are the deposit of the specific ideas of the faith and the vehicle of the influence — or at least of the perpetuation of the influence — of commanding personalities associated with the origin of the faith. But by and by, either by slow process or, perhaps, through sudden emergency, these writings are found to have assumed a representative character and a regulative force quite different from that simple esteem and natural influence which had always been accorded them. Mohammedanism, indeed, illustrates neither the natural evolution of such a literature nor the organic process of its canonization. Mohammedanism sprang up among a people whose leaders, at least, had the example of both the Old and New Testaments before their eyes. Mohammedanism was what has been called a book-religion from the beginning. That is to say, it was provided by its founder, within his own lifetime, with a revelation which was intended to be its specific sacred document. The Koran was to be to its adherents what Old and New Testaments were to Jews and Christians. For converts it was completely to supplant these or any other writings of the sort. In contrast it is to be observed that for the Christians the New Testament never took the place of the Old. At most, it took a place beside the Old Testament, or, if you choose, beyond it, as the further stage, the completion of that revelation which the other had contained.

But as we were saying, the usual order of events is different from that which we have thus observed in the case of Mohammedanism. The normal case is this. Writings which, outwardly, have had the most natural origin as incidental to the progress of a religious movement gather to themselves a reverence, not necessarily greater than that which men had for them from the first, but certainly different from that earlier reverence. Confucianism, Zoroastrianism, Buddhism, each in its own way, illustrates this law. Those documents which, however naturally they may seem to have come into being, are deemed by the men of the later time to be the original and characteristic records of the faith, are collected into a body of literature, which is then held sacred and apart from all other literature. This new sacredness comes to attach quite as much to the collection, as such, as to the individual documents which comprise the collection. In fact, the new sacredness may come to be reflected back upon a given document simply because it is comprised in the collection, men never asking how it came thus to be comprised in the collection. This new sacredness tends to obscure differences among the documents which were once clearly felt. In truth, all the facts pertaining to the human origin of the books tend, for the believer, to retreat into the background behind the overwhelming sense of the divine guidance of the believer's cause, which guidance these books record, and of which they enshrine something of the creative force.

It is not that the religious community has suddenly invented a treasure which it will henceforth find valuable to possess. But it has suddenly become conscious of the treasure which in this literature it has always possessed. Future ages come to regard these documents as alone setting forth the pure idea and feeling, as incarnating the primary impulse of the faith. These alone record with original authority the facts to which the adherents of the faith refer, and preserve the tenets from which they may not depart. Nay more—and whether the human authors were aware of it or not—these writings of theirs are now seen to have come into existence under a divine purpose and inspiration, in order that the need of future ages might be thus fulfilled.

The literature of the Christian origins, as we said, is not alone in having traversed this course. But in the case of the most of the sacred literatures, in some measure even in the case of the Jewish literature, the process is obscure. The documents themselves often reach far back toward the dawn of history. And even the later process of their canonization cannot always be traced. It may cover long intervals of time, and have left no record. In the case of the Christian literature, on the contrary, the thing happens at the very heart of civilization. When it begins to take place at all, it takes place with astonishing rapidity and leaves abundant evidence. It transpires, so to say, in the full light of day. This is not the least interesting aspect of the study which we have begun, that is, its aspect, as furnishing a basis for inference concerning the history of other religions.

In the large sense of a growing feeling for the treasure which, in a certain portion of its early literature, the Christian church possessed, the church may be said to have begun the process of canonization very early. It is not easy to say how early a vital process does begin. The Christian community was moving in an unconscious way toward a goal long before it deliberately set itself that goal. That goal was the sharp separation of a certain portion of the early Christian literature, as inspired and sacred, from all other literature, as uninspired, if not profane. The Christians felt that separation long before they declared it or made a duty of furthering it. The church had, in fact, a Canon long before it had any decrees concerning the Canon. The church had a Canon before it had the idea of a Canon. But, if we may be allowed the paradox, the earliest Christian Canon was nothing written. It was the tradition of the words of Christ. And indeed, if we should go still further back, we should have to say that it was Christ himself who took the authoritative place. Documents, later, took that place only because they alone seemed to enshrine the Christ.

Primarily, the literary impulse was foreign to Christianity. It received no such impulse from Jesus, who wrote but once that we have record of, and then in sand. It was not likely to receive the literary impulse from eleven peasants, fishermen, and publicans. It did not work much at the first among literary people. Even Paul, keen as was his intellectual interest, and transcendent as is the worth of such interpretation of Christianity as chances to be lodged in his letters, yet wrote genuine letters and not treatises, and was absorbed in the practical exigencies of his missionary work. We are so used to reading, writing, printing, that it is difficult for us to make real to ourselves a state of things in which the oral was the usual way of gaining influence for personality or currency for ideas. No less than three of the schools of Hellenic philosophy got their very names from places where, under conditions of physical freedom, oral instruction was conducted. The like would have been still more true in Palestine, or, again, of the stratum of Gentile society which Paul's mission mainly reached. Then also, the expectation of the end of the world in the lifetime of men then living, an expectation which Paul undoubtedly shared, was not just the thing to put men upon writing memorials of the past or regulations for a future which was not to be.

Now it is precisely in accordance with these facts that we find that the earliest Christian writings were purely occasional in their character.

The more formal ones began then only to be written when some of the causes above alleged had begun to wane. None of the writings, judged impartially, sustains the supposition of a later time that they were written with the conscious intent of an apostolic regulation of the Christian institution for all time. In truth, most of them were written when as yet there was nothing in existence under the Christian name, which went beyond the simplest and most rudimentary form of institution.

Nothing is more obvious than that Jesus quotes the Old Testament in the spirit of the Judaism of the time. He cites it most freely and devoutly. It is to him revelation from God and of divine authority for the life of man. But Jesus does not raise certain questions, literary and historical, concerning the Old Testament, which we inevitably raise. He does this no more than, on the other hand, he raises certain questions touching matters of physical science which are inevitably present to our minds. His language, in the one case, is simply the traditional, as in the other case it is merely the phenomenal, language. His criticisms of the Old Testament and his enormous advances upon it are exclusively within the realm of his own sublime intuition of moral and spiritual truth. His most impressive self-assertion, as over against the Scripture of the Old Testament, has not for its purpose to discredit that Scripture. Sometimes he seeks to free it from misinterpretation. Again, he aims to indicate the deeper, the more spiritual, the universal sense, lying behind a mandate which, he says, was but partial, and given for conditions which at the time prevailed. No one could speak of a book with greater reverence than does Jesus of the Old Testament. No one could be more anxious than is he, and that not in small and timid, but in great and vital way, that the movement which he inaugurated should be regarded as the fulfilment of the one which the Scriptures of his race record.

Paul, despite his Asiatic birth, his Roman citizenship and, possibly, some Hellenic elements in his earlier education, never spoke more truly than when he said of himself that he was a Hebrew of the Hebrews. He moves, in his interpretation of the Old Testament, almost exclusively within the atmosphere and employs the methods of his rabbinical training. Steeped in the Old Testament as he himself is, he assumes relative familiarity with that Testament on the part even of the Gentile communities to which he writes. For the most part, the earliest churches grew up upon the soil of the synagogue. If that was true so often even in the case of Paul's mission, we may assume that it was still more true in the case of the labors of the rest. Even the Gentile converts thought Christianity somehow the fulfilment of Judaism. All these things tended to hand on the Old Testament intact into the Christian church, and to cause to be accorded to it there a position similar to that which it held in the Jewish synagogue.

Now, if you will think of it, this is a very singular fact and an immensely important one. Of the earliest Christian churches, even of the overwhelmingly Gentile ones, after the bitter struggle with Paul's Judaizing opponents, and after the destruction of Jerusalem, to Greeks and Romans, to Asiatics and Egyptians, to Spanish Christians — if there were any — the literary basis and the sole written authority was the Old Testament. There was nothing written beside it.

This throws some light upon the controversy which has been waged, as to whether Christianity was, or was not, from the beginning a book-religion. Certainly the Christian religion had, from the beginning, a book which was to it sacred Scripture, inspired oracle, revelation of God. But, strangely enough, that book was the Old Testament. It was the book of another religion, Judaism. It was a Christian book only under an interpretation which no Jew would have allowed. But, of course, the proper sense of that question is not met by the answer given above. Did the Christian movement have from the beginning a certain sacred and authoritative literature of its own, to which it referred? That is the sense of the question. To that question we must answer, that Christianity certainly had not from the beginning such a book. It had in its earliest period no such relation to any book as Mohammedanism bore from the beginning to the Koran. It had not from the beginning a specific written authority indigenous to Christianity and in turn formative of the earliest Christianity. All that came later.

On the contrary, its specific and characteristic inspiration was from the beginning that of a personality and a life. Its authority was Christ himself. Its substance was a life, the life in imitation of Christ. For the believer, the essence of Christianity consisted, not in the acknowledgment of a book, not in adherence to an organization, not in the confession of a creed, but in the imitation of a life. Documents acquired authority only because they enshrined a personality. Organization gained importance only because it brought men in contact with others who were trying to live out the spiritual life. Doctrine was of consequence only because it expressed the basal principles of that life. Christianity found its first expression, not in literature, but in men's lives as they tried to follow the Master of that life. It acquired a literature, an organization, a dogma, only as incidental to the development and necessary to the perpetuation of the spirit of that life.

For, of course, it is implicit in all that we have said, that the earliest Christians did have something which they placed side by side with the divine Scriptures of the ancient Covenant. They did have something of their own to which they attributed an authority equal to and even greater than the authority which they conceded to the Old Testament. That authority was the Lord himself, who had declared, Ye have heard that it hath been said by them of old time, . . . but I say unto you. It was the Spirit which had spoken at sundry times and in divers portions through the Prophets, which had spoken in these last days in a Son. It was the Christ himself while he lived. It was the oral tradition of him when he was gone. It was the written Gospel only when the men who had companied with him in his life were going. It was the Master himself and his mandate which occupied this great place. It was the reminiscence of the living Christ when he had ceased to walk visibly among men. It was certain documents because they alone came to be held authentically to enshrine that reminiscence.

The constant appeal in the early Christian literature is to the tradition of what Jesus had said. "The Master said," "the Lord Jesus saith," — these are the ever recurring formulæ. Nothing which we can think of in our modern life gives us an adequate sense of the authority for the Jew of Jesus' time of that which Moses and the Prophets had said. The measure therefore of the impression which Jesus had made may be found in this, that, contradicting, as he did, some things which Moses and the Prophets had said, amplifying and supplementing many more, it is yet his word, the word of Christ and, with it, the Old Testament, which is the authority to which Christians refer. Jesus' own manner of putting his authority over against that of the Old Testament, and the earliest Christian impression of his dignity, had involved such concession of the weight of his teaching from the first. Beyond all dispute to Paul is that of which he is able to say that he received it from the Lord. He puts away a doubt concerning the resurrection with a word of the Lord. And, in regard to an opinion of which he knows that it is his own, he yet believes that, in it, he has the spirit of the Lord.

It is not impossible that already in Paul's time a beginning had been made of the writing down of sayings of Jesus. But there is not the least evidence that Paul had before him any such writing containing words of Jesus. Much less is there proof that the words had weight with him because they stood in a given writing. It was enough that he considered them genuine words of the Lord, however he had come by them — whether out of the body of the tradition current in the Christian communities, or through his own inward and spiritual revelations of the mind of the Master, which he deemed no whit less authentic than the testimony of the disciples themselves. One beautiful saying of Jesus, which has not come down to us in any Gospel, appears in the address of Paul to the Ephesian elders : " Remember the words of the Lord Jesus, how he said, It is more blessed to give than to receive."[1] That single instance, and the manner of its occurrence, suggest that the oral tradition, the substance of preaching and of pious reminiscence, held more in solution than

[1] Acts xx. 35.

has anywhere been deposited for us. Everywhere, in the Epistles, in the Book of the Acts, in the Apocalypse, we find this same apprehension. It is to the Old Testament and the word of Jesus, that the Christian looks for his authority.

Meantime, it accords with all that we have said that in the Christian literature until the time of Justin's First Apology, about the year 152, the citations of the Lord's sayings are very varied in their wording. At times we could almost think that something written, a Gospel, or at least some source of our Gospels, had been in the hands of the authors. At other times, it is as if the writers quoted freely from memory. And again it seems as if one of them had cited in forms which were current in his own time or locality sayings of Jesus which have been handed down to us in some other form. It has been remarked that this looseness of citation of the words of the Lord is in striking contrast with the growing verbal accuracy that characterizes the quotations from the Old Testament which are made by these same authors of whom we speak. And always, thus far, we have to think of any Christian writings as cited because they contain the words of the Lord, and not of the words as cited because they stood in certain acknowledged writings. That is a vast and characteristic difference.

It is reasonably certain that early in this period of which we speak, not only the predecessors to whom Luke alludes, but probably many others also, had wrought for the literary preservation of the tradition of what Jesus had said and done. Precisely what shape these memorials of Jesus took, and exactly what is the relation of our canonical Gospels to one or more of them — these are questions about which there has been almost infinite debate. It is possible that this relation can never with absolute certainty be fixed. Some of these primitive and fragmentary memorials of Jesus were no doubt early lost altogether. Portions of one or more of them are probably preserved to us embedded in our synoptic Gospels, or at least may lie at the basis of that common element in the synoptic Gospels which gives to them that name. Fragments have also come down to us, either in citation or independently, of writings which perhaps represent this earlier stage of the making of the Gospels, and which were not at once supplanted in public use by the Gospels that subsequently became canonical. By the middle of the second century there can hardly have been any Christian communities of consequence which did not possess some revered document of this sort. And such written memorials of the fulfilment of the Law and Prophets in Christ would come naturally to be read in the Christian assemblages for worship, along with the divine Book of the Law and the Prophets whose words were thus fulfilled. Thus publicly read they would become the means of edification and the basis of instruction, since the Christian teachers were no longer in the happy position of the men of the elder time who could tell out of their own experience of the wonders of that fulfilment.

The manner of the one definite allusion which is made by Clement of Rome to the First Letter of Paul to the Corinthians is most interesting. Clement writes in the name of the Roman Christians to the Corinthian church on occasion of miserable strife in the latter church not unlike that painful situation to which Paul addressed himself. "Take again in hand that letter of the blessed Apostle Paul," he says.[1] The implication is just what we might naturally have supposed. The letters of the Apostle were not at first read in the Christian communities to which they were addressed in any other manner than that naturally fitted to accomplish the purpose for which they were written. But this also is suggested in the passage from Clement, that these letters came later to be taken up again, to be read often, or even regularly, for the guidance and spiritual profit which they were felt to contain.

One thing is entirely certain. The devout reading in the Christian assemblages, along with the Old Testament, of writings deemed to have been derived from the Apostles, of Gospels, that is, in the first instance, and then of letters, was the first outward step toward the canonization of these writings. When one reflects how rare was, probably, the private possession of books among mem-

[1] I Clement, 47.

bers of the Early Christian Communities, one can judge how much the solemn public reading would mean. The reading of the memorials of Jesus, side by side with the Old Testament books, tended ever to bring these memorials, as books, to the level of the Old Testament. But the Old Testament books had been oracles of God to the Christians from the first.

It is certain that the formal canonization of the New Testament writings, when it did finally take place, was not felt, in the large, by the Christian worshippers to command anything new and strange. It did but commend and confirm something which was already old and familiar in the attitude and practice of believers concerning the great mass of these writings. That literature which, in the end, was solemnly declared to be holy and authoritative for the Christian institution, was, with but insignificant exceptions, the same body of literature which had long and widely commended itself as holy and authoritative for the Christian life. Ecclesiastical declarations, when they came, destroyed little and created nothing, in this particular. Those declarations did not give character or position to the books. They simply recorded the position which the devout mind of the Christian communities had long since given to them. They merely asserted the character which the Christians had widely, and with growing clearness, felt that the books possessed. But, of course, such declarations are yet far in advance of the point in our history which we have reached.

Although letters were, in any case, the first apostolic writings in the hands of the Christian community, yet we have already seen the Gospels considerably in advance of the Epistles in the approach to that authority which was conceded to the Old Testament. This was surely because the Gospels were most nearly made up of the record of words and acts of Jesus. The intentness of the earliest Christians simply upon life permitted this. The words and the example of Jesus ministered most directly to the Christian life. But in the bitter conflicts of the second century and in the confusion in the churches, men turned back lovingly to the words of Paul. It was to Paul's labor and love that the institution, as institution, largely owed its origin. It is the apostolic words which have mainly to do with the church as institution. And so in the growing power and peril of the institution, the apostolic words began to come to the front, or at least to overtake the Gospels in the march toward canonization.

The great heretical movements of the second century drove the church to consolidation of its sentiment as to what were to be considered accredited Gospels. And, equally, through the license with which men like Marcion undertook to form religious societies of their own, they drove the church to consolidation of its sentiment as to what was apostolic mandate and usage. There must be some barrier against the excesses and vagaries of which Christians themselves, like the

Montanists, made themselves guilty. All of these things had their influence. Too much, however, has been made of the forces of antagonism and of their bearing upon the formation of the Canon. With the waning of the original productive impulse and enthusiasm, came, all of itself, the disposition to idealize the Christian past and to look for authority to that past. Quite apart from Gnostics and Montanists a New Testament would certainly have come to be.

The Pauline churches were almost always the great history-making churches, so well had the great missionary chosen the strategic places. After the storm of contumely which arose about Paul had died down, when the bigotry and bitterness of his opponents had been forgotten, when men had got far enough away from him to realize how great he was, there came, even in Jewish circles, a sort of rehabilitation of the memory of the Apostle to the Gentiles. But, indeed, the lapse of time was bringing tribute to all of the Apostles. Were they not the sole witnesses to that which the Lord had said and done? And were not their writings the only part of their witness of which men could be sure? So that phrases like these, "Christ and the Apostles thus spake," or, "Christ, through the Apostles, has thus ordained," — became almost formulæ for that of which the church felt confident. Differences among the Apostles are forgotten. The Apostles are one body. They constitute the one body to which Christ committed all the interests of his cause. Both Irenæus and Tertullian speak thus in terms which Justin, only twenty or thirty years before, would hardly have understood, concerning a weight of the Apostles, and an authority of the apostolic writings, because apostolic, which authority was to be decisive in all cases. These are now the signs of a new thing coming.

It was but a step for these men and for their successors to try to prove to be apostolic, writings which the church had long used to edification; or again to remove from a usage well-nigh immemorial some writings which, though dearly loved, could not be found to be apostolic. The men still stood face to face with the question, not yet altogether closed: What writings are to be read in the Christian assemblages for worship? One sees how the standard of decision of that question was changing from one of inward and spiritual quality to one of outward fact, or at least of supposed fact. The earlier time had answered: Those books are to be read which contain the spirit of Christ. Of their containing that spirit the Christian man was the judge. His being edified was the criterion. But, as time went on, the very problem was to train up new generations in the spirit of Christ. The writings read in the public services must be the great instrument in that training. It seemed to men that if only the apostolic origin of the writings could be made out, then the Christian spirit of them would be assured. But of questions of authorship only the leaders of the church, and they upon external and historical grounds, could be the judges. And if once the circle of writings of apostolic authorship could be made out, then no others should be publicly read. We see the reasoning and appreciate its naturalness. The movement appears inevitable. But it was one of far-reaching consequence.

One stands still in the face of a momentous issue like this which we see here preparing, and asks himself whether it was, for the cause of spiritual religion, an advance, or whether it was not a retrogression, that the church did thus create a New Testament, and transfer to it an authority which before had been ascribed solely to the spirit which was in Jesus Christ. But can any one dream that the tradition concerning Jesus could have propagated itself indefinitely in any other way than this, without being indefinitely corrupted? It was not possible but that the men of later generations should jealously guard even the letter of these memorials of an earlier and more privileged time, as the charter and constitution of the faith which they possessed. It was not possible but that, in the end, men should thus betake themselves to an outward criterion in the judgment of this literature. For the inward spirit which could judge of it was the very thing which, by this literature, men were seeking to create.

It does not follow that their judgments of history were, in all details, correct. But assuredly we have to think of the making of the Canon as also under the same divine guidance and inspiration which obtained in the making of the single books and in the inauguration of the Christian movement itself. That touch of the divine Spirit upon the human which we mean by inspiration is here seen, in the slow miracle of history, making a collection of books, and not simply putting it into the heart of a man to write a single book in which the truth of God should shine. We have to think of that impulse which goes forth from the spirit of goodness in Jesus Christ, as not confined to the revelation in the books, but as extending to the whole life of the church and of mankind, and as answering, then and now, out of the hearts of men, to the revelation which is here contained.

In the very moment of gravest import and of greatest opportunity for all the future of Christendom, that decisive work was done. The recognition of the unity and sacredness of this little body of literature as against all other literature, Christian or pagan, was obtained. In the first zeal of it, that recognition was obtained at the cost of the loss of some other early Christian literature which, as students of history, we can never sufficiently deplore. But we should need to know more than we do know in order to be sure that the loss could then, in the making of the history, have been avoided, and yet the results secured which have followed to the world from the influence of the New Testament.

We shall do well to spend the remainder of this first lecture in the effort to construct a sort of framework for our study. Indeed, there are two bits of outline which we need to have brought to our attention. The first of these is chronological in its nature.

The movement which we are to study may be roughly apprehended as having passed through three stages. Its history falls, therefore, easily into three periods. There is, in the first place, the period, roundly two generations of the second century, in which there was not present even so much as the idea of a New Testament Canon that was to be placed side by side with the Scriptures of the Old Testament. In this period the apostolic origin of a book was not thought of as conferring upon it, at once, a quality which was identical with the prophetical character of the Old Testament. In this period the words of the Lord have indeed their own supreme weight, from the beginning. But the written Gospels have their weight because they contain those words. The Epistles have indeed the affectionate and reverent acceptance granted to the personality of the Apostles, but no other. And, as it happens, the one prophetical book of the New Testament is not mentioned until almost the end of the time of which we speak.

There is, then, in the second place, the period, roughly speaking, the third and last generation of the second century, in which suddenly, under pressure from without and from within, and keeping pace with the rise of the idea of the catholic church, the thought takes supreme possession of the minds of men, that there is a body of apostolic literature, sacred and authoritative, which is to be placed side by side with the Old Testament. To this literature is attributed an inspiration which is apprehended in the same way with that of the Old Testament. This apostolic literature is indeed the specific Scripture of Christendom.

And then comes the third period, covering more than two centuries, in which the conception is indeed fixed, but in which the limits of its application vary. The fact is now universally assumed that Christianity, also, has its own volume of inspired writings. But what writings are to make up that volume? The interest centres mainly about a few books like the Epistle to the Hebrews, the Apocalypse, and some of the catholic Epistles, which notoriously had whole generations of conflict to obtain their recognition in both East and West as scriptural books. This is the period in which we begin to meet with lists in the writings of the Fathers, in which lists they express their own opinions and canvass the opinions of others. It is, finally, the period in which our matter becomes the subject of decrees of councils, in which decrees it is intended that the orthodox opinion shall be settled beyond all possibility of dispute.

The other rough outline which at this stage of our study we should offer, is an attempt at some sort of classification of the literature, outside of the canonical, with which, in this decisive time, we have to deal. The last thirty years of the second century are, by all, conceded to have been years of the very greatest significance for the history of the Christian religion. Perhaps never in the whole history of the faith has so much that was of moment been crowded into one generation. Not only are these the years in which, if our construction of the history is correct, men first apprehended, in all the clearness of it, the idea of a New Testament Canon, and began to make earnest with the authority of that Canon. But in those same years men seem first to have conceived of that form of organization and church government which had been growing up among them, as something given in the intent of Christ and the Apostles; as uniform and authoritative from the beginning and over all the earth. And in these same years men came first to apprehend those forms of doctrinal statement which had been gradually taking shape among them, as if these were held in uniformity by all the apostolic churches, and as if they had remained unchanged since the Apostles' time, an original sacred deposit of dogma, a faith, even the formal utterance of it, once delivered to the saints. In other words, now suddenly, in these significant years, we seem to have arrived at a New Testament Canon; at an outward institution which could with propriety be called a universal church; and, under this church and Scripture, at an admitted rule of faith, binding upon all Christians, which issues in what we know as the Apostles' Creed. That these three things have the closest possible relation the one to the other will immediately be surmised. As a matter of fact, they are all but expressions of the same tendency, manifestations of the same force, and phases of the same movement. In the sixth and seventh lectures we plan to study them in their mutual relation.

But it will easily be seen that these three things, the Canon as the only authoritative source of information concerning Jesus, the triumph of the episcopal organization, and the finding of the bond of union among Christians in a creed—these three things definitely close the period of the Christian origins. They mark, or shall we not rather say, they constitute, the rise of the catholic church. They end an era which had continued, with characteristics more or less unchanged, since Jesus' time. They begin a new era with traits and issues of its own, which, in some sense, may be said to continue to our day.

With this epoch begins the literature which is, properly speaking, ecclesiastical. Of this literature the church Fathers, rightly so called, are the authors—Irenæus, Tertullian, Clement of Alexandria, Origen, Cyprian, and the rest. On the soil of the Roman state and in the spirit of Greek education, there springs up a new world-literature, with its controlling impulse in the religion of the despised Galilean. That religion from this epoch begins its march toward the possession of a universal empire. Its outward victory is still nearly a century and a half in advance of it. But without its Canon, its bishop, and its creed it could hardly have won that victory.

But, before these men, who were churchmen writing in the consciousness of belonging to a great institution, there was a little group of scholars, covering about a generation in their activity, who differed from those others as widely as can well be thought. They were men like Justin Martyr, Aristides, Athenagoras, Tatian, and the rest. They were the Apologists. They, too, were educated men, among the first whom in any number the Christian movement gathered to itself. They had been pagan philosophers and teachers, many of them. Most of them were converted in maturity. Their aim was to justify themselves in the eyes of the men of their own class. It was their work to say the true word on behalf of Christianity in the ears of rulers, and to defend the new religion before cultivated pagans. Their literary models were among the philosophers. Their spirit was often that of the rhetoricians. Their impulse was sometimes that of an intellectual freedom which would have startled the churchmen of a later time.

And then, if we go still farther back, we come to the time, from that of the authors of Second Clement and of the Didachè back to the Apostles themselves, when the poor and simple people, slaves, and the down-trodden, constituted the great mass of the Christian converts. It was the time when the sense that the Christ of God, the Deliverer from sin and death, had come was nearly all of Christian faith; and being good and showing love was nearly all of Christian life. The type of the whole thing was dominantly Judaic. It was, at the first at least, that of the synagogues and of the little bodies of proselytes which gathered about them. It had but little to do with the great outside world. There is nothing in the whole literature of the period which for a moment reaches up to the intellectual level of certain parts of the New Testament itself. But the models of the literature are precisely those which we know in the New Testament. There are letters, some of them not altogether unworthy to be called apostolic in their spirit, like that of Clement, and like those of Ignatius and Polycarp. There is an apocalypse, the Shepherd of Hermas. There are gospels, numbers of them, of which fragments have come down to us, like that according to the Hebrews and that according to the Egyptians. And there is one book of composite type, a simple manual of instruction, called The Teaching of the Twelve Apostles, the Didachè.

It is evident that the external conditions which gave shape to the literature which we know as the canonical produced also many other works of the same general sort, in the midst of which the works later canonized long stood. Indeed, not a few of these other works were read in the services for public worship in the Christian community, on the Lord's day, along with, or even in place of, some books which afterward went to make up the New Testament. Beyond question our Gospels were members of a class and examples of a numerous type. The preface to Luke bears that upon its face. Quite naturally did other apostolic spirits write letters for warning and entreaty not unlike in form to those which Paul had written. Men did not, at first, feel the difference. And no one strove as yet to enforce a distinction of the literature deemed to be apostolic from all other literature in the manner which has remained familiar down to our own day. But from this point we must take our departure for the study of the next lecture.

LECTURE II

THE WITNESS OF THE EARLIEST CHRISTIAN LITERATURE TO THE NEW TESTAMENT

LECTURE II

THE WITNESS OF THE EARLIEST CHRISTIAN LITERATURE TO THE NEW TESTAMENT

A WELL-KNOWN historian of Christian literature has put forth the thesis that if that history would be true to its task, it should ignore the distinction between the books which ultimately found place in the Canon and the rest of the early Christian literary work.[1] He argues that this distinction was, as we have seen, in all the sharpness of it, a discovery of the last generation of the second century. The separation of these writings from all others was one which the earlier generations had not felt. The sense of their elevation to a plane unique the earlier Christians had not shared. Those generations had used other documents in the church services for worship, to some extent, just as they used these. The sharp limitation of the New Testament Canon and the attribution to it of the quality of Scripture was really the first dogma of the catholic church.

But while all this is true, we must reply that the distinction upon which that separation was

[1] Gustav Krüger, *Das Dogma vom Neuen Testament*, Giessen, 1896.

based had existed from the beginning, although not at first observed. There was an inspiration of the main body of these writings, the outward condition of which, at any rate, was the nearness of their writers to Christ, and the consequence of which was the unique relation of the more important of these writings to the formation of the Christian church. There was a Heaven which lay about the infancy of Christianity, which only slowly faded out into the common light of day. That Heaven was the spirit of the Master himself. The main ones, at all events, among these writings, do centrally enshrine the first pure illumination of that spirit. We are not interested in asserting that all of the books in the subsequent Canon contain that spirit in an equal degree. We are not concerned to say that some books which ultimately found themselves outside of the Canon contain it in no degree whatever. We know how long the outline of the Canon was a wavering one. We cannot hold that the outline of the Canon, when at last it was fixed, achieved exactly that which the men who fixed it had in mind. And yet even so, the New Testament is a fact. It is an historic magnitude, definite, and of incalculable influence. The canonization, we concede, was a purely historic process. The contrary issue of many steps of that process is thinkable. But, even if we should say that the Christians, at the end of the second century, might have failed altogether thus to separate this literature from the rest, yet it is a mere matter of fact that they did thus separate. And by that fact these documents became for Christians the regulative ones, and the others did not. It is a simple matter of history that to these documents the Christian church for more than seventeen hundred years has thus referred, and to the others it has not. From these it has drawn its life, by these it has guided its course, and by the others it has not. If one would understand Christianity, he is compelled to reckon with the New Testament as it is. And furthermore, he is compelled to recognize the validity of the central distinction which made the New Testament what it is, namely, the nearness of the body of these writings to the impulse which went out from Christ.

Nevertheless, there is for us, just this degree of unquestionable truth in the above contention. For us, in the discussion of the literature which in this lecture especially engages us, to carry back into the century from the death of Paul to the death of Justin, roundly the century from the year 65 to the year 165, a distinction of which Justin, devout Christian that he was, had hardly yet thought, would be eminently unhistorical. If we desire to gain for ourselves a realization of the way in which the literature which we know as the canonical appeared to the men of those generations, we must divest ourselves altogether of the notion of the New Testament Canon. We must realize that we have gone back to the time when there was no New Testament, and only the faint dawn of the idea that there was going to be one. We have gone back to the time when the Old Testament would not have been called the Old, because it was the only Testament.

The phrase, "the old testament," in so far as it was used, carried the sense of the book of the ancient covenant with the fathers. The phrase translated "new testament" could mean only the "new covenant," "new dispensation."[1] We have gone back to the time when there were many more collections of Jesus' sayings, fragments concerning his doings, beginnings of Gospels, and Gospels, than our four. Some of these were read in the services for worship along with or in place of some of the four. In not all places had the four been got together. Men loved the oral testimony to the grace and truth which had been in Jesus Christ better than they loved the written substitute. We have put ourselves back in the time when there were many more letters of apostolic men than those of Paul and Peter and the rest. The word apostle had for the time gained, and had not yet again lost, a sense which made the glorious company of the apostles far larger than that of the Twelve. The name was applied to any man who bore Christ's message to the world. Prophets came still claiming inspiration of the Holy Ghost, and spoke to the churches as Paul, in the Corinthian letter, lets them do. There was at least one apocalypse, much less

[1] 2 Corinthians iii. 6.

intensely Jewish than our Book of the Revelation, and almost as much loved where men loved that kind of thing at all. And where it was rejected our Apocalypse was rejected too. We have gone back to the time when the little isolated Christian communities were themselves the judges what books they found themselves edified in Christ to have heard read. It was the time when the bishop was a man from out the circle of the elder persons, with God's gift of a blameless life, who led the observance of the Communion, spoke the good word, and administered the little charity, when no apostle or prophet happened to be present. It was the time when as yet there was no creed, nor the beginnings of any, beyond the belief in Jesus Christ, through whom the will of God for our salvation was made known. Forgiveness, resurrection, the good life, the Holy Ghost in all men's hearts, — these were the tenets, which each man framed much in his own way. The bond of union was not book, bishop, creed, not any one, nor all of these combined. It was the bare being committed to the following of Jesus Christ. The great duty of the Christians was, in word and life, to bring to mankind the message in which they had been blessed. And yet out of these simple elements, these simple people gathered the conviction, each least upper-room conventicle of them gathered the sublime self-consciousness, that they were the representatives, the illustration, of the eternal kingdom of God upon earth. And over all swayed the vision that the toil and suffering were not for long. The Christ would come again. Not all of these traits which I have delineated can be noted equally in all places. Not all of them mark uniformly the whole time of which we speak. Some of them fade out toward the end of it. Nevertheless, in motive, in principle and atmosphere, this is the background against which we have to paint.

And of course, this being the case, we have to treat the writings which we later know as the New Testament ones, just as they stood, in the midst of other literature of their time. This is the more easy to do, because practically all of the literature of the period is of one or another of the kinds which we find represented in the New Testament. There are, namely, letters, apocalypses, gospels, and, just at the end, one little book of instruction for converts with the emphasis all upon life and not upon doctrine, "The Teaching of the Twelve Apostles," as it is called, a most suggestive contrast to the Apostles' Creed.

We may repeat what we said in the first lecture that it is not our task to speak in detail of the origin and content of the writings which afterward became New Testament. And yet, of course, we cannot pass by these altogether. Our main interest, however, lies with those writings of the period which did not become New Testament. And, in a general way, we may say beforehand that the questions which we shall seek to answer, by the aid of these writings, are two. We shall ask, Which of the books that afterward became canonical did each one of these uncanonical writers know? Then also, we must inquire, In what light did each regard those writings which he did know? We shall thus be able to observe how the fragments of what is to be the New Testament, one originating here, one there, and scattered up and down the earth, begin, with time, to find themselves together, and how there dawns upon the generations the sense of the unique thing which these books together constitute.

We begin with the letters. The oldest book in our New Testament is a letter, probably the first of Paul to the Thessalonians. The first spreading of the gospel was the work of persons. There is no letter, not even the most elaborate and doctrinal one of Paul, which does not bear full witness to this fact. And halfway down our period, not the least precious treasure of certain Asiatic churches were similar letters of two apostolic men, Ignatius and Polycarp. We have no cause to think of these men as consciously imitating Paul in their manner of writing. It was the manner in which they would naturally write, as they also faced perils and gave counsel to the flock of God.

The main letters of Paul were written, according to our best knowledge, between the years 48 and 58. Portions also of the Pastorals belong before the year 64. These Pauline letters contain a good part of all the information touching the life and thought of that time which has come down to us. But nothing could be more obvious than the casual and occasional character of these writings. First Thessalonians, indeed, contains the injunction that the letter shall be solemnly read to the whole assembly of the Christians.[1] At the end of the Colossian letter is an injunction that when it shall have been read to the Colossian community, it shall be exchanged for a letter which the Apostle has written to the Laodiceans.[2] But nowhere is an intimation which, in the remotest way, looks toward the position which these Epistles, later, assumed in the Christian church. So vivid are they in their delineation, so practical in their instruction, that oftentimes the emergency which called out a given letter can be appreciated by us even in considerable detail. On the other hand, we should be gravely mistaken did we deem that these are but such casual letters as a man might to-day dash off by quick delivery and to-morrow contradict by telegraph. Difficulties of communication may, perhaps, be thanked for the fact that these letters are no hasty improvisation. The profound reflection, the disposition of material, the skill in marshalling of arguments, the art in presentation, the fortunate illustrations, all betray that their author spared no labor, and that the letters were intended to produce permanent effect. All of this, which is the mark of the author's genius, and beyond these

[1] I Thessalonians v. 27.   [2] Colossians iv. 16.

qualities, of course, the greatness of their subject, serves to explain the fact that letters which, in one sense, are but products of occasion, have yet stood in the short index of the world's greatest literature. This they do, judged merely by the standards of literature. And the time came when the church looked back upon the production of these letters as part of the plan of God for the guidance of the race.

It is well known that the Tübingen criticism seventy years ago began at this point of the Pauline Epistles. The extreme writers of that school left but four Epistles to the Pauline authorship, namely, that to the Romans, the First and Second to the Corinthians, and that to the Galatians. Investigation since then, and more particularly in our own time, has worked steadily toward the enlargement of the area of that which is assigned to Paul. This trend is conspicuous in the main work upon the history of Christian literature in the first three centuries, which has appeared within the last ten years.[1] Beside the four letters named above, the First Thessalonians, Philippians, and Philemon are by the large majority, even of the left wing among critics, acknowledged as of Paul. On the other hand the Pastorals, that is the First and Second Epistles to Timothy and the one to Titus, are, in their present form, at any rate,

[1] Harnack, *Geschichte der alt-christlichen Litteratur bis Eusebius*, Leipzig, 1893; *Die Chronologie der alt-christlichen Litteratur bis Eusebius*, Bd. I., Leipzig, 1897.

defended by but few. Nearly upon all hands, it is deemed that the development of doctrine and of government which they imply, compels us to think that they have been rewritten. How lightly they may have been touched over, how much of genuine Pauline material lies behind and has been taken up into them, is of course another question. A good deal of such material seems assured. Colossians in some part, and Second Thessalonians and Ephesians in whole, are assigned by many to Pauline circles, to Pauline influence, but to dates later than the life of Paul himself. And yet, even concerning these, many of the best scholars are of the opinion that it is not impossible to answer the arguments against their Pauline authorship.[1]

As to the Epistle to the Hebrews, which does not even claim to be by Paul, we shall have occasion many times in this history to note how long and in how many quarters this letter was refused admission into the Canon because men knew that it was not written by Paul. In the end it found its place in the Canon, probably because men had come to think that it was by Paul. But for that supposition, in those later days, it would have been shut out. And yet Calvin truly said of it that, despite the fact that we do not know its authorship, there are few books in the Canon which for spiritual content are more worthy of their place. Men have surmised in Barnabas, in Apollos,

[1] See Jülicher, *Einleitung in das Neue Testament*, Freiburg, 1894, p. 34.

the author, and even in Priscilla the authoress. We have no difficulty in thinking that, of this noble and original, this profoundly spiritual interpretation of Christ's gospel, the author may remain forever unknown. Before the making of the Canon men had been edified by books concerning which they did not even ask the authorship. But, exactly in the heat and stress which created the Canon the principle of admitting books of unknown authorship would hardly have been allowed.

Of the seven little letters addressed to the Christian world at large, and hence called the catholic Epistles, four, as we shall see, had a hard time to gain their place in the Canon, and one of them, Second Peter, has no certain external witness for its existence before the time of Origen. First Peter has better evidence on its behalf than the others, and First John clearly stands with the Fourth Gospel. As to them all, we may say that the letters are of so small compass that the absence of citation from them in this or that period should not be given too much weight.

Several letters of Paul seem to have been lost. There is the allusion to the Laodicean letter of which we spoke. There must have been one,[1] and there may have been two,[2] other letters to the Corinthians. The author of the Muratori Fragment knows of letters to Laodiceans and Alexandrians, but he directly declares them to have had their origin within the heretical sects.

[1] 1 Corinthians v. 9.   [2] 2 Corinthians ii. 3.

Outside of the writings which have become canonical, the first letter is one of the Roman community to the Corinthian community on the occasion of strife in the latter church. The letter is an interesting index that the Roman church early felt responsibility, and assumed leadership of all the rest. The Epistle can hardly have been written after the year 100. The name of the bishop who wrote it does not appear. But there is nothing against the tradition that he was the Clement who stands as the third bishop, counting Peter. By no means secure, on the other hand, is the identification of this Clement with the Consul Flavius Clemens whom his cousin, the Emperor Domitian, put to death for base withdrawal from the service of the State. It would be interesting if the Christian propaganda had so early reached the highest places. Paul's phrase, "they of Cæsar's household," probably means only slaves.[1] But weary people in the highest station were seeking light and peace in those dreadful days as the old world began to decline. On the other hand, almost a fourth part of the Epistle which we are discussing is made up of Old Testament quotations. And such familiarity with the Old Testament would be astonishing in one born in imperial circles. It is easier for us to think of some freedman, who had the right to bear the Flavian name.

Almost the very occasion of the letter gives it a certain resemblance to the Pauline letters to the

[1] Philippians iv. 22.

WITNESS OF THE EARLIEST LITERATURE 53

same church. The author speaks of himself as one who follows in the footsteps of Paul, bearing upon his heart the interests of all the churches. Beside the Corinthians, Clement knows Paul's letter to his own church, the Roman. He knows also the Epistle to the Hebrews and has been very deeply influenced by it. There seem to be traces also of the First Epistle of Peter and of that of James. There is no disposition to place writings subsequently in the New Testament Canon, even though they are thus often quoted, on the same footing with the Old Testament. On the other hand, Clement of Alexandria holds Clement of Rome among the sacred writers.

Much the same state of things obtains as to the so-called Epistle of Barnabas. Clement of Alexandria [1] counted it among the sacred writings and Origen [2] called it a catholic letter. In the single Latin translation which we have, it stands next the Epistle of James. Until Eusebius no one seems to have doubted that it was the work of the companion of Paul's journeyings. And yet the misstatements in the book concerning Jewish ceremonial can hardly be attributed to Barnabas, who was a Levite. The book is marked, moreover, by the most extreme antagonism to everything Jewish. The author has used the letters to the Romans, Corinthians, and First Thessalonians, and gospel material of a type especially near to that of Matthew. Barnabas has the phrase, "He said,"

[1] Eusebius, *H. E.* vi. 14. 1.   [2] *Contra Celsum*, i. 63.

without any noun for subject, as if no name were necessary to introduce the word which Jesus used.

Under the name of Ignatius quite a number of letters have come down to us. The tradition names Ignatius as the second bishop of Antioch, and he is supposed to have died the martyr's death at Rome under Trajan, that is, before the year 117. There are seven of these letters, in the form of their transmission which is now most generally credited; namely, letters to the communities at Ephesus, Magnesia, Tralles, Philadelphia, Smyrna, and Rome, and a letter to Polycarp. They purport to have been written by Ignatius on his journey to Rome under an escort of soldiers. They give thanks for the kindness which has been shown him in the cities through which he has passed, and warn against division and errors in the church. The Roman letter speaks out his ardent desire for martyrdom. If we except the letter to the Romans and that to Polycarp, the resemblance of these letters the one to the other, the repetition of the main ideas in them all, and their artificial character, have caused some to doubt if we have not here to do with a deliberate forgery. But these qualities are, to say the least, not more likely in the work of a man who would undertake a shrewd deception, than in that of a zealous man of no remarkable ability. The eagerness of the writer on behalf of the government of a single bishop in the local church has made men doubt whether the letters can possibly be given such an early date. Curiously enough, nothing is said concerning the situation as regards administration in the Roman church. And as relates to the situation in the Asiatic churches, it is not easy to make out how far the author describes a condition which existed in his time, and how far he delineates a condition which he much desires to have exist. We know too little of the stages of the development of organization, and for that matter, even of doctrine, in the different portions of the empire in the early part of the second century, to make that knowledge, in more than very general way, the basis of inference as to the age of documents. To Ignatius' mind the testimony of the Apostles exists only in their letters. Most of the letters of Paul seem to have been known to him. He has not certainly any one of the Synoptists except Matthew. But a passage from the Gospel according to the Hebrews is cited as a word of the Lord. He thinks of the Christian inspiration as still common to all. It is not simply a quality of Apostles. It is a gift and grace of God which fits men for deeds and personal life, as well as for the writing of books.

Under the name of Polycarp there has come down to us a letter to the Philippians. Irenæus relates that he himself, as a youth, had often seen Polycarp and heard him preach and tell of his intercourse with the Apostle John and with others of the followers of our Lord.[1] Polycarp died a martyr on the 23d of February in the year 155,

[1] Eusebius, *H. E.* v. 20. 8.

at the age of eighty-six, or very possibly still older. For he answers to the proconsul who would persuade him to make concessions and thus save himself from the stake: "Eighty and six years have I served my Master. How then can I blaspheme my King?"[1] It is quite possible, therefore, that he means to say, that these years have elapsed since his baptism, rather than that they indicate the whole length of his life. The authenticity of the letter in our hands hangs together with the question of the Ignatian literature. According to Jerome, the letter was in his time, that is, at the end of the fourth century, read in Asia Minor in services for worship. It is written in a beautiful spirit, indicating to the Philippians the foundation of their faith and reminding them of the duties which rested upon all Christians, but especially upon the leaders in the community. He recalls to the Philippians that they have a letter of Paul in their possession. Besides large use of this Pauline letter to the Philippians, Polycarp cites nine others of the Pauline letters. He seems to have known also First Peter and First John. Words of Jesus are cited directly three times in forms from Matthew, and there are reminiscences from all the other Gospels. He quotes freely from Clement.

Passing now from letters to books of the class to which our Book of the Revelation belongs, we have to note the fact that, strange as it may seem

[1] Eusebius, *H. E.* iv. 15. 20.

to us, there was no type of literature which the early Christians of the West more dearly loved. To understand the type we have to think for a moment of the later Hebrew literature. The great prophetical books of the Old Testament had been books of moral insight. Their authors were often men of political significance, reformers and popular leaders. But with the desperate misery of the later time came the disposition to paint in glowing colors the external features of the hope and future of God's people in this world or in the next, the glory of the Jews, and the dreadful vengeance which would be taken upon their enemies. A considerable part of the Book of Daniel is of this sort. One recalls the Book of Enoch. Now, it would have been strange if in the times of the agony of the church under Nero, Domitian, and Hadrian, from among Jewish Christians, or from men familiar with this apocalyptic literature, something of the sort had not come forth. That our Book of the Revelation is a work of this kind no one can doubt. Many of its difficulties are considerably diminished, so soon as this fact is recognized. The first three chapters are only setting. The letters to seven Asiatic churches are most interesting, in light of the letters of which we have just been speaking. But then comes the great series of visions, so intensely Jewish in tone, so slight in the admixture of Christian elements, that it is small wonder if men have come to think this part of the Apocalypse to be actually a Jewish writing, only lightly touched over by a Christian hand. The concentration of all attention upon the future, the spirit of revengefulness, the mysterious outlines of falling states, are all explicable from this point of view. But yet passages like that of the praise of the one hundred and forty-four thousand are beautiful beyond almost anything that Christian poet ever sung. The general consensus seems to be that the book was written, that is, the Christian part of it, toward the end of the reign of Domitian, who died in 96 A.D., although a part of the book would seem to belong to the time of Nero or to the time immediately after Nero. Of the Jewish part, if we admit that it was a separate document or made up from separate documents, it is impossible to assign the date.

Since Justin's time at any rate, the book has passed for a work of the son of Zebedee. But in Alexandria about the year 260 Dionysius was sure that it must have been the work of another John, a presbyter. The Roman Caius ascribed it even to Cerinthus, the arch-heretic. In Asia Minor, the country of its supposed origin, the Alogoi rejected it. Strangely enough the Romans loved it, while the East, and especially the Greeks, would have none of it. No book in the New Testament had such varied and dramatic fortunes and so hard a struggle to gain a place in the Canon. The same remark might be made which we made as to the Epistle to the Hebrews,

WITNESS OF THE EARLIEST LITERATURE 59

that the book probably came into the Canon under the apprehension that it was the work of an Apostle. But we shall have abundant opportunity to observe that to a large part of the world that supposition came very hard.

Side by side with this Apocalypse of John, an Apocalypse of Peter seems very early to have been known in churchly circles, and long to have passed as Holy Scripture. The Muratori Canon has it in the list of sacred books. Clement of Alexandria commented upon it. Decisively rejected by Eusebius,[1] it was yet publicly read in church services in Palestine in the fifth century, according to Sozomen.[2] The book had been known to us prior to 1892 only in a few bare scraps of citation. But a considerable portion of it was found in the grave of a monk at Akhmim in Upper Egypt by Bouriant, and published by him in the year named. The work has very little in common with the Apocalypse of John. It suggests rather the Jewish (or Christian) so-called Sibyllines. It has little or no relation to the Gospel according to Peter, but many points of contact with the Second Epistle of Peter. It moves in a circle of ideas and pictures which are of Greek, presumably of Orphic, origin. The vision of the torments of hell prepares one for that in which the Middle Ages took such delight. The might of Dante and Milton have almost given this mythology a Christian standing. One turns the pages of this little book, and

[1] Eusebius, *H. E.* iii. 25. 4. [2] Sozomen, *H. E.* vii. 19.

muses and asks himself: What if it had found a place within the Christian Canon?

A book which we know much better than the one just named passes under the title, the Shepherd of Hermas. It was counted as Sacred Scripture by Irenæus, by Tertullian before he became a Montanist,[1] by Clement of Alexandria, and by Origen. On the contrary, the Muratori Canon says of it that, though many loved it, it must not be counted among the Scriptures because, the author continues, "We know that it was not written by an Apostle, but by a brother of our Roman Bishop Pius, almost in our own time." Eusebius deemed that it might be used in the instruction of the catechumens. Athanasius, expressing the same judgment, enumerates it with the Didachè and with some of the Old Testament Apocrypha. Yet it maintained its place in many Bibles far down into the Middle Ages. The book gets its name from the guide and interpreter of the author in his visions, a kind of Virgil to his Dante. The purpose is an energetic call, to the whole of Christendom, to repent of the lax and sinful life in which it is sunken, since the end of the world and the coming of Christ to judgment is nigh. The author was a Greek who had been a slave, and betrays extraordinary familiarity with the Old Testament. He seems to have written after the

[1] See Tertullian, *Orat.* 16, and cf. *Pudic.* 10. 20, *v.* See Krüger, *Geschichte der alt-christlichen Literatur in den ersten drei Jahrhunderten*, Leipzig, 1895, p. 25.

year 130. Apart from those from the Old Testament, there is not a verbally accurate citation in the whole book. It is as if the author quoted his Christian materials from memory. Curiously enough the Apocalypse is never mentioned. The synoptic tradition is used. There is almost nothing from Paul; but First Peter and James are known. The most extravagant reverence is accorded to the very letter of the Old Testament. What stands beside this inspiration of the Old Testament is the gift of the Holy Ghost to all believers, including indeed the Apostles, but extending to Hermas himself, the chosen prophet of God. It is not until after this sense of the inspiration of all men under the new covenant disappears, as it gradually does, that the notion of the exclusive inspiration of books of the New Testament, as such, arises.

Not any one of our canonical Gospels reaches back with certainty into the time before the year 70, the year of Titus' destruction of Jerusalem. But assuredly to this period before the year 70 belongs the fixing, in no small degree, of the oral tradition concerning Jesus in the form in which it reappears in our Synoptics. To this time also belong with some certainty written documents which are the antecedents of our Gospels. The main witnesses to the life of Jesus were for a long time within the Jerusalem community. The substance of the synoptic Gospels bears the marks of this origin in the midst of the mother community. From thence the story of the sayings and of the deeds of Jesus was carried through Palestine and beyond its borders, and the tradition carefully preserved. One must infer that, even in many regions covered by the missionary activity of Paul, the information concerning Jesus had already penetrated. Nothing is further from the purpose of Paul's letters than the conveying of such information. The life of the historical Jesus is hardly alluded to in his Epistles. Nothing leads us to think that Paul had previously conveyed this information to all, at any rate, of those for whom he wrote. In Rome there was a matured Christian life in a community which he had never visited at the time in which he wrote.

Eusebius preserves the ancient opinion that Matthew had written down in Aramaic "Sayings" of Jesus.[1] It is not possible to think that this statement refers to the Gospel of Matthew as we have it. But it may well describe the document, or at least one of the documents, which lies at the basis of Matthew and perhaps also of Luke. As to the problem of the relation of the three synoptic Gospels, the one to the other, and to common sources, the agreement, even verbal, among them is so great, and yet the differences are so striking, that the question may be said to be the most difficult to which Biblical criticism has addressed itself. The discussion has passed through stages and phases which it would be difficult even to enumer-

[1] Eusebius, *H. E.* iii. 39. 16.

ate. And yet certain results may be deemed to have emerged, which are, with tolerable unanimity, acknowledged. One of these results is the priority of Mark. Another, is the fact that the Gospel of Mark was a main source for the writers of both the Gospel according to Matthew and that according to Luke. At the same time, there is much that is common to Matthew and Luke which does not appear in Mark. This material is mainly teaching. One thinks at once of the "Sayings" above alluded to. And beside this, about a fourth part of the Gospel of Matthew and again of that of Luke cannot be referred to either Mark or the "Sayings," and is not common to Matthew and Luke. This fourth part many are inclined to refer to the oral tradition. Against this last opinion, in part, it should, however, be said that the discourses in Luke, which belong to the Peræan ministry of Jesus, have all the marks of having been taken from a written and not from an oral source.

In the Gentile churches the number of men who could claim to have been eye-witnesses had been, from the beginning, small. That the movement toward literary deposit of the tradition was gathering headway may be inferred from the preface to Luke. The old Judaic influence is strong in Mark and Matthew, the Gentile and Pauline influence is stronger in Luke. But the Fourth Gospel is the great enigma of gospel criticism. It builds upon all three of the Synoptics, particularly upon Luke, although Eusebius' story of the intentional supplementing of the Synoptics is hardly true.[1] It would seem that the Gospel must rest upon authentic reminiscences of Jesus. For spiritual insight and revelation of the personality, it surpasses anything which otherwise the tradition concerning Jesus holds. At the same time, this Gospel shows a reflection, an adaptation of Christ's ideas to the profoundest intellectual life of the time, the beginning of the movement toward giving Christianity a place in the system of the world's thought, which is very hard to think of as the work of the son of Zebedee.

It is hopeless to try to separate the prologue, and a few touches here and there from the narrative at large, and then to say that we have thus, on one side the interpretative element, and on the other the ancient tradition from the disciple whom Jesus loved. The opal coloring, the combination of elements in amazing perfectness of fusion, runs from end to end. The inestimably precious and original material, the most profound and moving which is given us concerning Jesus at all, has yet been worked over from a new point of view altogether unlike that of the other Gospels. The tradition has passed through a new mind. The interpretation of Jesus into the life of the world and of the ages has begun. The highest stage of the development of doctrine in the New Testament, and a stage higher than any which the church attained again for eighty years, is before us. But

[1] Eusebius, *H. E.* iii. 24. 11.

the personalities concerned in it are veiled from us. Therewith is not said that the Fourth Gospel is removed from the Johannine tradition which we assume as its basis, and which accounts for its name, by any wider outward interval than that which separates the First Gospel from a Matthew original, or the Third Gospel from one of the sources of Luke. Even the Second Gospel, although it is a source of the First and Third, is itself also possibly at one remove at least from an earlier source of its own. It is the new and profoundly original interpretation of material drawn from its sources, in which the Fourth Gospel stands altogether apart from the other three. There is a story in the Second Gospel which is commonly supposed to allude to the author of that Gospel, John Mark.[1] It is related that at the crucifixion one disciple, wrapped about in a linen cloth, dared to draw nearer to the divine mystery than did any other. But when pursued, he fled away, leaving his garment in the hands of those who would have identified him. That tale may be taken as the eternal figure of the problem which the Fourth Gospel presents. It seems safe to place the production of the Gospel not far from the year 100.

If we rightly understand Eusebius, a translation of the original Aramaic "Sayings" of Matthew, and our Mark, lay before Papias, the Bishop of Hierapolis, when, in the second decade of the second century, he set about preserving all the oral

[1] Mark xiv. 51.

testimony which he could still gather from aged and privileged persons like himself. He thought with this to supplement and to correct the written documents. There is something very touching in the figure of this old man, with his vivid sense of the force with which the personal testimony and the oral tradition had come to him in his youth. He feels himself to be the representative of an age which is past. No one of his contemporaries any longer thinks the oral tradition superior to the written one. And we are bound to say that the few scraps from Papias preserved to us verify that judgment. Several scholars have attempted, in recent years, to gather together all of the fragments of the teaching of Jesus which appear to have been picked up by ecclesiastical writers from unwritten sources, or at least from sources other than the Gospels.[1] The result of the investigation enhances our confidence in our Gospels in a high degree. Theoretically, there would seem to have been no reason why the addition to our knowledge concerning Jesus from such sources should not have been worthy of consideration. In fact, it is astonishingly meagre. Of the 165 citations brought in this way under discussion, 103 may be dismissed as undoubtedly apocryphal.[2] Of the 62 remaining debatable examples hardly 10 are above the

[1] James Hardy Ropes, *Die Sprüche Jesu*, in Harnack's *Texte und Untersuchungen*, Bd. XIV., 1896.

[2] Alfred Resch, *Agrapha*, *Texte und Untersuchungen*, Bd. V., 1889, and Bd. X., 1893.

level of being considered inaccurate quotations. And of these ten there are only two or three which can be said to be, in their content, an appreciable enrichment of our knowledge of the teaching of Jesus, and one of these is from the Book of the Acts.[1] So nearly do the Gospels that we have seem to have gathered all that, in the time of the latest of them, was credibly known.

Fragments of three Gospels have come down to us which are undoubtedly very ancient. Two of them may perhaps represent the period of the first reduction of the tradition concerning Jesus to writing. These are the Gospels according to the Hebrews, according to the Egyptians, and according to Peter.

The Gospel according to the Hebrews is mentioned first by Hegesippus in a fragment preserved by Eusebius, then by Clement of Alexandria, then by Origen, and after that by many ancient writers. The chief fragments which have come down to us are preserved in the writings of Jerome. Jerome seems at times to incline to the opinion that he has here in hand a source, or perhaps the original, of our canonical Matthew. Other writers seem to have confused this Gospel according to the Hebrews with a later and more elaborate work, a Gospel much in use among the Ebionites. But the real Gospel according to the Hebrews would seem, without doubt, to have sprung out of the Jewish com-

[1] Acts xx. 35.

munity in Palestine, and to have been used among the common people, but not among those distinctively identified with any sect. Perhaps it is based upon that Aramaic source of our Matthew to which we have referred. It seems, however, to have altered this source to the taste of stricter Jews, and to have enriched it from the oral tradition. At the same time it appears to have preserved some original traits as compared with our synoptic Gospels.

Of the Gospel according to the Egyptians there are fragments in Clement of Alexandria, in Hippolytus, and in Epiphanius. And the Gospel is mentioned by very many ancient writers. There is good reason to suppose that it represents the tradition of the Gospel current among Gentile Christians in Egypt, and that its very name suggests the contrast of this tradition with that which was brought to the Jewish Christian community in Egypt from Palestine. And both these names of Gospels, that according to Hebrews and that according to Egyptians, even if given to these Gospels by men of a later time, suggest that the provincial communities were not, at the time of the currency of these Gospels, familiar with that form of the tradition which passed under the names of great Apostles and claimed general acceptance among Christian men. The Gospel according to the Hebrews is ascetic in temper and speculative in character. It may have arisen in some one of the Encratite sects. The Sabellians seem to have approved it.

A Gospel according to Peter is referred to by Origen in his commentary upon Matthew. It is also alluded to several times by Eusebius. Until the autumn of 1892 this was the most that we knew of it. In that year the French archæologist Bouriant published a parchment found in the grave of a monk at Akhmim in Upper Egypt. This fragment contained a part of the Apocalypse of Peter to which we referred, and also the latter portion of a Gospel according to Peter. The scrap begins in the history of the Passion, at the point where Jesus is condemned by the priests, and ends with the appearance of Jesus by the Sea of Galilee after his resurrection. The author would seem to have known our synoptic Gospels. The Gospel has the peculiar quality, as compared with our canonical Gospels, that in it the author speaks constantly in the first person, naming himself "I, Peter," and saying "we" when he speaks for the twelve Apostles. The whole narrative suggests the docetic point of view, which made the earthly life of the Saviour but an appearance. This agrees in very striking fashion with what Eusebius relates concerning Serapion, Bishop of Antioch from 190 to 203 A.D.[1] On the occasion of one of his visitations to the church in Rhossus in Cilicia, Serapion found that community reading a Gospel according to Peter. He permitted its use. The inference from his letter is that neither he nor they deemed such use of other Gospels in any way remarkable. But when, later,

[1] Eusebius, *H. E.* vi. 12.

he read this Gospel, he wrote at once recalling his permission, because he found the book docetic and heretical. One gets a glimpse of the way in which the fourfold Gospel came, in the end, to displace all others.

Sometime after the beginning of the second century, the treatment of the Gospel material began to assume all manner of speculative forms and to be moulded to every doctrinal and sectarian purpose. The treatment ran out, at the end, into imaginative constructions and pure romance. Books of that first sort, handling the tradition with doctrinal and sectarian intent, and usually constituting the secret literature of schismatic bodies, got the name Apocrypha, which means simply secret books. These were of course energetically repudiated by the rising catholic church. And they passed on the name, at least, to all books rejected for whatever cause, although some of the books thus labelled were never the serious documents of any sect and were hardly above the level of pious romance. There were Gospels according to Thomas, to James, to Nicodemus, Gospels of the Infancy, Acts of Pilate, and many more things of the sort. But these need not detain us here.

One sees that up to the time which we have now reached, about the year 150, there were many more Gospels than four, and some of them stood in high favor with devoutest people. That the church, however, in the end, out of this confusion, came to possess four Gospels of like worth in the estimate of its adherents, and not simply one Gospel, must be owned to be an extraordinary fact. Analogies from other religions might suggest the possession of but one book of this sort, one biography of the founder and hero, one book to be read in the public assemblies and to which all the traditions had been reduced. The earliest Palestinian churches apparently had but one Gospel. The Gospel according to the Egyptians we assume to be the single form which the tradition took in the Gentile church of that land. The Syrians later even made, in Tatian's Diatessaron, the four Gospels into one, and preferred that. Only in the fifth century were they compelled to put the four in its place. Of course, we can understand that the provincial tradition, according to Egyptians, according to Hebrews, could never make stand against the might of Gospels bearing the great names of John and Matthew and the rest. But why the church paused at these four, instead of going on to their resolution into one Gospel, remains obscure. Some have thought of a kind of compromise, as if one Gospel were best loved here, and another there, and the only agreement possible was the agreement upon all. But there is no evidence to sustain, in any larger way, the theory that one of our four Gospels was in exclusive honor here and another there. Rather, it appears that, from the time when men began to know our four canonical Gospels at all, they soon came to know and to prize all of the four.

At least, the first three, the synoptic Gospels,

often make their appearance together. We may assume that from the time when men began to know our four canonical Gospels, all serious use of other Gospels save in remoter places, as in the case of Rhossus just given, fell away. And as regards these four, even if it be assumed that the reduction of them all to one Gospel, after the manner of Tatian's Diatessaron, was the logic of the situation, yet the force which prevented that reduction had been operative from the beginning. That force was, namely, the apprehension of these four as in some sense original witnesses. What takes place is a kind of arrest in progress. It is as if the sense of the unique sacredness of this material, and the fear of the loss or change of the least particle of it, overtook the men with some suddenness. It is as if, midway in the process of composition and recomposition, of the casting and recasting of this gospel stuff so freely, as it had been going on all these years, men said to themselves: But let us stop right here. We had rather have four Gospels, deemed to go back to witnesses; we had rather have four Gospels, even if they do overlap one another and present impossible problems in the attempt to harmonize them. We had rather have four Gospels, than one, which, if it were now made, would, after all, represent only the opinions of our own time as to how this unique material is to be combined. They stood still at the four. We can never be sufficiently grateful that they did so, and that no such attempt as that of

Tatian ever gained great currency, or took the place of the four in any wider way.

Certain it is that toward the end of the second century the fourfold Gospel was in supreme honor and authority in Rome, in North Africa, in Egypt, and in Gaul. Indeed to Irenæus' mind — and his training carries us back to Asia Minor, and as far at least as the year 155 — it was as much a part of the divine order of things that there should be four Gospels as that there should be four winds of Heaven or four rivers of Paradise. The process had begun which ended in the elimination of all Gospels but the four.

Acts of Apostles need not detain us long. The one canonical book is certainly by the author of the Third Gospel and is virtually a continuation of the history which that Gospel had begun. One source of the Book of the Acts is of extraordinary vividness and value. It is the so-called "We-section," the portion in which the narrator speaks always in the first person. It is the document which underlies a good part of the last half of the narrative. It is the story of an eye-witness and participant in many of the stirring scenes in the life of Paul. It is almost like the journal of a companion of his wanderings. Whether this companion was himself the author, the physician Luke, or whether the author has used the narrative of this companion, cannot certainly be made out. For the rest, we must say that while the author has clearly had written sources, yet many things in the earlier part of his history, that part which centres about Jerusalem, are difficult to make out. Indeed, for the author himself sharpness of outline is wanting. Things have faded out somewhat in the distance. The bitter antagonism revealed in Paul's letters is almost forgotten. Just why the book should end so tantalizingly as it does, leaving Paul in his own hired house in Rome, and telling us nothing of the issue of that glorious life, most likely we shall never know. It is not possible to think, with many of the ancients and some modern scholars, that the book was written in the year in which the narrative breaks off, that is, before the death of Paul. Certainly the Book of the Acts was written after the Third Gospel, and clearly that Gospel was written after the destruction of Jerusalem in the year 70. On the other hand, if the Book of the Acts was written soon after the destruction, it seems strange that the author should not mention so significant an event — almost more strange than that he does not mention the issue of the life of Paul. But the strangest thing of all is this, that although the author well knows the point of the Pauline preaching, and has given us several sermons which he puts into the mouth of Paul, yet there is not a single passage in any Pauline letter which can be regarded as a source for any part of these sermons. It cannot be directly proved that the author even possessed a single letter of Paul, although it would seem impossible that he did not. When one compares the use made of the

Pauline letters by Clement, Barnabas, Ignatius, and Polycarp, this fact is very striking. Even these men feel themselves in greater measure outside of the personal influence of Paul than does the author of the Acts, and are compelled to gain from his letters the knowledge which they have of Paul.

Just why no one has ever told us much of the missionary journeyings of the other Apostles is a question which we cannot answer. The fragments of early deposit of tradition here are small. The tendency to write romances with the Apostles for their heroes sets in later. The efforts to use one Apostle and another as stalking-horses for doctrinal peculiarities are of such late origin, and are such palpable inventions, that they can hardly be said to have any relation to the history of the Canon. The romance of Paul and Thecla, the devout woman who is described as journeying with Paul on his mission, is, perhaps, the only one of which we need even to give the name.

Eusebius[1] counted among the books not to be accepted, one known as the Teaching of the Twelve Apostles, Didachè. There were allusions in the writings of the Fathers to this or very similar titles. But until the year 1883 this was nearly all that we knew. In that year Bryennios, Patriarch of Constantinople, published his discovery, in a monastery on Mount Sinai, of a manuscript which since that time has been the subject of almost unending discussion. Then it became evident that many of the

[1] Eusebius, *H. E.* iii. 25. 4.

Fathers had extensively quoted this writing. It is a sort of manual of Christian morals to be used in the instruction of those looking forward to Christian baptism. In the second part, it contains also admonitions to maturer Christians concerning the rites of the church. Almost certainly the book is in part the redaction of older material. Perhaps in part a Jewish manual is here worked over by a Christian hand. As we have it, however, the work seems to have arisen in Syria about the year 150. The interesting thing for us is that there is not the slightest trace of the existence of the New Testament Canon. The authorities of the Christians are the Old Testament, and the Gospel, which is spoken of, however, as something written. The use of the singular number, Gospel, is to be noted. But our four canonical Gospels together are often by later writers spoken of as constituting one Gospel. And besides these written authorities we have the Apostles themselves, as those whom the Lord had commissioned to teach. Apostles, prophets, and teachers are still the real functionaries of the church. There are more bishops than one in a single community. There is no set order of worship such as appears already in Justin. And there is no trace of the rule of faith, and of the movement which issues in the Apostles' Creed. Words of the Lord are given in almost every chapter, seventeen times in the form of Matthew, four times in the form of Luke. The Gospel according to John seems also to have been known. Apostolic letters appear to have been known to the author. But not once is material from them cited as apostolic teaching.

On the other hand, that which is put forth as the tradition of apostolic teaching in the church could never have been put forth under that name if the apostolic letters had had scriptural authority, as yet, in this part of the church, or even if they had been much read. That judging of the spirit of the prophets which Paul commands, the Didachè forbids. This is surely a sign that the authority of these prophets was waning. But, as we have seen, where this sense of prophetic inspiration of living persons was still present in force, and these could claim the supreme authority of God and Christ, there could be no talk of the authority of New Testament Scriptures as such.

In that sermon of some unknown preacher in Rome in the middle of the second century, which has come down to us under the name of the Second Epistle of Clement, the authorities of the Christian are the Old Testament and the Apostles. But, again, it is the Apostles as the tradition knows them, the living witnesses to Christ, and not the books of the Apostles, as yet, to which the author thus refers. It is the will of the Father which Christians are to do, it is the commandment of the Lord which they are to remember and keep. And despite the fact that these phrases sound so much like famous phrases in the Fourth Gospel, only Matthew and Luke are adduced in their support. The author has made extensive use of an apocryphal Gospel, most likely that of the Egyptians. There is almost nothing in this attractive little homily which shows any trace of the influence of the writings of Paul.

We have finished our task. We have touched upon those writings of the earliest Christianity which belong to the types, and, roughly also, to the times which produced the New Testament. If we have gained one single clear impression, we may be satisfied. It is this impression, that for the time of which we speak, that is, until about the year 165, the literature which we know in a closed body or collection, and under the definite apprehension of it as inspired and sacred Scripture, did not yet exist as a collection, and did not exist under that apprehension. That apprehension existed. But it was applied only to the Old Testament. The authorities of the Christian were the Old Testament and Christ Jesus the Lord. The spirit of Christ was deemed to be everywhere abroad in the hearts of Christian men. The Apostles were beginning to be looked upon as the sole authoritative witnesses to that which Christ had said and done. And also, the Apostles were beginning to be felt to exist as witnesses only in their writings. But those were the signs of the new thing which was coming. Those were the traits of the time which was to be.

LECTURE III

THE NEW TESTAMENT AT THE END OF THE SECOND CENTURY

LECTURE III

THE NEW TESTAMENT AT THE END OF THE SECOND CENTURY

By the middle of the second century the Christian movement had reached the stage at which, as a mode of life, it must explain itself to the civil authorities, and, as a form of doctrine, must justify itself to the mind of the educated world. The men who undertook one or both of these tasks are known as the Apologists. Up to this time the great mass of the Christians had been drawn from among simple people, from the poor, and even from the ranks of the slaves. And even now it is noteworthy that scarcely one of the Apologists was born of Christian parents. These men were for the most part pagan philosophers and rhetoricians, converted in maturity. They were men able to assert their rights under the Roman Empire. And they were impelled to explain their conduct to men of the class with which they had just parted company. Without doubt, the large majority of the Christian adherents still continued to be from the lower orders of the people. But the work of the Apologists makes plain that the Christians themselves were rising to self-consciousness, to self-respect in their new position; and with these traits came the impulse to self-defence. No less does the work of the Apologists make plain that the world about the Christians was beginning to discover that Christianity was not to be ignored as merely one new oriental superstition added to the many which were then current in the West. Nor was it to be regarded as merely one of the many contentious sects of Judaism concerning which one might say with Pilate, "Am I a Jew?" or, like Gallio, might care for none of these things.

The Apology, therefore, differs markedly from those types of literature which preceded it, and with which we have thus far dealt. These all had been produced by the same impulses which gave shape to the writings which afterward became canonical. The Apologies, on the other hand, took not merely their form but also in good degree their substance from impulses all their own. The Apology shows also a distinction from the type of literature introduced a generation later by such men as Irenæus and Tertullian. To the minds of these men the Christian church which they represented had become a great institution with an organization of its own, with a growingly distinct form of doctrine to assert, and with a sacred literature to which to refer.

These discriminations are broadly true, despite the fact that a few of the men overlap this classification. They transcend it, indeed, in either direction. Tatian, for example, beside writing an Apology, prepared a redaction of our four Gospels, the general use of which redaction in the Syrian churches shows that there, at any rate, for two centuries, the canonical way of thinking of the four Gospels did not obtain. And, on the other hand, Origen, busied with the maturer development of theology in the middle of the third century, reaches back to answer the aspersions of Celsus, who had written his assault upon Christianity during the last generation of the second century. The apologetic literature falls, however, mainly, into the period between the years 145 and 180.

The writers of this literature were for the most part of the type of training which we usually associate with the name of the Greek sophists, whose art and mode of life had undergone a curious revival in the Roman Empire of this time. They were men who themselves had found in the Christian faith and hope and love a satisfaction which, in the speculation and the ceremonies of their time, they had sought in vain. Their works are cast in a form which shows either that they were intended to be heard, and not read, or else, that the authors followed the fiction of the schools that such works should be written as if they were to be heard rather than read. With this trait goes, often, the unfortunate rhetorical manner which the Apologists affect, and that degree of unreliability which always accompanies the conscious striving after eloquence. The writers take their departure from the current popular philosophy. Justin is fully aware of this fact, in his own case. Tatian, on the other hand, roundly abuses philosophy, since he has become a Christian, but takes his departure from it none the less.

One of the best loved forms of argument is that of the appeal to antiquity. If a religion is divine it must be ancient; the more ancient, apparently, the more divine. The reproach had obviously been made against the Christians that their religion was but of yesterday. The attempt of the Apologists is, therefore, to prove that Christianity, through Judaism, of course, is much older than the Greek and Roman paganism. The earliest exponents of paganism, lawgivers and others, had but borrowed from Moses, and often borrowed very badly. As against Judaism, the attempt is to prove that the Christians alone really understood Judaism. This argument from antiquity had the curious effect that it threw the Old Testament into the foreground in a measure even greater than that which we have thus far observed. What was new and characteristic, in the teaching of Jesus and of the Apostles, was obscured, or, rather, because it was so unfortunate as to be new, it was treated as if it were of less worth. The Old Testament was even more than ever apprehended as a Christian book of oracles, and this both by those within and by those outside of the Christian community. Attention was withdrawn from Christian writings; and a movement to collect those writings and to familiarize the public with them was, in so far as the influence of certain Apologists was concerned, retarded. When Marcion and others like him presently rejected the Old Testament altogether, and pronounced the God of the Old Testament not even the same God with the God of Jesus, this was, in part, only a natural reaction against the strange overestimate of the Old Testament within the Christian community and neglect of elements which were new and characteristically Christian.

The foremost of the men who attempted thus the mediation between Christianity and the culture of the pagan world was Justin the Martyr. He was born in Palestine, at Neapolis, the ancient Shechem, of heathen parents, about the year 100. He was converted probably about the year 133. It would appear that in Ephesus he first came into sympathetic contact with the Jewish community and acquired his knowledge of rabbinical teaching. In Rome, under Antoninus Pius, he lectured in Greek in his own auditorium as teacher and apologist for Christianity. Acts touching his martyrdom assign his death to the prefecture of Rusticus, 163 to 167 A.D., in the city of Rome. Two Apologies, beside the Dialogue with Trypho, are deemed genuine. But the Second Apology, so called, is hardly more than a postscript to the First. It contains but an application, in a fresh instance, of the principle set forth in the First. It may have been handed in to the Emperor Antoninus Pius along with the First Apology. At all events, the assertion of Eusebius that the Second Apology belongs to the reign of Marcus Aurelius cannot be true.

In this First Apology, written after the year 150, Justin declares it to be unworthy of the Roman state that the Christians should be persecuted and punished as if simply for the bearing of that name. One has the sense, as he listens, that in Justin an advocate has arisen for the dumb multitudes who have suffered silently thus far. He boldly defends the Christians against the accusation of atheism. The accusers probably meant that the Christians had no images. He declares them not guilty of horrible immoralities alleged. Charges such as were current throughout the whole period of the Apologists, for example, that of eating human flesh and drinking blood, may have arisen out of phrases used by the Christians in connection with the Eucharist. But they were taken in dreadful literalness by the pagan multitude. One recalls the tragic misunderstandings between Jews and Christians in the Middle Age. Justin denies that the Christians are in antagonism to the State. The notion of that antagonism may have originated in the withdrawal of the Christians from the public service, or, less justifiably, from their refusal to do homage to the image of the emperor. Justin declares, on the contrary, that the Christians are most valuable citizens because of their pure moral life and charity. Over against these, he satirizes bitterly the doctrines of vulgar paganism, and points to the corruption of the heathen life. He describes the worship of the Christians in their conventicles, to allay the jealousy of the state against all secret assemblages which might become the hotbeds of political intrigue.[1] That jealous watchfulness spared only the mutual benefit and burial societies among the simple people. And in truth the Christian church existed, through a certain period, under the apprehension, on the part of the authorities, that its purposes were those of such a guild. We have thus touched in this place upon certain points which explain the whole apologetic literature.

In the Dialogue with Trypho, written apparently between 155 and 160 A.D., there is a touching account of Justin's own conversion, which occurred as he wandered about the world in the pursuit of truth. Justin never laid aside the garment or the mode of life of the wandering philosopher. The defence of Judaism in the Dialogue is feeble. There may have been an actual Rabbi Tarphon; but one has the feeling that Justin's Trypho is a man of straw. Justin's argument is, in a general way, that of the Epistle to the Hebrews, only by no means so well conducted.

But everywhere in Justin the great weight of argument is on the fulfilment of prophecy. Jesus is to Justin what he is because he fulfils the Prophets. The Old Testament is honored as a book of divine oracles. Opinions concerning Jesus' person and work are always sustained with proof

[1] Justin, *First Apology*, 65 and 67.

texts from these oracles. Rarely indeed are such opinions made to rest upon historical evidence taken from the works which are to become New Testament. The Prophets are cited verbally. The fulfilment of the prophecies, on the other hand, is related in words from the oral tradition, from extra-canonical writings, and from our Gospels, quite at random, and with no emphasis upon the wording. Never are any writings except those of the Old Testament spoken of as inspired. Only Old Testament citations have attached to them the phrase, "Thus saith the Holy Spirit." Old Testament quotations have the names of books or authors' names appended. This latter honor is bestowed upon the Apocalypse alone of all the New Testament books. And this is assuredly because the book was thought of as the continuation of the Old Testament prophecy.

Of interest, on the other hand, is Justin's declaration, in the course of his account of the Christian services, that apostolic memorials concerning Jesus were publicly read in the conventicles every Lord's day in connection with the reading of the Old Testament.[1] But Justin does not himself apprehend this as the putting of new Scriptures beside the old. It is simply the putting of the facts of the fulfilment of prophecy alongside of the words of the prophecy which was to be fulfilled. In the one case the emphasis is all upon the facts, however the statement of them may be worded. In the other

[1] Justin, *First Apology*, 67.

case the emphasis is all upon the sacred words. Only the words of the Lord, and not the writings which contain them, have authority like that of the Old Testament. Fulfilment of prophecy is the criterion of truth of the statements in the Gospel. The historic test of the truth of such statements in themselves is never applied. The grace and truth which were in Jesus Christ himself, appealing to the hearts of all men, constitute no argument. It is this grace and truth, as forecast in concrete manner by the inspired men of the ancient covenant, which alone have weight.

But, after all, for Justin these authoritative words of Jesus exist only in written documents. They are no longer a living voice as they had been for Papias. The word Evangelium, the Gospel, describes this whole mass of tradition concerning Jesus as the Christians knew it. Even the Jew Trypho uses the expression, "in the Gospel." On the other hand, toward the outside world this tradition is called the "apostolic reminiscences." But in this fixed magnitude, the Gospel, is included, beyond question, the Gospel according to Hebrews, and perhaps also those according to James and to Thomas. The Gospel according to John, although known to Justin, does not appeal to him. Everything outside of the Gospels is in the background. Letters of Paul — Romans, and Galatians, at any rate — are known to the Apologist. But the impulse of Paulinism is hardly felt at all. Antipathy to Paul is indeed everywhere found. Yet the erroneous doctrine against which Justin argues is clearly not that of Paul.

On the whole, we may say that although Justin knows many of the books of the later Canon, yet of a Canon of New Testament Scriptures, inspired writing in the sense of the Old Testament, there is at most but a bare beginning. That beginning may perhaps be discerned in the fact that under the phrase "our writings," Justin includes Gospels as well as the Old Testament.[1] With passages from the Gospels, moreover, he uses the phrase, "It is written," which men before Justin had used only of the Old Testament.

Tatian, according to Clement of Alexandria and Epiphanius, was a Syrian. A phrase of his own bears the possible interpretation that the place of his birth was in Assyria, that is, to the eastward of the Tigris River. He was of Greek education and had already made a name as a rhetorician when he was converted to Christianity in Rome before the year 152. He was a pupil of Justin until the death of the latter. Probably about the year 172 he broke with the Roman church, and went over to the ascetic sect of the Encratites and maintained a doctrinal position which was deemed heretical. He returned to the Orient; but the place and time of his death are not known. His Apology addressed "To the Greeks" would seem to have been written some time after his conversion and in justification, to former associates, of that step. It

[1] Justin, *First Apology*, 28.

contains a bitter and sometimes unjust critique of current Hellenic morals and religion, and, as well, of philosophy and art. It is the work of a man of information rather than of learning. But one has the feeling always that we have here to do with a man of character. Passages from Paul and John are touched upon. The writings of Justin have been used.

But much more interesting to us than Tatian's Oratio, is his Diatessaron, or Harmony of the Gospels. We cannot be sure of the date of this endeavor, but it was certainly after the year 172, that is, after Tatian's departure from Rome for the East. Eusebius says that it belonged to the time when he served as the head of an Encratite community. The Diatessaron may have been written for a Syrian church. On the whole, it is likely that the original was in Greek, that is, that the harmony was made from our Greek Gospels and then translated into Syriac. The kind of piecing together of texts from different sources without much grammatical reconstruction, which is here involved, would, indeed, be easier in Syriac than in a language so highly articulated as the Greek. But the Latin rendering, associated with the name of Victor of Capua, bears evidence of having been made from a Greek text, rather than from the Syriac. No Greek text of the Diatessaron is preserved to us. Ancient Armenian versions show that it was widely used. There is also an Arabic rendering from the Syriac.

Tatian's idea was to do away with the repetitions and divergences which our four Gospels present, leaving out what could not be brought within the unity of plan. He achieves thus something like a running biography. The genealogies of Jesus have been omitted. The text begins with the first verse of the Fourth Gospel. But then follow the two accounts of the birth, first that in Luke and then, after it, that in Matthew. The conflict between the two narratives by no means disappears. Tatian's faithfulness to his sources, after all, sets a limit to the thoroughness of his proceeding. It has been said that the disposition of material is that of the Fourth Gospel. Rather, it appears that the scheme is that of Matthew, and that the author then brings in the material from the Fourth Gospel as best he can. Tatian uses great freedom in the accomplishment of his purpose, at least in so far as relates to that which he omits. But in that which he retains and rearranges he keeps close to the letter of the texts. It has been said that the word diatessaron is a musical technical term for accord, or harmony, and that the term does not itself imply that only the four canonical Gospels were employed. But there is no evidence that material other than that drawn from the four Gospels was used. It is clear, therefore, that the four Gospels held a unique position in Tatian's mind, and very likely also in the minds of those for whom he worked. But the attempt, with such freedom, to made one narrative out of the four, together with the fact that this narrative was long publicly used in at least one national church, shows that the full canonical sense about the four did not there as yet obtain. Eusebius says that in his time, that is, before the year 340, the book was used in Syrian churches as the sole book of the Gospels. In the second half of the fourth century the first vigorous efforts were made to remove the Diatessaron from the churches and to put the four Gospels in its place. Ephraem Syrus wrote, before the year 378, a commentary on the Diatessaron, although he was quite aware of the controversy concerning it. Theodoret, Bishop of Cyrrhus, about 450 A.D., removed two hundred copies of it from the churches of his diocese and caused them to be burned.

Such a procedure as this which we have described, on the part of Tatian, was, in its essence, an interpretation. The judgment that two sections of the narrative are parallel, and that one of them may therefore be omitted, is a private judgment. The arrangement of chronology and the adjustment of localities so as to make a running story — these also express judgments of the writer. Moreover, the thing could hardly be achieved without the insertion, at one point and another, of small scraps, at any rate, of which we may assume that Tatian was himself the author. All this constitutes the subjective element which appears in any Life of Christ, although that Life may be written in the best of faith.

Although ecclesiastical writers denounced Tatian as a heretic, and although his services as an Apologist were almost forgotten in the aversion to him as a Gnostic, no one ever asserted that the Diatessaron was an interpretation of the Gospels contrived for the sustaining of his heresy. This accusation would have lain very near at hand had there been ground for it. That was a procedure in which many Gnostics had indulged. The work seems, on the contrary, to have been done in the interest merely of simplicity in instruction. To Tatian, and to some others in his time, the divine thing in the Gospel was still simply the tradition concerning Jesus. The incomparable worth was in the substance and not in the words, as yet. We must in fairness say that only to some men, and only in certain quarters, was this still, in Tatian's time, the case. In certain other quarters, even then, such an attempt as that of the Diatessaron would have found no favor. We may be grateful that neither the work of Tatian nor any similar work prevailed. Had this really happened in wide measure, we might have lost the four Gospels. We should thus have been committed to what was, after all, only an interpretation of the Gospels, a construction of them by a later hand and in the light of a new time.[1]

Upon the witness of the minor Apologists we can but touch. Aristides, whom we now know to

[1] See Zahn, *Geschichte des Neutestamentlichen Kanons*, i. 387 f. and ii. 530.

have written under Antoninus, and not under Hadrian, will have none of the praise of Judaism which is so constant in Justin. The character of the Old Testament as revelation is even denied. Of the arguments from antiquity and from prophecy no use is made. Tobit, an apocryphal book, is the only Old Testament work which is cited. But the synoptic tradition also is scarcely alluded to. It is material from Paul, and perhaps also from the Fourth Gospel, which the author mainly uses, and which he describes as gospel writing.

Melito of Sardis, in the time of the Roman Bishop Soter, 166 A.D., seems to have been a man of great influence in Asia Minor. He addressed an Apology to Marcus Aurelius of which fragments only are preserved to us in Eusebius. His attempt was to show the blessing which Christianity had brought to the Roman Empire, and to move the Emperor, whose interest in the good he recognizes, to view the Christians with favor. His Eclogæ was an interpretation of certain passages " out of the Law and the Prophets touching the Saviour and our whole faith."[1] In this work he enumerates the Old Testament books, and calls them explicitly by the name, the books of the ancient covenant. He is the first Christian who directly uses that whole phrase. It would seem as if the conception of a body of literature of the new covenant which he might enumerate lay close at hand for him. But he does not say so much as

[1] Eusebius, *H. E.* iv. 26. 13.

that. And the only New Testament book which we know that he commented upon was the Apocalypse. He was himself a prophet.

Athenagoras addressed an Apology to Marcus Aurelius and Commodus, in the years, therefore, between 176 and 180, defending the Christians against the accusation of immorality and pointing out the injustice of the attitude of the government toward the Christians, which was different from that which it observed toward any others of its citizens. He wrote also in the spirit of the Platonic philosophy a work on the resurrection, in which he quoted words of Paul from the fifteenth chapter of the First Corinthians precisely as he had cited certain words of the Prophets. But he never calls the authors of Epistles "bearers of the Spirit," like the Prophets. He cites the Gospels without name of book or author, simply with the phrase, "It says," or "He says." Here is the old point of view of the authoritative word of the Master.

Theophilus, Bishop of Antioch, writing before the year 190, is the first to cite a Gospel under the name of its author and in such a manner as to lay the weight upon the personal testimony of the author.[1] It is the testimony of the Apostle John in the Fourth Gospel to the matter involved in the paschal controversy. And he first speaks of the authors of the Gospels as also bearers of the divine Spirit, precisely as the authors of the Old Testa-

[1] *Aa Autolycum*, ii. 22. See Holtzmann, *Einleitung in d. N. T.*, 3 Aufl. 1892, p. 109.

ment had been the bearers of that Spirit. Strictly speaking, it is still the authors rather than the books of whom this assertion is made. But it is a small step for him presently to use, concerning the Fourth Gospel, the word "holy writing" which he has often used of prophetical books. And in one place he cites Isaiah, Matthew, and the Epistle to the Romans all in one sentence, with the phrase "the divine word commands." He quotes Paul more frequently than does any other of the Apologists. In this he stands more nearly with Ignatius and Polycarp. For him the letters have almost reached the same apprehension which before had obtained for Gospels and Prophets only.

In the Acts of the Martyrs of Scili in Numidia of the 17th of July, 180 A.D., a North African Christian is related to have been asked by the proconsul, "What do you keep in your strong box there?" He replied, "Our holy books, and besides, the letters of the Apostle Paul."[1] That Gospels as well as the Old Testament are here meant under the phrase "our holy books" we may certainly assume. The Pauline material is not yet quite on the same footing with these. Nevertheless it was preserved in the churches.

Allusion has been made to the fact that Origen in his time answered the great attack upon Christianity which the philosopher Celsus had made about 175 A.D., under the title of The True

[1] J. Armitage Robinson, *Texts and Studies*, i. 2, Cambridge, 1891, p. 113.

Word. The work itself has been lost, as have so many others of the writings of the early opponents of Christianity. But it was answered in such detail, that no small part of it has been reconstructed out of the argument of Origen. We gather that it was the most formidable literary attack which Christianity had suffered until Origen's time. In some sense it was the embodied answer of the ancient world to Christianity. Celsus was especially bitter against the Christians because, following their superstition, they are withdrawn from the service of the state in the dark time which he sees coming on. After exhausting the resources of his scorn, he yet ends with an exhortation which has some pathos in it, that the Christians shall yet return to reason and join hands with all good men against the evils which threaten to overwhelm all. Celsus' information concerning Christianity is gathered from oral testimony, but partly also from Christian writings which he has read. He seems to have read everything of which he could hear. He declares that the Christians had four times and even oftener rewritten and changed the form of their narrative concerning Jesus.[1] But from the four Gospels he does not distinguish apocryphal material. The gnostic literature is for him as truly Christian literature as the rest. There is for him no official literature of the church to which he can hold himself, that is, no Canon of the New

[1] *Contra Celsum*, ii. 27. See Holtzmann, *Einleitung*, 3 Aufl., 1892, p. 111.

Testament beside the Old. And yet, in large part, his citations are drawn from the synoptic Gospels.

In speaking of the exaggeration of the worth of the Old Testament on the part of some of the Apologists, we intimated that it was a natural reaction against that exaggeration, and but the continuation of certain anti-Jewish tendencies in Christianity itself, which came to its expression when certain other men of this very time rejected the Old Testament altogether. And if the over-emphasis upon the Old Testament retarded for a moment the growth of a Canon of New Testament writings, yet, on the other hand, inevitably, with the rejection of the Old Testament, the collection of New Testament writings and the appeal to these as alone authoritative became natural and necessary. We may be sure that a Canon of the New Testament would have arisen in the rising catholic church, quite apart from the influence of the heretical sects. But it is interesting to note that within those sects a movement in the direction of the formation of a Canon was going on, which was the direct parallel of the movement in the body of the church itself. And indeed, in some respects, this heretical action anticipated the action of the church itself. If one had no Old Testament, then, the more, must one have a collection of authoritative Christian writings. The time was past when the movement could get on altogether without documents. And if one allowed himself to differ in capital matters with the leaders of the church, then, the more, must one have apostolic documents wherewith to sustain those differing opinions. The leaders of the heretical sects made instant and consequent use of the principle with which the leaders of the great body of the church operated only timidly at first. In some degree, the shaping of the Canon within the church became necessary in order to refute the claims which the heretics were already making concerning New Testament Scriptures.

The gnostic leaders all sought to give sanction to their peculiar tenets through the fiction that Jesus had committed certain more intimate truths to certain chosen ones only of his Apostles. These truths were then handed down in a secret tradition different from that common in the body of the church. These truths might pertain to phases of life and doctrine which were not for every man to know or strive to follow, but which concerned only those Christians who cared for this kind of illumination. In earlier times neither the man within the church nor the man outside of it, would have had need thus to trace back his new ideas through supposed secret tradition to the Apostles. He would simply have said that he himself had a revelation. But the time of such spontaneity, or, rather, of any general credence in such spontaneity, was past. The notion of two ideals of wisdom, the notion of salvation by wisdom at all, as distinguished from salvation by character, was as far as possible from anything which Jesus ever taught. But it was a notion widespread in the Hellenic world. The church did at this time nobly declare that there had been no such secret tradition, that the Gospel was for all, and the kingdom of Heaven was open to all believers. But the later ecclesiastical notion of the priest, as the sole rightful interpreter of the Gospel, is only this same gnostic idea to which the heretical leaders had sprung in an instant, but at which the great body of the church was slow to arrive, and of which it has been still more slow to get rid. It was a Gnostic, Marcion, to whom is ascribed the first collection of New Testament writings under the apprehension of them as his sole authoritative documents for reference. And Marcion's reference to them had for its main purpose the sustaining of such theories as these which I have just described.

Marcion was a Pontian, born in Sinope on the Black Sea, a ship-owner, and a man of means.[1] He seems to have come to Rome about the year 140 and to have been a member of the Roman Christian community. The account in Hippolytus of the sins of his youth is to be received with some hesitancy. These things were easily alleged after a man became a heretic. No one mentioned them at the time of his reception into the Roman community. Already in the time of Justin's First Apology he was deemed a dangerous heretic. He was the head of a sort of school, which, after

[1] See the article, *Marcion*, by Gustav Krüger, in Herzog, *Real-Encyklopädie*, 3 Aufl., 1903, xii. p. 266.

his breach with the Roman community, became the nucleus of the Marcionite church. Tertullian and Epiphanius refuted his writings, and much that we know concerning Marcion must be gathered out of the argument of his enemies. There seems, however, to be no doubt that he attempted a thoroughgoing treatment of the Christian tradition in the light of theories which he had accepted, and with the suppression or alteration of those documents which did not accord with his theories. For his gospel he took the Gospel according to Luke. He removed from it, or altered in it, all that bore upon the connection of Christianity with Judaism, or, again, upon the reality of the human life of Jesus. The God of the Old Testament was not the same God with the God of the New. If the Christian faith were rightly understood, there could be nothing but contradiction between it and the Old Testament. The second part of Marcion's collection was made up of the Pauline Letters, except the Pastorals. But these letters were also in good degree rewritten, and filled with glosses interpreting them in the Marcionite sense. The revelation of God which came to Jesus was at once corrupted by the Jewish element in the Christian church. Paul was the only one who had ever really understood his Master. But even his letters had been interpolated and falsified by Judaizers. Marcion was the only one who had ever really understood Paul. Marcion's opponents accused him, not without good ground, of interpolating and falsifying apostolic documents. He held that it was at his hands that these documents were reduced to their true compass and restored to their purity. It is a singular frame of mind in which a man can allow himself such arbitrary procedure with documents, and then demand of himself and of others such absolute faith in the documents which he has thus emended. But this strict appeal of the Marcionites to certain apostolic documents as against others is not without its relation to the very process by which the church, a little later, set up what it took to be apostolic writings against all other writings whatsoever.

The conflict was unceasing, from the time of Justin onward, with the gnostic movement. The strife was with systems of thought which were indefinitely more erratic than was this of Marcion, and of far less moral earnestness as well. Marcion was indeed misled by his fanatical antagonism to everything Jewish, and no one could defend his procedure with the apostolic writings. At the same time it appears that though he was a man of narrow nature and of mediocre mind, he was yet intensely concerned with the ethical content of these documents and their meaning for men's lives. It was not that he, in mere speculative interest, wrested the documents to sustain fantastic theories of the universe, as so many others of the Gnostics did. The church soon found itself compelled to bring into some sort of catalogue those writings of apostolic men which were to be read in the catholic churches. In the fixed texts of these books the church came to seek the basis of its theological development, as against the vagaries of gnostic doctrine and the flood of apocryphal documents and of separatist interpretations. In the struggle with Gnosticism the Canon was made. No man, after the end of the second century, ever seriously attempted to put forth new documents as apostolic and authoritative, or to emend old ones in the way that Marcion had done. The body of that which Christians would admit to be Scripture was substantially made up. And this body of literature became a universal inheritance. It was the inheritance of the orthodox and of the heretical sects alike. No man might part with that inheritance altogether and still claim to be a Christian. However widely men might differ, henceforth, as to the interpretation of this body of Scripture, it was the same body of Scripture which they all henceforth claimed to interpret.

There was indeed one moment of reaction before the church definitively parted with that idea of immediate and general inspiration of the Holy Ghost which it had cherished from the beginning. The subjects of this immediate inspiration, the men who spoke because they were filled with the Holy Ghost, had stood in the earliest church in place of books and even of the ascended Christ himself. Such men and women were preëminently the bearers of the new revelation and the interpreters of the old. But that state of things could not last. Vagaries were inevitable. The first great moral impulse received from Jesus had spent itself. That impulse could be made fresh again only by contact with Christ such as men could now find only in the Gospels. The theory of immediate inspiration had had consequences which the Apostle Paul himself deemed very questionable. A little later, imposture had been not unknown, and the evils of fanaticism not unfelt. It was a theory which in the extreme form of it, at any rate, was bound to give place with the lapse of time, with the waning of the first enthusiasm, and with the presence of reflecting and cultivated people in the Christian church. And when this sense of immediate inspiration gave way, something must take its place. That thing was the body of the apostolic writings, viewed as the authoritative witness to Christ, as oracles of God and the depositary of the divine wisdom.

Shortly after the middle of the second century there appeared in Phrygia one Montanus, supported by two women, Maximilla and Priscilla. Montanus claimed to be the Paraclete whom Jesus promised. He professed to be perfect, and exhorted men to perfection. The age of the Law and of the Prophets was but the childhood of man. Even the time of the Gospel in Christ was but man's youth. The new period of the Paraclete was to be the full maturity of the race. Montanus made but little use of Scripture, except of that passage in the Fourth Gospel in which he recognized his own commission. He is alleged by others to have favored the Apocalypse. The end of the world was soon coming at Pepuza. Stringent fasting and penitence were enjoined. Hatred of all art and learning characterized the new movement. The leaders, and perhaps the body of the adherents generally, were excommunicated from the churches. Maximilla survived the other two for some years and under her able leadership the movement made inroads upon the church of Asia Minor, and at one time seemed likely to sweep everything before it. It drifted into fanaticism, and in some cases, no doubt, into gross immorality. Yet the movement had wide success, and that far beyond the land of its origin. Tertullian became an adherent. It had confessors and martyrs of whom the church might have been proud. It did not wholly disappear until the sixth century.

Nor can it be denied that the movement, even in its distorted form, embodied a primary principle of Christianity. Movements like this have recurred, now and then, throughout the Christian ages. But there is this difference. Montanus had no New Testament Scripture, in the sense in which we understand that word. He had no canon of inspiration to which his own must be referred. He had no Christian sacred book already acknowledged, and along with which his own new revelations must be read. The New Testament Canon came into existence, as canon, partly to control such wandering inspirations as his own. It became a part of the faith of subsequent Christendom to give to the inspiration of the Apostles, and to the revelation as it came through Christ, a specific sense and an altogether unique quality, and in this sense to say that the age of revelation was past. The Christians would have said that what we, under the guidance of the Holy Ghost, have henceforth to do, is to interpret into our own life and time the Scriptures of the New Testament.

The very incarnation of this new spirit of authority are two writers whom we have already often named. These are Irenæus and Tertullian. Irenæus was an Asiatic, but spent his whole later life among the Greek-speaking peoples in the valley of the Rhone, and died as Bishop of Lyons. Tertullian, on the other hand, wrote in Latin. He was a native of North Africa, and a Roman in spirit through and through. The lots of these two men would seem to have been cast far apart; but in thought they are close together. Both had strong feeling for the rising catholic church. Both used the Canon, as they came to conceive it, as the divine instrument in the consolidating of the organization of that church.

Irenæus speaks more than once of his boyhood in Asia Minor. But he seems to have left that country before 155 A.D. He was teaching in Rome at the time of the death of Polycarp. He appears to have succeeded the martyr bishop Pothinus in Lyons, after the year 177. Even before that time he would seem to have been in high honor in the churches of the Rhone valley, having been chosen to bear to Rome the touching letter concerning the persecution, which was written on behalf of the churches in Lyons and Vienne. He died about 200 A.D. He was a man much beloved and possessed of qualities of leadership. In all the great controversies of his time he had his part. But with all his zeal he exerts an influence for peace in the midst of those controversies. Characteristic is his appeal to Victor, Bishop of Rome, beseeching Victor not to excommunicate the Asiatic Christians for their attitude in the paschal controversies. He is known to us chiefly through his writings against the heresies of the age. For Irenæus the fourfold Gospel is assured.[1] Two Apostles and two pupils of Apostles transmit to us thus, beyond dispute, the tradition concerning Our Lord. It was Irenæus also who made a beginning of the use of the four living figures named in the Apocalypse, the ox, the lion, the man, and the eagle, as symbols of the four Evangelists. Every departure from the sacred number of the Gospels, whether for the acceptance of a greater number or for the rejection of one of these, is heresy. The letters of Paul belong also unequivocally to the new Scripture. The new Scriptures are as truly the gift of God for the guidance of the church as were the old. It is interesting to note that in all of Irenæus' New Testament citations — and he has

[1] See Jülicher, *Einleitung*, p. 303.

more than two hundred from Paul alone—he knows well whence his citations are taken, and lays weight upon the naming of his sources. On the other hand, as to the Old Testament quotations, he frequently does not know what book he quotes. The apostolic writings are to the Christians what the Law and the Prophets had been to the Jews. Up to Irenæus' time the word Scripture had been the solemn distinction of the Old Testament; in Irenæus, however, the word is used for the books of the new covenant as well. Only the title New Testament does not yet occur. It was the Apostles who truly delivered the oral tradition. It was these alone who transmitted to us the written record. These records, therefore, take the place of the Apostles as the witness of Christ in the church. For Irenæus the core of the apostolic part of the New Testament, as distinguished from the Gospels, was of course constituted by the Pauline Epistles. How many letters other than the Pauline letters Irenæus knew, it is not possible for us to make out. Certainly he had First Peter and First and Second John. But there is at any rate no such fixed determination of a canonical number of Epistles as we have seen above in the case of the Gospels.

Tertullian was the earliest of the Latin ecclesiastical Fathers in the same sense in which Irenæus had been the first Greek Father of the church. He was born in Carthage, the son of a soldier, and was an advocate by profession. He was converted, perhaps in Rome, before the year 197. He became presbyter in Carthage, and at some time between 202 and 207 he broke with the catholic community, to become a Montanist. He was a man of education. But when he became a Christian he could never speak with sufficient contempt of æsthetic culture and secular learning. He is perhaps the most original of the Christian writers before the Nicene age. He presents the singular contrast of a man who was, at times, intensely a legalist in his appeal to Scripture and the episcopal organization as his authority, but who, again, was uncompromising in his adherence to what he deemed a higher law. It was under this last impulse, of course, that he gave himself up to Montanism. His use of the word Scripture is the same with that of Irenæus. The weight of the New Testament is derived from the fact that it was written by Apostles who had diligently handed on that faith which they received from Christ. He calls the apostolic writings "the divine literature." He has a particular fondness for the lawyer's word, "Instrumentum," the legal record in a case, the document in evidence, the means of proof. He has the phrase "the whole Instrument of both Testaments." He uses this word Instrument even of the parts of the apostolic writing; for example, "the Instrument of Paul," to which, by the way, the Hebrews does not belong, and is therefore of less worth. But not even Tertullian has the actual title, "the New Testament." He, as well as Irenæus, speaks of the Old Testament usually under the title, "the Law and the Prophets," as also of the New under the title, "the Gospel and the Apostles."

The actual title, "the New Testament," for the books, as distinguished from the same phrase in the sense of the new covenant in Christ, seems to occur for the first time in a passage which Eusebius has preserved from some unknown writer against Montanism, who has been assigned approximately to the year 193.[1] That title occurs in this significant phrase: "The doctrine of the New Testament, to which it is impossible that anything should be added, and from which nothing should be subtracted by one who has resolved to live according to the Gospel." The title occurs soon afterward in Clement, in Origen many times, and with all subsequent writers. It need not be said that for those who use this title, the reckoning of the New Testament as on the same level with the Old Testament is a thing achieved.

To these testimonies from the western church at the end of the second century we must add that of the Muratori Fragment.[2] This Fragment is a portion of a list found in 1740 by the famous Milanese librarian, Muratori, embedded in a manuscript of Ambrose, with which manuscript it is needless to say that the Fragment has nothing to do. It contains a list of the books of the New

[1] Eusebius, *H. E.* v. 16. 11.
[2] See Zahn, *Gesch. d. N. T. Kanons,* ii. 1-143.

Testament and, presumably, had been preceded by a list of the books of the Old Testament, as well. It is in barbarous Latin, which perhaps is due to the copyist, if the original was in Greek. Greek was certainly the prevailing language of the Roman Christian community until toward the end of the second century. The origin of the Fragment in Rome is reasonably certain, and the time of its appearance can be determined with comparative accuracy. Probably it was written before the year 190. It is interesting to us, because it is the first document which we possess which makes a business of enumerating the books in order, and concerns itself exclusively with the question which occupies us in these lectures.

The first line of the Fragment is broken and begins with the mention of Mark. But there is no doubt that the author knew also the Gospel according to Matthew. He mentions no other Gospels than the four. He has thirteen letters of Paul, but no mention of the Hebrews. He discusses letters of Paul to the Laodiceans and Alexandrians, which he deems spurious. There is no mention of First or Second Peter, of James, or of Third John. Besides the Apocalypse of John, he himself would accept the Apocalypse of Peter. In regard to Hermas, on the other hand, he knows that some are inclined to receive it. He himself rejects it, as not being of apostolic origin. One might infer from this last sentence that apostolic authorship was the principle of admission to the

THE END OF THE SECOND CENTURY 113

Canon. But that principle is not consistently carried through. Notable is the coincidence of this list with that which we have gathered from Irenæus and Tertullian. One sees how widespread is the agreement which is manifest, thus before the year 200. In Gaul, Carthage, Rome, and Asia Minor we find this sacred body of apostolic writings, which are to be read on the Lord's day along with the Old Testament in the Christian churches.

If we should turn for a moment to Alexandria, in this same last decade of the second century, we should discover that the Alexandrine Canon differed not a little, both in the idea and in the compass of it, from that which we have seen current in the West. Clement, who had been born of pagan parents, possibly in Athens, was the great teacher, along with Pantænus, in the school for catechumens in the church at Alexandria, before the year 190. He was driven out by the persecution in 202 or 203, and seems to have died in the Orient, some time before the year 215. He was a man who had read and travelled much. He was the first to work out a system of Christian doctrine in something like a harmonious way. He was the defender of learning, and insisted upon the need of it to the noblest Christian life. The influence of Plato upon him is everywhere evident. Thoughts like these are cardinal for him: the Logos of God is the teacher of man, and the purpose of God is the education of the race. His Protreptikos belongs in the class of the Apologies. But in the skill of its composition, and as well in the beauty of its language, it far surpasses most of these. His Paidagogos, or Teacher, is one of the most charming of the early Christian writings. It is filled with the truest spirit of learning, with deep piety, and with tender interest for the welfare of others. It is with reluctance that one gives up those beautiful hymns which have been assigned to Clement. But the opinion of most scholars is against their Clementine origin. The best known of them is in many of our hymn books: —

> Shepherd of tender youth
> Guiding in love and truth
> Through devious ways,
> Christ our triumphant king,
> We come thy name to sing,
> Hither our children bring
> Tributes of praise.

For Clement, as for Irenæus and for Tertullian, the four Gospels make up that portion of the Canon. The Gospel according to the Egyptians he deems less trustworthy as a source of information concerning Jesus. But he cites, as from Scripture, words of the Lord from other than canonical sources. He has fourteen letters of Paul; that is, he includes in this number the Epistle to the Hebrews. In fact, he frequently alludes to the Hebrews as a work of Paul. Of the catholic Epistles he has First Peter, First and Second John, and Jude. Besides these he has, of course, the Book of the Acts, and also the Apocalypse. He cites Hermas as divine revelation. The letters of Barnabas and of Clement of Rome are writings of Apostles, and the Didachè is Scripture. From all of this it is very evident that Clement took a more generous view of writings outside of the subsequent Canon than did Irenæus or Tertullian. He manifests more understanding than does either of these of the conditions under which the Christian literature had grown up. He realizes that the process of the formation of the Canon was a more or less conscious selection. He recognizes many books outside of the Canon as inspired. Even the Sibyl was a prophetess of God to the heathen. It is as if to him the Canon were but the centre of the sphere of revelation, and as if the lines of that revelation went out into all the realm of knowledge and of life. This is a position absolutely unthinkable to the narrow and legalistic mind of Tertullian. Clement knows that even the Canon itself had a different content and area in different lands which he had visited. This, also, Tertullian would hardly have owned.

And now that we have reached the turning-point in our discussion, we may pause to consider for a moment the forces which we have seen leading up to the canonization. How the thing looked to the great theologians of the later church we may learn from two striking examples.[1]

That zealous exegete and commentator, Theodoret, who died in 457 A.D., elaborates the well-known

[1] Given by Jülicher, *Einleitung*, p. 307.

theory of the Song of Solomon, that it is an allegory of Christ and the church. He well knows that there are those who dissent from this interpretation, and who would take the book in its obvious literary sense as a praise of faithful love. But to these he replies, that we ought to remember how much wiser and more spiritually minded than we, were the blessed Fathers who had put this book in the class of sacred Scriptures, canonizing it as a book to be read for the spiritual profit of the church. Certainly they would never have done this, had they taken such a commonplace view of the book as that which his opponents suggest. We might say in passing that we have here clearly before us the situation in which, even as regards such a book as the Canticles, men no longer ask themselves in natural way as to the meaning of the book and its claim to a place in the Canon. But they find the book in the Canon and attribute to it a meaning accordingly. And this, which happens to an Old Testament book, befell the New Testament books as well. The whole allegorical method of exegesis is only a method of finding an extraordinary meaning in a book whose ordinary and natural meaning does not seem exalted enough to suit the character attributed to the Scripture as a whole. But the main point for us in this citation from Theodoret is his acknowledgment that the origin of the collections of Scripture was in free choice, and that that choice was guided by a spiritual intent.

The same general notion of the way in which the Canon came to be may be gathered from that which Origen says in reference to the preface to the Gospel according to Luke. He declares that, just as in the case of the Old Testament the gift of the discriminating of spirits operated to make the collection what it was, so was it also in the case of the New Testament. " Many set out to write Gospels. But those who were responsible for the guidance of the church would not receive all of those works. They chose out these four, and these only, to give them place and honor in the Christian church." Here is the clear sense that the New Testament had come to pass by process of choice, and that the church itself, through its leaders, had exercised that choice. These leaders are assumed to have been guided by the divine Spirit in that exercise of choice. Nothing could be truer than is this apprehension of the history which we have reviewed. The New Testament Canon is the work of the leading thinkers and practical guides, the bishops and theologians of the second and third centuries. The influence of single personalities was unquestionably great. The feeling and custom of individual communities was operative. The practice of other communities was no doubt consulted. But the decision was with the bishops, we may be sure.

And no such remarkable unanimity of choice as that which we have observed is thinkable except we suppose that, from all sides, like forces were making for the decision, and essentially similar points of view for the canonization prevailed. Nothing is more striking than the fact that there were no great councils, synods, or decrees touching the Canon until long after the time to which we refer. There is an obscure allusion in one of Tertullian's tracts, as if in an African provincial synod which he mentions, the matter had been subject of debate.[1] But this is an isolated case. Synods and councils had no influence which we can trace in the making of the Canon. They simply registered the Canon after it was made. Even when Origen discusses differences of opinion in the several national churches, he nowhere intimates that there were conferences of the church leaders to secure a compromise of these differences. That compromise came to pass, that uniformity was secured, apparently through usage and personal influence.

It is important to remember this, because in the excess of zeal with which the historical view of this matter has been taken up, some have allowed themselves to speak as if the Canon were somehow the arbitrary and intentional contrivance of shrewd church leaders to secure ecclesiastical ends. The question is sometimes debated as if it were possible that the most valuable books were those which had been left out of the collection, and then destroyed in order that men might not know how valuable they were. But it is not evident how we can ever know that just the most valuable books were those

[1] Tertullian, *De Pudic.* 10. See Holtzmann, *Einleitung*, p. 138.

which have left no trace. It has been hinted that the determination to sustain a given doctrinal view may have guided the selection. But in truth, when one reflects, what chiefly impresses us is the great variety of doctrinal views which are included within the New Testament collection. It is difficult to see that one doctrinal view dominates the New Testament. Or if any such view were intended thus to dominate, it is not easy to see why the traces of the others were not more diligently removed. Variety of doctrinal type was just the trait of the second generation of the second century. And this was the generation which in good part fixed the usage of the New Testament books. It is true that the moment at which the church became conscious of this body of literature as New Testament, was proximately coincident with that moment in which the Roman baptismal symbol was carried back to the Apostles as the rule of faith, and bishops came to deem that they ruled by a divine right, in the name of the Apostles and of Christ. But this body of literature, although not yet under the apprehension of it as New Testament, had been in use in the services for worship in the Christian communities, with but insignificant additions or subtractions, already a generation before the doctrinal or the ecclesiastical issue became acute.

It cannot have escaped us in this study of it, how profound and vital the movement was, how inevitable and irresistible it was, how far it was from being merely a superficial arrangement, an artificial convention, an ecclesiastical design. The movement, in its decisive character, was already far on the way before even those leaders who had greatest insight cherished any design concerning it. It was far on the way before the great mass of the Christian people so much as knew what was happening. And yet it was the mass of the Christian people who, out of the depths of their religious life and need, were furnishing the very force by which the end was being achieved. Time was when historians were disposed to credit the great makers of history, and even masses of men, with full consciousness of all that they accomplished. Every great movement in human history proves the contrary. Here, for example, we see that the Christian movement had within itself, all unconsciously, both the goal toward which it moved and the force by which it was ceaselessly propelled toward that goal. Men were the free and voluntary bearers of that impulse. They were, without knowing it, the incarnation of that impulse. And yet it would be altogether false to say that any one of them perceived the full issue at the beginning, or, until later stages, deliberately set himself to further that issue. It is just such movements as these which impress us with the sense of the guidance of God in the life of man.

LECTURE IV

THE CLOSING OF THE CANON IN THE WEST

LECTURE IV

THE CLOSING OF THE CANON IN THE WEST

IN the preceding lecture the Muratori Fragment engaged our interest as being the first list which has come down to us in which the attempt is made to outline the New Testament Canon. It is the first formal endeavor to mark the boundaries of the new collection of writings which were fast coming to be regarded as sacred Scripture, parallel to the Old Testament, and indeed, for Christians, of authority greater than that of the Old Testament. The purpose of the author — whom, by the way, Lightfoot thought to have been Hippolytus — was to declare what books belonged to this new body of Scripture, and what books, even though in use in Christian communities, were to be deemed as not belonging to that body. We assumed that the fragment was written at some time before the year 190.

But the Muratori Canon is still more interesting as revealing to us some, at least, of the principles of discrimination, as these lay in the author's mind. It gives us a measure of insight into the motives which prevailed with him in his decision concerning this book or that. And these motives are, in a way, much more interesting than are the decisions themselves. We may therefore pause at this point in our narrative and, taking up the Muratori Canon once again, ask ourselves questions concerning it, of a different sort from those which before engaged our thought. The fragment reveals some of the forces which were operative in the minds of the men of that age. It lets us see what constituted the claim of some of the major books, at all events, and what was the quality upon which the Christian acceptance or rejection of a given book as Scripture was made to depend. For of course this list, even if we suppose it to have been written by some authoritative person, is not a decree. The author simply registers what he deems to be the prevailing Christian sentiment, and puts forth reasons with which those whom he addresses are supposed to be familiar. The issue of the application of these principles, he acknowledges, may not be the same for all men's minds. But the point of view is that which he supposes everybody shares. And this point of view, these motives of the canonization, are far more important for us to consider than is merely the boundary of the Canon as, by the Fragmentist's time, and in that part of the world with which he was familiar, that boundary began to be achieved. Compared with these guiding apprehensions of the matter the question whether this or that book was by a given author included in the rising Canon is of minor consequence.

The Muratori Canon remarks certain differences among the Gospels. The author has reflected upon the fact that not all of the Evangelists speak as eye-witnesses of the life of Jesus. He is therefore careful to assert that those two who were not of the Twelve, namely Mark and Luke, give us their narratives under the authority of Apostles, namely of Peter and of Paul. The author thus belongs to the time which has begun to reckon Paul, to all intents and purposes, as one of the Twelve. The antagonism of the Twelve to Paul has been forgotten. It is well known that the tradition never did take any account of the election of Matthias to take the place of Judas. The author has, however, not reflected upon the fact that we have no knowledge that Paul was an eye-witness to a single event in the life of Jesus. Or, rather, the author belongs to the time in which the inspiration of the Apostle was held to take the place of his having been an eye-witness. He explicitly says that the great facts are guaranteed in all the Gospels, and are complete in all, through the influence of the one controlling divine Spirit. The origin of the Fourth Gospel is ascribed to the fact that the Evangelist John was urged by the other Apostles and by the bishops to make this addition to the knowledge of the world concerning Jesus. Andrew, indeed, had special revelation that he should make of John this same request. Emphasis is laid upon the fact that the author of the Fourth Gospel describes himself, in his First Epistle, as one who had seen and heard that of which he told. The being an eye-witness is evidently the main matter with reference to the authorship of Gospels. And yet, as we have seen, the distinction is not rigidly carried through. According to the Muratori Fragment the Book of the Acts also confines itself to that which Luke himself had witnessed. This is the reason why the narrative breaks off as it does without relating the death of Paul.

The letters of Paul are placed in a curious order, beginning with the First Corinthians. They are, indeed, addressed to seven different communities. But that very fact, that their number is thus the sacred number of completeness, is evidence that the letters were intended by their author for the instruction and edification of all the world. The fact that there are also seven letters in the Book of the Revelation shows, by that same round and mystical number, the destination of these, and of the book in which they are embodied, for the edification of all Christendom. How surely would the author of the Fragment have added here the interesting fact that there are also seven catholic Epistles, if all of the seven had been known to him. The four letters of Paul to individuals do not so easily fall into a scheme. But these have become the property of all the world because they deal with the universal problem of church government; a statement which, by the way, is hardly true of the letter to Philemon.

But, after all, this scheme of sevens is not to be taken too seriously. It is only a devout afterthought. For the writer rejects letters of Paul to the Laodiceans and to the Alexandrians, which he knows to be current, not because they do not fall in with his scheme, but because to his mind they were palpably manufactured by heretics. He says that they cannot be put with the genuine letters, as gall cannot be mixed with honey. In all of this, however, one sees what it is at which the author aims. He is seeking to find a reason why these books should be deemed to have a universal application, whereas they bear upon their very face the evidence that their original destination was a limited and specific one. The author has not risen to the thought that these books have a universal significance because they enshrine so much of the original Christian inspiration, no matter what was the conscious intention of the authors as they wrote. The Fragmentist does not perceive, what is to us so obvious, that, in the large, the Christian church accepted these books because of its feeling for their spiritual content, and only afterward reasoned about their authorship, their original destination, and other concrete facts of the same sort.

But what the author says concerning Apocalypses is most interesting. For himself he accepts, beside our Book of the Revelation, the Apocalypse of Peter, although he knows that there are many Christians who will not suffer it to be read in the churches. But the Shepherd of Hermas, though many love it, may not be placed upon the same level with the revelation of the Apostle John. It has been written within comparatively recent years, and by a man whom some of the Fragmentist's readers may have known. It may still be read privately for edification. But the inference is that only such works as are deemed to have been written by Apostles, or, at least, within the apostolic circle, are to be read in the services for public worship. There is no place for the Shepherd among the writings of the Prophets, that is, in the Old Testament, because the number of the Prophets is, for all time, complete. That assertion, by the by, no man of the time of the author of the Shepherd would have admitted. And, as we have seen, Athanasius did put this book and the Teachings of the Twelve Apostles with certain Apocryphal books of the Old Testament. It escapes the Fragmentist, for the moment, that the Book of the Revelation is a prophetical book within the limits of the New Testament.

When the author of the Muratori Fragment comes to speak of books current among the Valentinians, among the Marcionites, and in other sects, it is with the explicit purpose of causing the Canon, as accepted within the church, to stand out in contrast with those works which had weight in communities which he deemed to be Christian only in name. What the Fragmentist says of the

Apostles, as being the witnesses, "at the end of the dispensation," would seem to be aimed at the Montanist assertion of continuous Christian inspiration and of a new revelation to the Montanists themselves.

If now we proceed to inquire how these motives of the canonization lay in the mind of Irenæus, we shall find that, from the nature of his writings, it is not so easy to get an answer in detail. But some things are clear. The church is "built upon the foundation of the Apostles." This is the thought which Irenæus constantly reiterates. Through the unbroken series of the bishops from the Apostles' time the church is secured against the loss of its sacred inheritance. You might almost expect to hear Irenæus say that, because of this unbroken tradition through the bishops from the Apostles, the church has the less need of a Canon of Scripture. But that is by no means the case. On the contrary, it is of supreme importance that the Christians should be able to compare the doctrine and order of the church, in any age, with that outlined in the apostolic documents, and so to prove the identity of the latest with the earliest Christianity. The Apostles and the bishops are, in their succession, the living bond between the church and Christ. But the Apostles' works are the guarantee which all men may read that the leaders of the church have not departed from the apostolic ways. There is no dissent of the apostolic writings one from another. There are no divergences, in order, life, or doctrine, among the apostolic churches. There never have been such divergences. The same Spirit of God which spoke through the Apostles in their lifetime, speaks now and teaches through their written word. The same Spirit of God which spoke through the Apostles in their lifetime, speaks and teaches now through the living leaders of the church. And these teachings are one. The writings of the Apostles contain therefore infallible truth, whether they transmit the narrative concerning Jesus, or warn against heretical teachings, or give counsel concerning the life of the believer, or touch upon the organization of the church. This series of ideas is repeated by almost all the western Fathers from Irenæus onward.

You might almost expect the rule to be laid down that, as everything in the Old Testament must be from prophets, so everything in the New Testament must be from the hands of Apostles. But to a consistent declaration of that sort we do not come. At times it is to the undoubted credibility of the eye-witness that his book owes its place in the Canon. Again, it is the spiritual gift with which he was endued, which gift the hearts of those who listen to his word must own. The question whether all the writings thus acknowledged had Apostles for their authors is not sharply answered. The question whether the Apostles wrote other books than those which the church thus used in its services for worship is not directly discussed. It appears that reflection, in any larger way, upon the conditions of the canonization, then first began when the Canon was already practically an accomplished fact. Reflection shaped itself to a theory concerning books which were already being devoutly read in the public worship of the church. It is not as if ordered and conscious reflection, at this time, and on the basis of some theory, decided what books ought to constitute the sacred Scripture of the New Testament, and then demanded that those books should be read. When men began consciously to reason, in any larger way, upon this matter, the magnitude with which they had to reckon was already mainly given. The burden of proof was on the side of him who would have withdrawn anything which was being read. And, equally, it was on the side of him who would have added anything which was not being read. First after the men had a New Testament do they appear to have asked themselves, why that New Testament which they had, took precisely the shape with which they were familiar. In consequence of this state of things the answers which they give appear to us, often, mere justification of existing circumstances. The theory is being stretched to meet the situation. The document is apostolic because it is read, and is not, as they continually say, read because it is apostolic. Or, again, the argumentation is so remote and fragmentary, so fantastic often, so inadequate, that one has to remind himself how irrefragable is the thing which was being argued for in so inconsequent a manner. With a kind of inevitableness and with irresistible force the Christians created their Canon. In unconsciousness they worked; or, if you choose, in that condition above the ordinary consciousness of mankind in which great works of genius are wrought, great events shape themselves, epochs are prepared, and great history, especially popular history, is made. We can hardly expect to be led by the church Fathers into the workshop where this thing was executed, and have explained to us the principles from which they wrought. They did not fully know the principles from which they wrought. Just why the New Testament appeared exactly at this juncture, and so rapidly, and in precisely the shape in which it appears, is a thing which no one of the contemporaries has been able fully to tell us. It is, sometimes, as if the men already indulged the naïve assumption that there had always been a New Testament; and supposed that men had always viewed the apostolic writings just as they now viewed them. There is much in the history of which we may be bold to say that we, at this distance, read it more accurately than did the men who participated in the making of that history.[1]

Despite its intimate relation to Judaism, and so to the Old Testament, Christianity was, after all, a new religion. And that new religion could not

[1] See Jülicher, *Einleitung*, p. 312 f.

be expected to go on indefinitely with only the old book. The Christians had not felt the lack of a book of their own at the first. So long as men had Jesus and the Apostles, so long as they had even prophets and teachers in every Christian community, who told of that which they themselves had witnessed, or spoke out of what was to them full and conscious inspiration of the Holy Ghost, no one thought of New Testament books. But the immense impression which Jesus had made lost something in being conveyed, even by those first witnesses, to others. Or, rather, it became evident that that impression could not always be conveyed in the manner in which the early witnesses had transmitted it. The immediate certitude was gone. The first enthusiasm waned. Christians "left their first love," as the Apocalypse poetically puts it. The sense of original inspiration was diminished. Speakers or exhorters in a given community were often wanting. Men were perhaps no longer present whose authority in questions of life and doctrine all would concede, and upon whom, beyond question, the Spirit of God rested. The Christians sought to make that good. The stronger was the sense of their own lack, the greater was the tendency of these men of the new time to preserve, and to defer to, everything written that had come down to them from the earlier and more favored generation. When men came to admit, despite the fact that the remains of the apostolic literature were scanty, that they yet gathered, in the rule, more inspiration for the Christian life out of this apostolic literature than out of the Old Testament plus the interpretation and the reminiscences of living teachers or of wandering prophets, then the placing of new Christian Scriptures beside the old sacred books had become inevitable.

Moreover, the richer the content of a religion in the realm of thought, the more that religion claims to be a complete system of truth, the more necessary is it that, sooner or later, it shall have a body of literature to which all can refer, and which has for all an acknowledged and regulative force. To ask when the New Testament arose is simply to ask when the necessity for such an external authority and the feeling of dependence upon the elder generation, gained ascendency over the fresh consciousness of spiritual power which had marked the earliest Christian time.[1] If this point had been reached soon after the death of the Apostles, it would not have been strange, when one remembers over what wide areas, and those in part areas by no means well prepared for it, the new Gospel spread. But the exigency would be felt with ever increasing force, as men of every nationality, of every sort of antecedent, and of every grade of culture thronged into the Christian church. The exigency would be felt with ever increasing force as Christianity began to draw to itself the attention of serious people, the world over, and men

[1] See Jülicher, *Einleitung*, p. 314.

began to ask, What is Christianity? It would be felt with ever growing urgency as Christianity began to assimilate to itself the elements of culture, and to transform with its spirit whole phases of man's life. It would be felt with ever growing urgency as men with strong interests, speculative and ascetic, approached Christianity from the outside and sought to appropriate its force for their own purposes. That this situation became acute in the conflict of Christianity with the Gnostics and with the Montanists is evident. A church in conflict with opposing elements would feel the need of documents and authorities earlier, possibly, than one which went its way in peace. But a church whose march was one long triumph, a religion whose superiority was on all hands conceded, if we could imagine such a case, would yet need to give an account of itself to others, and to come to an understanding of itself, as in the long run it could do only through documents and authorities. Quite apart from Gnosticism and Montanism the New Testament would certainly have come to pass.

We said that some of the Apologists, through their excessive veneration for the Old Testament, exerted an influence which retarded the growth of the New Testament. But on the other hand, it is obvious that the apologetic influence, in the large, would work to further the growth of the Canon. One could not expect Emperors and the learned among the pagans to understand what Christianity was and what it proposed, if one could refer only to the Old Testament and to the words of enthusiastic people. We have seen how a man like Celsus, being a man of books, would instinctively ask himself, What literature have these Christians? We have seen that, to some extent, the caricature which he drew was due to the fact that he described the whole movement as he saw it, and took, as acknowledged and representative, writings which many Christians would not have admitted to be such. Origen was at a great advantage, in answering Celsus, over any Christian who might have attempted the answer in Celsus' own time, in that he was able to point out this fact. He was able to say that such and such documents only were acknowledged among Christians as setting forth the pure ideal of Christianity. Of the rest, some were viewed with greater aversion by the Christians than they could possibly be viewed by Celsus himself.

We have seen that it was upon the regular reading of the apostolic literature in the public services of the Christians for worship that the hallowing of this literature followed. The later generations would have said that they read these books because they deemed them inspired and sacred. So we say to-day. The earlier generations read them because the books told of Christ and took the place of the Apostles. They came to deem sacred and inspired, writings which did thus tell of Christ and take the place of the Apostles, and which they had been accustomed to read, along with the inspired writings of the Old Testament, in the services for public worship. The Muratori canon shows how easily the one of these notions passed over into the other.

At the same time, we have more than once noticed the fact that in the Christian assemblages some books were long read, other than those which ultimately attained canonization. And men sometimes speak as if, at the point of our history which we have now reached, we had to think of a grand process of separation. Men write as if, in the canonization of these writings which had grown dear to the Christian heart, a great mass of other writings had fallen a sacrifice and been driven out of use in the Christian church. But in this respect it is easy to exaggerate. As, after the year 160, the New Testament began to grow apace, without doubt one writing and another was rejected in order to carry out the distinction of sacred and apostolic writings as against all others. But on the other hand, there is abundant evidence that, as one Christian community or province became cognizant of the differing practice of another, as churches compared their books with those read in public worship by neighboring churches, the growing canonization had the appearance, in some cases at least, of an enlargement of the area of the literature of devotion rather than that of a diminution of that literature. It may well have been some time after the outline of the Canon was tolerably fixed, before every church possessed every writing which belonged to that Canon. We must remember, also, that the books would naturally appear as separate rolls of parchment, or more likely of papyrus. Manuscripts of the whole New Testament, which we think of as a continuous book, in a few rolls at the most, are not talked of until the time of Constantine. It is doubtful if anywhere we have to think of a great reduction of the number of books as a thing suddenly resolved upon and authoritatively carried through. In the generation in which the notion of the Canon had been growing up and taking possession of the minds of men, the question of the limits of this body of literature, to which sacred character was to be attributed, had also been gradually settling itself. We have not to think of the abstract notion of the Canon as being first fully matured and then, in this matured shape, suddenly applied to all the literature treasured in the Christian communities here and there. The contacts of the churches one with another, and the comparison of their mutual practices, had already done away with the most striking differences. The debate within the church touching the boundary of the Canon continued indeed for almost two hundred years. But it was a debate which had been reduced to very narrow compass. It touched, after this time of which we speak, but a few books, and those not the most important ones.

That the final boundary line of the Canon fell

somewhat arbitrarily, no one denies. That that line failed to follow absolutely the distinction which it was supposed to register, all must admit. The men supposed themselves to be operating with the principle of apostolicity. As a matter of fact, they vindicated that which had vindicated itself as of spiritual worth in the Christian experience. In the large, we may say that the writings which had failed to vindicate themselves in public and solemn use as of spiritual worth were not put out of the Canon. They never got into the Canon to any great extent. One can clearly see, on the evidence offered by our own New Testament itself, that the maxim of its formation has not been to receive as little as possible. Rather, the disposition would seem to have been, to lose nothing which by any possibility might be apostolic, of all those writings which had proved themselves useful to edification in any important part of the church. It was this disposition which also inclined men, later, to take an unduly favorable view of the apostolicity of some books which they canonized, as, for example, in the case of the Hebrews, and surely in the case of Second Peter as well.

And, indeed, the Gospels and fragments of Gospels which have come down to us outside of the Canon do not make upon us the impression that the class to which they belong, even if we possessed it in far greater fulness than we do, would have added much to our knowledge concerning the Gospel of

Jesus. The fragments of the Gospels according to the Hebrews, according to the Egyptians, according to Peter, are either very meagre in their content, or they show a tendency to interpretation of their subject in far greater measure than do the canonical Gospels. The Gospels to which the preface of Luke refers were not put out of the public devotional use. They never got into that use in any larger way. There is no apocryphal Gospel whose wide dissemination can be proved. And if we speak of letters, we must own that the wandering argumentation of First Clement and, still more, the contentiousness and puerilities of Barnabas, have but little of that immediateness of religious feeling and communication which is so wonderful in Paul.

Surely we must marvel at the spiritual tact, and appreciation of the true issue which was involved, with which the Christian men of the generation before the Canon proceeded in the choice of books which should be publicly read. For it was these men who left relatively little for the later generation deliberately to reject. The makers of the New Testament in the final and authoritative stage proceeded not radically, but very conservatively. The Canon, as it was finally declared, is really only the codifying and legalizing of what was traditional. Whatever literature was read in the leading Christian communities from Sunday to Sunday in the last decades of the second century, that, after a time, men came to regard as divine Scripture, being led up to that idea by the long process which we have reviewed. That high authority which they found this literature, for inward and spiritual reasons, to possess, they soon came to conceive in outward fashion, and to explain in the manner in which they had already reasoned concerning the authority of the Old Testament. They ascribed it to an oracular inspiration of the book itself. This was the idea which the men of that generation, probably all unconsciously, put in the place of that other and simpler idea which the Christians had always had—the idea of the inspiration and authority of these Christian books as drawn from the Christ whose holy spirit they enshrined.

But, of course, when once the Canon had been thus conceived, the church grew sensitive to differences, and more eager that those differences should be blotted out. One might leave to the individual church the decision as to what was edifying to be read. That decision always had been left to the individual church. But one could not thus leave to chance, as it seemed, the declaration as to what was and what was not divine. The men did not see that, while it is easy to make an authoritative declaration concerning the apostolic origin of a given book, or concerning any similar external matter, the witness of the divineness of a book is, after all, its influence upon the hearts and lives of men. Where this influence is present no declaration is needed. And where this influence is absent no declaration is of any avail. But the formal decision of questions as to the apostolicity of this book or that, and the effort to coerce the churches to acceptance of these decisions, belong to a period long subsequent to the time of which we now speak.

We noted the fact that Clement, the representative of the Alexandrine church about the year 200, shows a truer appreciation of the nature of the Canon and more sense for its history than do his Roman and Latin-African contemporaries. His idea of the meaning of inspiration is less mechanical and external. The central body of literature which he deems sacred rays out at the edges and its spiritual quality passes off by gradation toward other Christian writings than those which became canonical, and even toward oracles not Christian at all. Moreover, the writings which to him are canonical possess the spiritual quality in varying degrees. They are therefore, in varying degree, of spiritual import to their readers. This lack of sharpness of outline and of legalistic quality remains characteristic of the canon of the Greek church, at all events until the time of Athanasius.

The sect of the Alogoi, in Asia Minor, about the year 180 or 190, denied the authenticity of the Apocalypse. They disputed the doctrine of the Logos in the Fourth Gospel, and from this fact derived their name. That strenuous opponent of Montanism in the Roman church about the year 200, the Presbyter Caius, according to Eusebius, described the Apocalypse as a forgery of the heretic Cerinthus, it being the book which, according to Caius, was most in favor with the Montanists.[1] From still another point of view the Apocalypse was drawn into question. It seemed to favor the chiliastic doctrine, of the thousand years' reign of Christ on earth before the general resurrection.[2] This view had been shared by Papias, and was not uncommon in his time. Justin adhered to it; Irenæus and Tertullian argued for it. Caius seems to have been the first who vigorously assailed it; Origen refuted it.[3] It was now repudiated. It must therefore, in the judgment of those who objected to it, receive no countenance from a book which was supposed to be of divine origin. Or, rather, a book which does countenance this doctrine has no right to a place in the collection of books which are held to be of divine origin and authority. In general, we may say that the Johannine portion of the Canon, in one or another of its fractions, Gospel, Apocalypse, or Letters, was the most disputed element in that very portion of the world, Asia Minor, where John was held to have lived and to have ended his days. These protests against the Apocalypse do not show that the Canon containing that writing

[1] Eusebius, *H. E.* iii. 28. 2.   [2] *Revelation* xx. 4.

[3] On Chiliasm, see Harnack, article "Millennium," in *Encycl. Brit.*, 9th ed., 1883, XVI. p. 314 ff. See *Dogmengeschichte*, 1st ed., Bd. I, p. 114, and note.

was not yet in existence. But they do prove that that Canon had not yet been so long in existence and in authority that the objection to one or another of its parts seemed monstrous. Men who had witnessed the growth of the Canon had no hesitation in subtracting this or that book from it if they saw fit. In the new emphasis upon the Apostles, such writings as were deemed to be not apostolical were everywhere to be removed from use. We recall the episode of Serapion, Bishop of Antioch, and the matter of the use of the Gospel according to Peter in the church at Rhossus.[1] The bishop withdrew his permission of the use of that Gospel when he discovered that it contained heretical doctrine. He does indeed say, in his letter, that the church has no tradition of any Gospel according to Peter. But his rejection of the book is not based upon the fact that he has investigated the question of its authorship. He judges it heretical, and determines its authorship accordingly. The distinction between these two points of view is one at which the men of that age never arrived. They did not realize the danger of moving in a circle. They did not perceive the risk of determining the type of apostolic doctrine from writings which chanced to be already acknowledged as those of Apostles, and then of rejecting other writings because they contained doctrinal apprehensions of a different type. There was the danger that they might accept as

[1] Eusebius, *H. E.* vi. 12. 2–6.

apostolic, writings which were much used and loved in the Church, if only these writings did not diverge too widely from the accepted doctrinal type. No one imagines that in this case of the Gospel according to Peter any error was made. But it is the point of view which we need to note.

A similar use of writings other than those which became canonical probably went on for some time in out-of-the-way places. Methodius of Olympus, the great opponent of the Origenist movement, about the year 300, had the Apocalypse of Peter and probably also Barnabas and the Didachè in his canon. And no one can read the passages in Eusebius in which he shows such zeal for the rejection of certain books without inferring that in his diocese of Cæsarea in Palestine the effort to compass their rejection had not thus far been altogether successful.[1] In general, debates concerning some such questions lived on in the East long after they had died out in the West.

Meantime, however, the Greek church had had in Origen its greatest ecclesiastical writer and one of the greatest theologians of all ages. Origen was the head of the catechetical school in Alexandria, over which Clement had presided at an earlier date. His position with reference to the Canon is interesting in itself, and of great importance also because of Origen's influence both upon his own time and upon the next succeeding gen-

[1] See Jülicher, *Einleitung*, p. 323.

erations. Unfortunately many of his works are lost, and many others exist only in unsatisfactory Latin translations. The man who before 250 A.D. was the greatest ornament of the Greek church, and to the description of whose life and work Eusebius enthusiastically devoted the greater part of the sixth book of his Church History, the ecclesiastical authorities of the sixth century condemned for heresy and, through the destruction of his works, did everything in their power to put an end to his influence.

He was called by the ancients the Adamantine, because of his iron diligence. He was born about the year 185, of Christian parents, in Alexandria. His father, Leonides, was his earliest instructor both in religion and in philosophy. He enjoyed also the instruction of Pantænus and of Clement. His father died the martyr's death in 202, and the family estates were confiscated. Origen was scarcely restrained from giving himself up to death at the same time with his father. He was enabled by a rich woman of Alexandria to continue his studies. He aided himself by teaching. Before he was seventeen years old he was an instructor in the school for catechumens. In the year 203 he was appointed by the bishop Demetrius to succeed Clement as the head of that school. Here he worked and studied for fifteen years. Accomplished in the Greek philosophy, he won over many pagans of the educated class. Held back from preferment, as he conceived, by jealousies in

Alexandria, he allowed himself, in the year 231, to be consecrated a presbyter, in Cæsarea, upon one of his journeys. For this offence against discipline he fell into controversy with his bishop. A synod, in the year 231 or 232, removed him from the presbyterate and banished him from Alexandria. He returned to Cæsarea and established a school somewhat similar to that in Alexandria, which became a centre of Christian learning. The popular exposition of the Scriptures in the public services for worship was a task to which he seems to have given himself with enthusiasm. From the persecution under Maximinus Thrax he made good his escape to Asia Minor. But in the persecution under Decius, while imprisoned in Tyre, he suffered injuries from which he died, probably in Tyre, in the year 254. The legend asserts that he wrote six thousand works. Certain it is that his literary activity was almost unexampled. But many of the writings which entered into any such extravagant enumeration must have been sermons and addresses. Even his letters were for a time preserved. We have alluded to his apologetic work, Contra Celsum. We should name his Principles, which we gather was his great dogmatic work, and also his Stromateis, a book in which it appears that he endeavored to show the agreement of Christian and philosophical teaching. But his incomparable service was as an exegete. Whether in more formal commentaries or in his homilies for popular instruction, he shows himself a master of interpretation. He set an example, and fostered in others a zeal for the study of the Scripture which has rarely been surpassed.[1]

Within the Holy Scriptures Origen knows no difference of value between the Old Testament and the New. He writes commentaries upon Matthew, John, and Romans as he writes upon Exodus and Leviticus. Of his mode of thought one sentence may serve for an example, "It is ours to study day and night the law of the Lord, and that not only in the new words of the Gospels and of the Apostles and of their revelation, but as well in the ancient writings of the Law, which had the shadow of good things to come, and in the corresponding testimony of the Prophets." All are inspired books and of infallible truth. It makes no difference for Origen's argument whether his proof texts come from the Old Testament or from the New. He often uses for his Canon the title, The New Testament, in contradistinction from the Old. It is possible that in this use of the title by Origen we have the first unquestionable application of it to the writings, as such, and that the phrase as it stands in Clement and the Antimontanist still refers to the new dispensation under Jesus, including, of course, the literature of that new dispensation.

That there are but four Gospels to be acknowledged is clearer to Origen than it had been to

[1] Eusebius, *H. E.* vi. 2. 3, 8, and especially 16 and 19.

Clement, and he has but one Apocalypse.[1] He says that the New Testament has place for apostolic writings only. Hence Hermas is not Scripture although it is revelation. He has fourteen letters of Paul, that is, he assigns the Hebrews to Paul. Yet he himself, in other places, expresses doubt about the Pauline authorship of the book. In one place he says of it that its author is known only to God. It is with him a favorite book.[2] He has all seven of the catholic Epistles, but speaks once of the "so-called Epistle of Jude." He knows that five out of the seven, namely, all except First Peter and First John, are not extensively in use, and in some places are rejected. He says, "What but the judgment of the ancients can decide concerning a work wearing the name of an Apostle and not discredited by heretical tendencies?" Accordingly he arranges all the works which come within the compass of his discussion in three classes, namely, those which are everywhere accepted, those everywhere rejected, and those which are still in doubt.[3] Rejected are such books as the Gospel according to the Egyptians, the Gospel which is in use among the adherents of Basilides, and the Gospel of the Twelve. Doubtful are Second Peter, Second and Third John, and probably also James and Jude. Sometimes it seems as if he would put Hermas

[1] Eusebius, *H. E.* vi. 25. 3 and 4; and vi. 26. 2.
[2] Eusebius, *H. E.* vi. 25. 11.
[3] Eusebius vi. 25. 3-14.

in this class. Unequivocally acknowledged are, of course, the four Gospels, the Acts, thirteen letters of Paul, and the Hebrews, though more often he says simply fourteen letters of Paul. Finally, in a statement which very much surprises us, he says that the Apocalypse of John belongs also in this class. And after all this classification one still finds Barnabas cited as a catholic letter, Clement of Rome in high honor, and a passage from the Didachè quoted as teaching of the Holy Scripture.

The Latin church, with its two foci at Rome and Carthage, possessed no man who for learning and insight was to be mentioned with Origen, in the period of which we speak. No man in the West showed a like interest in the history of the Canon or like appreciation of the fact that the Canon had a history. No man in the West showed a like knowledge of the actual state of things as it existed in different communities, or a like sense of the larger meaning of the New Testament.

Hippolytus was the bishop of a schismatic community of the Romans who, in the year 235, with the Roman bishop Pontianus, was deported to Sardinia, and probably died there in the mines. He was the author of several works of importance. He wrote still in Greek, and gives us a fair notion of his Canon. It is that of Irenæus and of the Muratori Fragment, except that Hermas and the

[1] Origen, *de Princip.* iii. 2. 7.

CLOSING OF THE CANON IN THE WEST 151

Apocalypse of Peter have disappeared altogether. The Apocalypse of John, on the other hand, is to him a much loved book and he defends it against Caius. He has but thirteen letters of Paul. The Epistle to the Hebrews he knows, but does not use it as Scripture. Quite as conservative is Cyprian; and Cyprian's writings, even more than those of Hippolytus, are of such a character as to give us a fair knowledge of the Canon as it existed in his mind. Next after Tertullian he was perhaps the most influential man in the development of the mode of thought and speech characteristic of the Roman Catholic church. Born in Carthage, in the early years of the third century, of a family of some distinction, he became a teacher of rhetoric in Carthage. He was baptized in the year 246. A few months thereafter he was consecrated priest. In the year 248 he was made bishop of Carthage. He escaped the earlier stages of the Decian persecution and set a shining example in the discipline of the community in that trying time, and in the organization of his church for charity toward the heathen in the period of the plague. He was in continual conflict in the church, however, both with men who, like Felicissimus, judged the conduct of those who had lapsed during the persecution too leniently, as Cyprian deemed, and as well, with men like Novatian, who judged the lapsed with too great severity. Cyprian was excommunicated by the Roman bishop Stephen, because he denied the validity of heretical baptism. He in turn denounced Stephen, and in a synod at Carthage in 256 A.D. he solemnly declared that the Roman bishop had no primacy over the other bishops. He was beheaded in a new outbreak of the persecution under Valerian in 258 A.D. He was a man less original than Tertullian, but of better balance. He was a pastor and teacher and practical executive rather than a theologian. Some of his tractates, and eighty-one letters, have come down to us, revealing a beautiful character and a great personal force. The titles of some of these little works are suggestive. They touch upon the treatment of the lapsed, upon the unity of the church, upon the Lord's Supper, upon good works and almsgiving, upon the fact that Christians, as well as heathen, died in the plague, upon the accusation that the atheism of the Christians was the cause of the evils of the time, upon fearlessness in face of martyrdom. The Apocalypse was in high honor with him. The Epistle to the Hebrews he never mentions. Of the seven catholic Epistles he has only two, namely, First Peter and First John.[1]

In general, for the whole Latin church, and so late as 395 A.D., we may say that only Lucifer of Cagliari desired to exclude the Apocalypse. And he had been long in banishment in the East, where he had learned of the oriental repudiation

[1] See especially, the quotations of Scripture in Cyprian's *De Exhort. Martyrii.*

of the book. It was obvious that despite the protest of the East, the West would never give up the book. On the other hand, as regards the Epistle to the Hebrews, the eastern churches had given it a secure place, in some cases, though by no means in all, under the direct assertion that it was the work of Paul. But the Latin church during this period either did not know the book or deemed it not the work of Paul. Some western writers left the question of its authorship an open one, or suggested that Barnabas might have written the book. But in the West, more than in the East, uncertainty concerning the authorship of a book had weight to keep it out of the Canon, even though the content of the book might be approved. In general one may say that where the Apocalypse was accepted the Hebrews was rejected, and conversely where the Hebrews was accepted the Apocalypse was in dispute. But to this statement one must record so distinguished an exception as that of Origen, alluded to above. The number of the catholic Epistles varies and grows but slowly. First John and First Peter are everywhere known. But the other five Epistles which we have seen so largely current in the East made slower progress in the West. And before the fourth century there is no evidence in the Latin church for the presence of Second Peter at all.

The Latin church had stronger feeling than had the Greek for the necessity of a sharp outline of the Canon. It was less conscious than was the Greek church of the gradation of spiritual quality among the books which it accepted. It was more often disposed to declare that the books which it rejected possessed no spiritual quality whatever. Classifications like that of Origen are almost never heard of. To these men a book is either inspired or else it is not inspired. It is either sacred or else it is profane. And if it has falsely claimed the sacred quality, then it is even worse than other profane books. A book is either Scripture, holy and beneficent, or else it is not Scripture, and hence indifferent, or even injurious. Hilary of Poictiers, who died in 366 A.D., speaks out the prevailing spirit of the Latin church of his time when he says, "What is not in the Book, of that we should take no notice whatever."[1] And yet Hilary himself never mentions the five catholic Epistles which we have seen so much in dispute. But he cannot have been ignorant that many others counted these Epistles as belonging to the Book.

The closing of the Canon in the West falls after the year 400. Rufinus of Aquileia, who died in 410, Jerome who died in 420, and Augustine who died in 430, are the men through whom the end of the discussion is chronicled, or even in some small measure brought to pass. Rufinus is the only man in the West who even seems to have been aware that Origen had divided the literature into three classes. But to Rufinus that division is purely a

[1] Jülicher, *Einleitung*, p. 335.

CLOSING OF THE CANON IN THE WEST 155

matter of antiquarian interest. To his mind all twenty-seven of our books would belong beyond question to Origen's first class, namely, that of the books which no one disputes.

Jerome was a man whose knowledge of the literature of the church was considerable and whose travels had been extensive. His knowledge of Greek was good; and such knowledge was somewhat rare in the West in his day. His knowledge of Hebrew was fair; and such knowledge, among Christians, was then even more rare. He belonged in a way to both East and West. He was born in Dalmatia, but educated in Rome. He had lived in Trier, in Germany, and was for years in a monastery in Bethlehem. Long occupied with secular studies, he later gave himself to a harsh ascetic life. He was a voluminous commentator. It is not a strong showing which his learning makes when compared with the illustrious achievement of Origen. If some one in Jerome's day and with Jerome's advantages had done thoroughly the thing which he, in his Lives of Famous Men, has done in somewhat untrustworthy fashion, he would have placed the world under obligation. The attempt was to preserve the main facts touching the biography of many Christian leaders. It is painful to find that many of Jerome's statements are not correct. The material from which we might have corrected those statements has perished forever. His controversial works reveal such self-consciousness and irritable temper that we do not wonder that the sharpness of his speech exposed him and his little monastic circle, more than once, to personal violence.

But Jerome's title to immortality is his contribution to the translation into Latin of the Scriptures, both of the Old and of the New Testaments. The revision of the existing translation, the so-called Itala, was committed to him by Damasus in 382 A.D. Jerome's version is the foundation of the Vulgate, the authorized Latin Bible in the Roman church. Jerome knew that certain books had been long in dispute. He says of Second Peter and Jude that many rejected these books; of James that it was alleged to have been written in the Apostle's name; and of Second and Third John that many deemed them to have been written by the presbyter. He had learned in his travels that Hermas and Clement were much loved in certain portions of the East. He himself was deeply interested in the Gospel according to the Hebrews. He certainly knew the grounds which Dionysius had alleged against the Johannine authorship of the Apocalypse. He must have known that a good part of the world had never believed that Hebrews was written by Paul. But, as conversant with the usage of both churches, he settled the long dispute concerning Hebrews and the Apocalypse by the method of the inclusion of both. Apostolic writings alone, he repeatedly asserts, are to be canonized. The inference is that, in the case of all the disputed books, he him-

CLOSING OF THE CANON IN THE WEST 157

self accepts the tradition which assigns them to the Apostles named.

Jerome found within the church divergent traditions concerning the Canon of the Old Testament. In the synagogue also in his time, Palestinian Jews held to the Canon of thirty-nine books with which we are familiar. Alexandrine Jews included many books besides, as the Septuagint translators had done. The Christian use of the Old Testament was, in the Gentile Christian churches, prevailingly on the side of this larger, so-called Alexandrine, Canon. Jerome protested against the use of the Canon of the Seventy. But, by the influence of Augustine, the additional books which we know as the Old Testament Apocrypha were admitted to the Vulgate and appear in Roman Catholic Bibles. They appear in many versions and editions in Protestant countries also to this day, although the Protestant bodies in the main made a point of rejecting the Old Testament Apocrypha and of returning to the Palestinian Canon for which Jerome had stood. The more impressive therefore, when we consider this attitude of Jerome and of Augustine toward the Old Testament Apocrypha, is the fact that there was no divergence of opinion concerning any New Testament Apocrypha. None appeared in the Vulgate. There was no body of dissentient opinion concerning the compass of the New Testament Canon of which Jerome or Augustine needed to take note. There was no single New Testament apocryphal book which they deemed it advisable to translate and append to the collection, even with the statement that it was apocryphal. So absolute was the unanimity concerning the outline of the Christian Canon which had been attained.

Few men who have borne the Christian name have appealed more powerfully to the imagination of all generations than has Augustine. Born at Tagaste in Numidia in 353 A.D., of a pagan father and of a saintly mother, a youth of ill-regulated ambitions, and of unbridled lusts, a man of power and persuasion in the career which he had chosen, he sought rest in the violence of Manichæan self-discipline and light in the secret doctrines of that sect. Disappointment and despair taking possession of him, he rescued himself temporarily through the Neoplatonic philosophy. In Milan, in pursuit of his calling, he came under the influence of Ambrose, and on Easter eve, 387 A.D., was baptized along with his natural son, Adeodatus. Returning by way of Rome to his native city, he was chosen, in 391, against his will, a presbyter by the community of Hippo Regius. In 395 A.D. Valerius, the Bishop of Hippo, had him elected his own coadjutor. From that time it may be said that Augustine ruled in the might of his genius the whole African church. He illustrated in himself that glorious phrase of his Confessions, "Thou, O God, has made us for Thyself, and our hearts are restless till they find their rest in Thee." If ever a man vindicated his own prayer, it was he;

CLOSING OF THE CANON IN THE WEST 159

"Give, O God, what Thou askest, and then ask what Thou wilt." He dedicated all his strength and charm to the new life which opened to him after his conversion. There were few things which transpired in the Christian world within the thirty years of his ceaseless activity which did not in some way bear his stamp. A man of affairs as truly as a thinker, a great theologian as also a consummate administrator and a genuine saint, he was a good lover, a hard fighter, a man of astonishing prevision, and consumed with zeal for the kingdom of Christ, that "City of God" of which he wrote. He died in 430 A.D., in his own see of Hippo, during the siege of the city by the Vandal hordes. Deepest of mystics, he was yet one of the most relentless of controversialists and one of the most practical of ecclesiastics. His derivation of the state from the might of sin among men, and his uncompromising demand for the subjection of the state to the church, was the theoretical basis for the mediæval apprehension of the relation of the two, and in no small part the dogmatic foundation of the claims of the papacy. But no less, his antithesis of nature and grace, his emphasis upon election, his doubt of free will, his assertion of salvation by faith and not by works, made him almost the typical predecessor of Luther and Calvin, forerunner of the Reformation, and saint of Protestantism as well.

His contribution to the matter of the Canon is perfectly characteristic. The great debate of so many generations was practically over. But it remained for some one to say that it was over. It remained that some one should solemnly declare what the church was to regard as its sacred body of New Testament writings from that day forth. It was Augustine who, in three provincial synods, cast his weight for that which Pope Damasus had suggested in 382, and outlined that which Pope Gelasius did for western Christendom in the year 492. These synods, under the influence of Augustine, were held, one of them in Hippo in 393, one in Carthage in 397, and again the last of them in Carthage in 419 A.D. They all of them passed canons ordaining that the twenty-seven books which we know should constitute the Christian Scripture, the oracles of God, and charter of the faith under the new covenant. The only difference to be noted in these decrees is that, in those of 393 and 397, the phrase runs, "Thirteen letters of Paul and the letter to the Hebrews, by the same," while the decree of 419 reads simply "Fourteen letters of Paul." In this the synod of 419 had but followed the example of Rome. For in a letter of Innocent I to the Bishop of Toulouse, in the year 405, twenty-seven books of the New Testament were cited, fourteen of them being letters of Paul. In the same letter of Innocent and in the three African decrees, three letters of John are cited, showing that the attempt which Damasus had made in 382 to assign First John and the Gospel to the Apostle, and Second and Third John, with the Apocalypse, to that illusory personage, the Presbyter, had failed.

Twenty-seven books, no more, and no less, is henceforth the watchword throughout the Latin church. That same letter of Innocent of the year 405, after citing by name the principal rejected books, says of them that they were not only to be excluded from the sacred Canon, but they were formally to be condemned and the faithful warned against them. The authority of Augustine in the occidental church was immense, and all serious resistance from this time forth ceased.

These canons put forth under Augustine are the first general decrees touching the matter in the Occident. They are the first formal decrees concerning the Canon in the church at all, if we except a canon of the Council of Laodicea, assigned to the year 363. But this canon of Laodicea is sharply disputed, and we shall speak of it in another place. One curious and confirmatory exception to the uniformity which henceforth prevails in the West may, however, be cited. The Goths and Visigoths had learned their Christianity from missionaries of the Greek church. They were oriental Bibles, or translations of Bibles out of the Orient, which these hordes, in so far as they were Christian, brought with them in their conquering invasions of France and Spain. These Bibles, of course, had no Apocalypse. And Spanish synods after the year 600 struggled against those who denied the Apocalypse.[1]

[1] Jülicher, *Einleitung*, p. 340.

Directly, and by formal utterance of the Roman pontiff on behalf of all the world which acknowledged the leadership of Rome, the Canon was closed by the decree of Gelasius, "De libris recipiendis et non recipiendis." This phrase is so interesting in itself, and is so closely parallel to the phrase which introduces the famous "Index librorum prohibitorum," the list of forbidden books, throughout all the history of the papacy, that it is impressive to remember that the phrase first occurs, so far as we know, in this formal fashion, in a decree concerning books which are to be regarded as canonical New Testament, and concerning those which, not being thus regarded, the faithful are warned against. Gelasius was pope from 492 to 496, A.D. We do not know more nearly the year of his decree. The list rested indeed upon that of Damasus of the year 382, and it was repeated by Hormisdas, who was pope from 514 to 523. But there is no change except in the order of a few books. The Gelasian index of books prohibited included the Gospel according to Peter, Hermas, the so-called Apostolic Constitutions, and some books which since that time have altogether disappeared.

After this time in the West, not only does the discussion cease but the remembrance of it vanishes. The sense for the true history of the Canon, the realization of the meaning of it and of the long struggle through which it had passed, gradually disappears. The New Testament was there.

Not a voice was raised to say but that it had always been there, and had always been just what it now was. Usage had become unvarying. The church had spoken. And so passed a thousand years.

LECTURE V

THE CLOSING OF THE CANON IN THE EAST. THE RENAISSANCE AND THE REFORMATION

LECTURE V

THE CLOSING OF THE CANON IN THE EAST. THE RENAISSANCE AND THE REFORMATION

WE spoke in the last lecture of the Alexandrine view of the Canon. We endeavored to define the position of the greatest of Alexandrine teachers, Origen. We noted his division of the material under discussion into three classes. There was, firstly, the group of books acknowledged by all in the Christian communities as sacred Scripture. Secondly, there was the group of books repudiated by all. And, finally, there was the class of writings which Origen knew to be still in dispute. We said that in this distinction, and in Origen's whole handling of the matter, there survived far more of the true historic sense about the New Testament than we should have found at that same period anywhere in the western world. This historic sense persists in no small measure in what Eusebius has to say touching the Canon. And Eusebius writes more than two generations after Origen.

The Father of Church History, as he has often been called, Eusebius stands at the end of an era in the life of the Christian movement. He witnessed the new epoch which was made by the conversion of Constantine and the elevation of Christianity to a position of supreme power as the religion of the state. He himself lived through that transition, the greatest transformation which the outward relations of the church could possibly have undergone. It was a greater external change than the men of the previous generation would have dared to look forward to. And there followed after it, speedily, a change in the spirit of the institution as well.

Origen also had stood at the end of an old period, or, rather, just over the boundary of a new one. Origen also looked back upon a momentous transition which immediately antedated his own work. Indeed, when we reflect, we must say that the transformation of the Christian institution which Origen in large measure registered, had immeasurably greater spiritual significance than had that whole dramatic change which the Emperor with such pomp inaugurated, and which Eusebius, in the last books of his History and in his Life of Constantine, with some obsequiousness records. We are not quite sure that Origen himself appreciated, in all the breadth of its meaning, the change to which his own works bear such overwhelming testimony. It is not altogether clear that he realized how different was the Christianity in which he lived and moved from the religion of Christ and of the Apostles. And it is quite certain that Eusebius and his contemporaries regarded the acknowledgment of Christianity by the state, and the

CLOSING OF THE CANON IN THE EAST 169

appropriation of the state by Christianity, as by far the most momentous event in Christian history. But to us it seems otherwise.

The alteration in the status of Christianity which took place in the first quarter of the fourth century was indeed a stupendous one. But it was, for the present, at any rate, an alteration only in status. It was an alteration, primarily, only in the conditions of the Christian life and thought and work. On the other hand, the change which passed over Christendom in the last two decades of the second century was a change not merely in status, but in nature. It was nothing less than the metamorphosis of Christianity itself. The contrast between the despised and persecuted church of the catacombs and that church whose bishops were the chosen advisers of the master of the world, and scarcely forbore to sit with him upon the throne, was indeed a great one. The change was accomplished with dramatic suddenness. It had all the paraphernalia which make such events impressive. But certainly the gulf which separated primitive Christianity, the original unorganized personal enthusiasm and inspiration, from that superb and world-subduing organization which we know as the catholic church, and which in all of its distinctive principles was present at the beginning of the third century, was greater still. That change too had been long preparing. It also came, at the last, or seemed to come, with startling suddenness. It came almost as crystallization happens when one jars a vessel in which a solution has been slowly coming to the saturation-point. One moment all is transparent fluid, and the next, there are those wonderful forms as hard as adamant and as permanent as the elements which make the earth.

A simple popular movement, with a thousand centres, and under natural forms of voluntary leadership, is far removed from that compact organization which conceded the supremacy of bishops who, to all intents and purposes, were monarchs clothed in the authority of Christ and God. Men whose bond of union was the sustaining of a moral discipline, and who found themselves in the world of culture as best they could, were in far different case from those whose tie was a confession, the binding formulary of a faith once for all delivered to the saints. A church whose authority was Christ alone, and which cherished writings for no other reason than that those writings enshrined its Christ, is sharply contrasted with one which found infallible authority in sacred apostolic documents, and had a Canon of inspired Scripture where it once had only the spirit of its Lord. The metamorphosis which in these three sentences has been described is surely far more significant than that other. The fundamental difference in character between primitive Christianity and the catholic church is of incomparably greater consequence than the mere contrast in the outward fortunes of the church which indeed was, at one moment, trampled under the feet of every provincial governor, and upon whose brow, in the next, the Emperor himself had set the crown. That first change touched the essence of the matter. This last touched, primarily at all events, only its state.

And yet the transition which Eusebius witnessed was also momentous. Misunderstood, despised, oppressed thus far, discriminated against in every fashion, the objective point of every popular tumult, and viewed with hostility more often by good rulers than by bad; doing its work in large degree in secret, barely tolerated even in the times of laxest administration, and at the last fiercely persecuted because, in the judgment of such a straightforward pagan as Diocletian, it constituted an intolerable menace to the state; the church suddenly overbalanced, in the shrewd estimate of statesmen and of soldier-emperors, the pagan elements against which it had been weighed. It was seen for what it was, the true moral and conservative force with which the civil authority must ally itself if it would save the world from utter dissolution. For, whatever we may think of Constantine's motives, and however true it may be that in doing as he did he followed his own interest, it was at least a self-interest which reckoned with moral magnitudes and desired to have moral forces on its side. Marcus Aurelius, also, had reckoned, in pathetic loneliness and bitterness of spirit, with those moral magnitudes. But Christianity had apparently never been seen by him in any light save that of its ignorant fanaticisms, the very light in which it was most repulsive to the lofty spirit of the Stoic. Christianity had seemed to offer him no help as, in deep moral solicitude, he bore the weight of the whole world. One lets his imagination play with the question, Might the civil authority at least have postponed its own dissolution, would the course of the decay of the ancient civilization, the decline of the ancient world, have been materially different, if that authority had earlier and in hearty fashion struck alliance with the moral forces which Christianity unquestionably did represent? Answer to that question, in part at least, is furnished by the mournful comment that, no sooner had that alliance in the time of Constantine been struck, than Christianity came to represent a great many things beside moral forces.

When one thinks of the atrocities of the persecution under Diocletian and Galerius and Maximinus, of the scant tolerance of the edict of the year 311, no greater change can be imagined than that which took place when, in rapid succession, after the year 313, Constantine forced from his unwilling colleague Licinius one concession after another in favor of the Christians, and, after the death of Licinius in 324, declared himself a Christian upon the throne of the Cæsars. Thousands of those who had really been convinced of the truth of Christianity, but had not dared to ally themselves to it, now found themselves not merely safe, but honored in so doing. Ecclesiastics became the Emperor's chief counsellors. Adventurers, male

CLOSING OF THE CANON IN THE EAST 173

and female, deemed it good policy to get themselves converted. From Constantine to Julian the number of Christian adherents is said to have increased tenfold. That tells a good part of the tale. An emperor called the first ecumenical council, presided at some of its sittings, gave his seal to the settlement of doctrinal questions which was there arrived at, and offered his sword for the execution of the same. When Constantine transformed the old city of Byzantium on the Hellespont into Constantinople, he did this as a practical measure for sustaining his authority in the far East. We, who look back upon it, see that that step facilitated the disruption of the marvellous fabric which the genius of the Cæsars had built up. It left the Pope more than ever to his own devices. It increased the certainty that the day would come when the church would really be the Roman Empire, after the state, as such, had fallen before the hordes of the barbarians.

Measure of the change may be gathered from the fact that, whereas Diocletian had declared that no Christian church should be left standing, Constantine is credited with having paid out of the public treasury for the erection of Christian basilicas at one place and another, all the way from the Holy Sepulchre at Jerusalem and from the shores of the Bosporus to Trier in the valley of the Mosel. Whereas the same Diocletian had decreed that all Christian books were to be burned, Constantine is said by Eusebius to have given orders for fifty manuscripts of the Holy Scriptures of incredible sumptuousness. Whereas Galerius had ordered, as indeed Decius had done before him, that leaders in the Christian community were everywhere to be sought out, condemned to the sword or to the stake, or thrown to the wild beasts, Constantine's ministers, even in secular affairs, were often church dignitaries, and he was pleased to regard himself as, in some sort, an ecclesiastical functionary by the special call of God.

The evils of the system thus inaugurated no one seems to have forecast. Religion had been always in antiquity closely associated with the state, and the state with religion. It was because of this close association of religion with the state that the Christians had been compelled often to withdraw from the service of the state. It was because of this close connection of the ancient religion with civil functions that the heads of the state became so often the persecutors of the church. But the catholic church, as, during the century and a quarter from Irenæus to Eusebius and in the teeth of fiercest opposition, it had organized itself, was a factor to be reckoned with in a sense in which the ancient religion had never been an independent factor. It was an organization in a sense in which the ancient religion had never had an organization. It was a moral and ideal force in a sense in which the ancient religion had never been a force. And even in the mingled and perverted forms which the moral and ideal elements in Christianity now largely took, the gigantic force remained. Of the magnitude and virulence of the evils of the system thus inaugurated, the church itself was in the next thousand years the witness. And the church, in all that pertained to true religion, was itself, and in hardly less measure than was the state or the world at large, the victim of those evils. That for a time the progress of civilization may have seemed to be furthered by this alliance, may be admitted. But that, in the end, the cause of religion itself and, as well, the causes of political liberty and of enlightenment, were retarded and at times almost crushed, no one will dispute. But at present we have only to chronicle this amazing revolution which Eusebius saw.

Eusebius, bishop of Cæsarea in Palestine, was born probably in Palestine. He was the friend of Pamphilus, the head of the school in Cæsarea and defender of Origen. In the persecution under Diocletian Eusebius fled to Tyre, and later to Egypt, where he was imprisoned. Returning to Palestine, he became bishop of Cæsarea in 313. He was a friend of Constantine. At the Council of Nicæa, in the year 325, he stood at first upon the side of the Arians, as did most of the Origenists. He strove long and vigorously for some kind of compromise, but at last subscribed to the victorious formula of Athanasius. He died in 340 A.D. The notable library which Pamphilus had gathered at Cæsarea may have given to Eusebius his literary impulse. Certainly it constituted, in part, his opportunity. His ventures as an author in the department of theology are of no great consequence. His Life of Constantine, which is really the continuation of his history of the church, is written too much in the spirit of a courtier's adulation. His Martyrs of Palestine is deeply impressive, and perhaps we may pardon him for writing in such heat as he betrays. But his great work is his Ecclesiastical History. He set out to delineate the Christian movement from the beginning to the year 325. The great value of this work lies in its use of archives which in Eusebius' time were in many places extant, but since then have perished. Eusebius was familiar also with much Christian literature which has not come down to us. For certain later parts of the narrative he was an eye-witness of the stirring events of which he told. That he should have possessed the full critical spirit in the use of his sources is not to be expected. But his disposition to fairness and reality cannot be denied. His work remains an incomparable treasure, although it is also an unending problem. It is the mine out of which all students of Christian history must dig.

We have seen that Eusebius' point of departure in all questions of scholarship was that of Origen. His general view of the Canon is almost precisely that of Origen. He devotes the whole twenty-fourth chapter of the third book of his History to a discussion of the order and composition of the Gospels. The twenty-fifth chapter then begins with these words: "This seems to be the proper place to give a summary statement of the books of the New Testament." And these two chapters are embedded in the history at the point where the author has just been speaking of the life and death of the Apostle John, and before he comes to tell of the Ebionites, of Cerinthus, of the Nicolaitans, of the martyrdom of Simeon, of the edict of Trajan and of the epistles of Ignatius.

This fact in itself is highly interesting. For although the description which Eusebius gives of the state of the case concerning New Testament writings, is that which fits no time until the time of Origen, yet he interjects this description at a point in his narrative which brings it close to the lifetime of the Apostles themselves.[1] In other words, because the literature in question belongs, for the most part, to this period in the history, it is not made clear but that the collection of this literature into a New Testament and the assigning to it of a scriptural authority was also achieved at this same point in the history. Direct answer, to this effect, beyond question Eusebius would not have given. On the contrary, he was familiar with numberless facts which made against any such supposition. His own writings are the source of a good part of all our knowledge of these facts. Nevertheless, there is here, even in the work of a man so learned as Eusebius, this curious effect of

[1] Cf. with Eusebius, *H. E.* iii. 24, and 25, especially *H. E.* vi. 3-16, referred to above.

foreshortening, by which the fact of the growth of the New Testament tends to be overlooked and the New Testament appears as if moved backward, *en bloc*, toward the Apostolic Age. And if even a man so truly learned as Eusebius did not escape, in a moment of unconsciousness, the working of this illusion, how much more certainly may we expect to meet that illusion in the minds of men not learned at all.

In his catalogue Eusebius names in the first instance, of course, four Gospels, then the Acts, letters of Paul, whether thirteen or fourteen he does not say, but Hebrews he does not otherwise mention, First John and First Peter, and then, curiously enough, at the end of the list he says, "and, if you choose, the Apocalypse of John." In the arrangement of Eusebius it is the middle class which is the class of the disputed books. These books are James, Jude, Second Peter, Second and Third John, the same five minor catholic Epistles which were with Origen in dispute. To the third class, that of the books falsely alleged to be apostolic, belong Acts of Paul, Hermas, the Apocalypse of Peter, Barnabas, the Didachè, "and finally, as some will have it, the Apocalypse of John." This indecision concerning the Apocalypse is curious. Origen had positively accepted the book, although he knew of the dispute concerning it. Eusebius knows of the dispute, and appears inclined to reject the book.[1]

[1] See especially Eusebius, *H. E.* vii. 25.

In the end, however, we have this contradictory statement, which puts the book in two places in his classification.

Since Eusebius speaks in other passages in his History of one and another of the matters here involved, and since his statements do not always agree with that which he has here put in tabular form, his real position has been somewhat in question. It is possible that the whole table represents the overwhelming influence of Origen upon Eusebius, and that his own opinions may be gathered rather from that which he has elsewhere said. In general, however, one sees how completely we have come to the basis of apostolicity as the ground of decision in reference to books. But often the argument runs like this: Either the books contain heretical sentiments, in which case they cannot be apostolic; or else they have come down from the ancients as apostolic, and we see no heretical sentiments in them, therefore they may be accepted by us also as apostolic. Often his procedure is almost like a counting of heads. And sometimes the authorities thus to be counted in the settlement of the Canon are communities, and again they are individual authors. It is no wonder if by this method inconsistency in statement sometimes results.

Eusebius diligently counts the votes of the ancients, for example against Clement and Barnabas. But he puts the wrong interpretation on that vote. As a matter of fact, the real reason for the exclusion of such books as those of Clement and Barnabas was not that the men of the earliest time doubted that such books were from the authors whose names they bore, although it is sometimes open to us to have doubts upon this point. Still less would the men of that earliest time have denied that Barnabas and the rest stood near to the apostolic circle, and might conceivably have shared, in some measure, in the original spiritual impulse. The real reason was that the content of these books had never commended them in a measure which brought them into general use. They had never been used in public worship in anything approaching universal way. Their exclusion from the Canon was, therefore, upon the surface, a judgment merely upon the basis of rejection in fact. Deeper down, however, it was a general judgment of the quality of the books. It was that kind of a judgment of masses of men and successive generations concerning great literature which the world has come to regard as nearly infallible. It was that kind of a judgment of a moral and spiritual magnitude, uninfluenced, unreasoned, or at least unconscious, which, when from millions of men, and these widely severed both in time and space, it converges upon some one object, we are wont to say can never make mistake. Of this sort was the historic Christian judgment concerning the main Christian books. But when no longer acceptance, or the spiritual quality which lay behind the general acceptance of a book, but, instead of these, apostolicity became the ground of decision, then the middle class, that of the disputed books, could no longer be maintained. The great public could hardly leave such a question forever unsettled. Either the books, like the five minor catholic Epistles and the Hebrews and the Apocalypse, must be declared apostolic, and therefore placed in the Canon, or else they must be declared false, forged, pretenders to apostolic quality. In that case they must be put out of the Canon, and that with a contumely which would not have been their lot had the claim of apostolic authorship and authority never been made on their behalf.

Uncertain, for Eusebius, is really only the Apocalypse.[1] The discussion of this matter he introduces with a letter of Dionysius, Bishop of Alexandria, who died in 264 A.D. Dionysius could not believe that the opening verses of this book were intentionally misleading. At the same time his critical judgment, as he compared the Apocalypse with the Gospel and the First Epistle, convinced him that it could not be the work of the author of those books. The name John was a common one in Ephesus, he says. Tombs of persons of that name had been shown to him. This book must have been written by another John, a holy and inspired person, whom men then confused with the Apostle. At the same time, as to the contents of the book, Dionysius conceded that they

[1] Eusebius, *H. E.* vii. 25.

were too high for his understanding. The acknowledgment of the spiritual worth of the book could be only a matter of faith.

This was good for scholars like Dionysius. But the people knew only one Apostle John. If this new presbyter, John of Ephesus, stood in some such relation to the Apostle John as that in which Mark was alleged to have stood to Peter, then his book might come into the Canon. But in that case it would be the Apostle John who was responsible for it, after all. Dionysius had said that it was difficult to read. But if it was apostolic it must be read, and, if need be, it must be allegorized. This it was which men did with other writings which they did not understand. But if it was not apostolic, then it should be removed from the Canon. For the popular mind, we may be reasonably sure, the judgment that it was not apostolic would have removed the book from the Canon. But it was in the Canon. It was much read and loved in the West, and the West was dominant. Therefore, in the end, the book came into the Canon in the East also. And its remaining in the Canon amounted to the confirmation of its apostolicity.

By this curiously inconsequent series of arguments the Greek church, after Eusebius, satisfied itself to do that which the Roman church had long since done, namely, to canonize the Apocalypse. It came to deem that it had not the full collection of the apostolic writings until it possessed the twenty-seven which we know.

What Eusebius wrote belongs before the year 340, and part of it, perhaps, before 325. We have a list from Cyril of Jerusalem of about the year 348. We have one from Athanasius in an Easter epistle of the year 367. We have a list from Epiphanius of the year 403. There are also two metrical lists. One of these is of Gregory of Nazianzus, who died in 390 A.D., and the other of his friend, Amphilochius of Iconium, the date of which latter list we do not know. There is a curious absence of synodical decrees. The eighty-fifth of the so-called Apostolic Canons may belong to this general period. But that is by no means certain. The sixtieth Canon of the Council of Laodicea, possibly of the year 363, is believed to be a later addition. It seems to be a mere supplement to the fifty-ninth decree, which had forbidden the reading of uncanonical New Testament books. Some later editor of these Canons then seems to have felt that the books which might be read should be named. Of these various lists, that of Amphilochius alone puts the matter in statistical form as Eusebius and Origen had done. According to Amphilochius fourteen letters are of Pauline authorship, but by most Christians the Apocalypse is deemed not genuine. Cyril, Gregory, and the sixtieth Canon of Laodicea all have but twenty-six books. The Apocalypse is wanting. But the seven catholic Epistles are spoken of as if the very memory of the long dispute concerning them had faded from men's minds. The famous synod of the year 692, known as the Quinisexta, had two decrees touching the Canon, one with and the other without the Apocalypse.

Similar to that of Cyril is the general judgment of Athanasius except in the one particular. He has the Apocalypse. Athanasius had lived long in Trier in Germany, and may there have learned to know and value the book. At least he may there have learned the value of agreement between East and West, and been convinced that the West would never surrender the Apocalypse. Undoubtedly the personal influence of Athanasius did much to carry through this decision in the eastern church. And yet Chrysostom and Theodoret were against the book. Arians everywhere rejected it. Its conquest of the East was very gradual. Photius, Aretas, and the great men of the revival of the Greek church in the eighth and ninth centuries all had it. But even in the tenth century one finds manuscripts which have no Apocalypse and writers who declare that there are but twenty-six New Testament books.[1]

The life of Athanasius, Bishop of Alexandria, was so completely taken up in the great contest with Arianism that his biography might be said to be the history of that strife. He attended the Council of Nicæa as deacon, and secretary of the aged Bishop Alexander of Alexandria. But, despite his subordinate position and his youth, he

[1] Jülicher, *Einleitung*, p. 342.

was easily the intellectual leader of the party which triumphed in that assembly. So early as in 328, he succeeded to the bishopric of Alexandria. In the long interval until his death in the year 373 he contended, unwearied, for the Nicene statement concerning the person of Christ. Five times Athanasius was banished from his city. Twenty years all together he spent in exile from his see. But from the time of his return to Alexandria in 366 A.D. he was able to hold the field. Athanasius was more than a controversialist. He was a true shepherd of souls and a man upon whom the practical issues of religion and the demoralization of his flock, through the long frenzy, weighed most heavily. It is mainly his practical writings which are for our purposes significant. And we should not be mistaken if we said that it was the practical emergency created by the Trinitarian controversy which made men, of both parties probably, in that dreadful time, to feel that continued uncertainty as to what constituted the authoritative body of Christian writings was insufferable. And yet apart from his opinion, above cited, concerning the Apocalypse, it was not much that Athanasius contributed to the closing of the Canon. Rather, we may still observe in Athanasius the lingering of the Alexandrine tradition. The Wisdom of Solomon and other Old Testament apocryphal books, and beside these, the Didachè and Hermas, although he says of them distinctly that they do not belong to the Canon, might yet be read for the instruction of the catechumens.

There was never an authoritative last word spoken in the East, as the Gelasian decree had been the last word in the West. There was in the East no generally acknowledged authority which could have spoken such a word. On the other hand, there was never any such awakening of men's minds or a reopening of the question in the East such as we find in the time of the Renaissance and Reformation in the West. Still less has there been a movement of scholarship in the Greek church to be compared with the rise of New Testament criticism in Europe and America in the nineteenth century. In the general stagnation of intellectual life in the Christian Orient after the ninth century the last word had been spoken, none the less. And it remains practically the last word in the Greek church to this day. Cyril Lucar, in 1645, enumerated the twenty-seven books, and a council of Jerusalem in 1672, without naming the books, declared that such works must be reckoned as belonging to the New Testament as the acknowledged Fathers and the orthodox Synod have thus reckoned.

Extremely interesting are some illustrations which have been given of the way in which men, as the night of the Dark Ages drew on, seemed occasionally to forget that the New Testament was closed, and sought to bring into it other books which they had come to believe to be apostolical, which were read in churches, which were useful for the Christian life, or which for some reason were regarded by them as inspired writings.[1] Thus a manuscript of the New Testament found in the cloister of Bobbio, which belongs, very likely, to the seventh or to the eighth century, solemnly counts twenty-eight books. It has added something under the name of the Book of the Sacrament. It can hardly be doubted that this means the Book of the Mass. What we here have is the canonization of ritual. It is the apprehension of liturgy under the same idea of sacredness and inspiration which belonged to Scripture. The point of view of the New Testament as the original literature of Christianity, created under the immediate impulse of Jesus, has been lost. Or should we say that the liturgy also is carried back in the naïve thought of the writer to the Apostles' time? But this impulse, because of the use of the ritual in churches and because of a vague sense of its inspiration to include this also in the New Testament, is almost an isolated case in the West.

On the other hand, in the Greek church, cases which illustrate the same principle are not altogether uncommon. The so-called Apostolic Constitutions, books forged in the name of Clement of Rome and added to from time to time from the fourth to the sixth centuries, are several times enumerated as part of the New Testament. The interest here, however, is in church government,

[1] Jülicher, *Einleitung*, p. 343.

and not, as before, in worship. This drift to the inclusion of books of ecclesiastical law with the Scripture goes so far that an Æthiopic New Testament, of unknown date, contains thirty-five books, the additions being all of the nature of canon law. In truth, if men had identified the notions of the canonical and of the apostolic, and then came to believe in the apostolic origin of such books as the so-called Apostolic Constitutions, it is not altogether strange that some should have thought to place these also in the Canon.

The same logic might have led men in the western church to put the Apostles' Creed in the New Testament Canon, in the days when the great interest of the western church was in its creed, and when men had come firmly to believe that this elaboration of the Roman baptismal formula went back to the Apostles themselves. But it must be remembered that in the occidental church there had always been a much sharper sense of the boundary of the Canon than in the East. Before the state of things which we have described descended upon the West, the New Testament Canon had been authoritatively closed in that portion of the world. In the East that had, indeed, never been the case. But in the East men had had, prevailingly, not the Apostles' Creed, but the Nicene and Athanasian creeds. And although of course men held these to be, for substance, identical with that which the Apostles taught, yet they never attributed them directly to apostolic authorship,

CLOSING OF THE CANON IN THE EAST 189

and so they could not place them in the New Testament Canon under the Apostles' name.

Once again we must speak of the Syrian church as having had, in this matter of the New Testament Canon, a slower development than had either the Latin church or the Greek. We noted that still in the time of Theodoret the Syrian church, in its use of Tatian's Diatessaron, occupied a position which the Greek church had left behind it two hundred years earlier in the acceptance of four Gospels. The famous Syriac translation, the Peshitto, which can hardly be older than the time of Eusebius, still has but twenty-two books, that is, not Jude, not Second Peter, not Second or Third John, and not the Apocalypse. This, again, is a point in the discussion which the Greek church had passed almost a century earlier. And one must remember that the church of Eastern Syria, after the Council of Chalcedon in the year 431, held to Nestorianism, which had been condemned, and so came to be separated from the great body of the church, both East and West, more completely than ever. A manuscript of the year 1470, probably of Nestorian origin, closes the New Testament solemnly after the Pauline letters. The author then says, "We append also letters of Apostles not acknowledged by all." These are, namely, Second Peter, Second and Third John, and Jude, and the two so-called Clementine Letters on Virginity. The Apocalypse is not so much as named. This curious survival indicates how men in monastic ages sometimes went on copying out opinions, not realizing that those opinions had been for a thousand years already obsolete.

The Renaissance, with its awakening of men to the historical and literary sense, caused students in most unexpected ways to feel, as if by instinct, that much which they had accepted as beyond question was very questionable, and much which they had deemed fixed had, at any rate, not always been thus fixed. The influence of Constantinople upon the revival of learning in the Occident was enormous. Byzantine scholars flooded Europe and introduced the West afresh to treasures, both classical and ecclesiastical, in the Greek tongue. But the influence of these men upon their own portion of the church was insignificant. The hope, cherished so lately as the beginning of the seventeenth century, by a few enlightened spirits under the patriarchate, of a reunion with the Protestants, seems to us now utterly chimerical. Though the genius of the Renaissance was the Greek spirit, yet that spirit scarcely touched the Greek church.

The Reformation, with its general assault upon the principle of tradition, touched the tradition of the Scripture Canon, along with many others. The very emphasis which Protestantism laid upon the Scripture should have had, as one of its corollaries, the most thoroughgoing investigation of the Scripture upon which such exclusive reliance was placed.

And indeed, in the hands of the first and greatest among the Reformers, this inquiry for a time bade fair to be inaugurated. But the times were not ripe for it. The state of general knowledge did not really permit it. Practical interests, in no small part the political interests, of the Reformation, fully occupied men's minds and filled their hands. A generation later the exclusive authority which the Protestants attributed to Scripture, with their external way of apprehending that authority, the apparent necessity of finding it an infallible authority as over against the infallible authority of the Roman church, made Protestants, of all men, for the time at least, those who were most unlikely to initiate a great critical movement which should ultimately do for the tradition of Scripture exactly what the Reformation had done for the tradition of the church. That this was the logic of Protestantism no one can doubt. But that logic has been long in asserting itself. For quite intelligible reasons, nowhere has this inquiry been at times so much resisted as in Protestant churches. But on the other hand, nowhere has the movement for the fearless investigation of Scripture been fostered to such an extent as among Protestants; that is to say, by the very persons whose acknowledged and sole basis of faith it is which is being thus rigidly investigated. Underneath temporary hesitations and despite occasional fears, the real spirit of Protestantism has been and is that of entire reliance upon the truth, and of the search for that truth, whithersoever that search may lead. If the fear, which was born of the realization how much is, for Protestants, at stake in the investigation of the Scripture, has sometimes held men back, yet the love of the Scripture and the real trust in it have driven them forward. Underneath has been the conviction that God is Himself the truth, and all study of the truth must lead us but to God. Underneath has been the divination that, as the dissolving of the mediæval way of thinking of the authority of the church brought men more truly under the mastery of Christ himself, so the discovery that the inspiration of the Scripture is the inspiring Christ, and the authority of Scripture is that of truth and of God Himself, will be to us not a loss but an immeasurable gain.

So long ago as in the time of Nicholas of Lyre, a Franciscan monk, professor of theology in Paris until 1325, reminiscences of the struggle concerning the New Testament Canon had been present to men's minds. So vividly were his words remembered that some of Luther's opponents, by way of impugning Luther's originality, had said that if Lyre had not played, Luther would not have danced. The Cardinal Cajetan, whose commentary was finished in 1529, had learned, as any one might easily have learned through Jerome, that Hebrews, James, Jude, Second Peter, Second and Third John, and the Apocalypse were very possibly not to be attributed to the Apostles whose names they bore. Certain it was that in the ancient

THE RENAISSANCE AND THE REFORMATION 193

church they had not been always thus attributed. Erasmus, who died in 1526, was deeply in doubt concerning Second Peter and Jude. He ascribed Second and Third John to the so-called presbyter. He was uncertain about James. He did not believe that the Hebrews could have been written by Paul. He made current again a good part of the substance of the ancient arguments against the Apocalypse. But, in his own ironical fashion, he proclaimed himself ready to submit his judgment, should the judgment of the church be to the contrary. Other Catholic writers of note continued to express with no great originality these historic doubts.

Deeply interesting is the fact here brought to light, that this great discussion in the modern world comes to life again, after a thousand years, upon precisely the point where a millennium before it had died out. The only wonder is that, with the writings even only of Jerome before men's eyes, it had not earlier been revived. The question was again merely the minor one as to the boundary of the Canon. It was only the query whether six or seven books, and these surely not the most important ones, do or do not belong to the New Testament. Or, to put the issue still more accurately, and since these books by right of much more than a thousand years of acceptance, do belong to the New Testament Canon, the question was solely whether they belong to it for the reasons which the Fathers had been pleased to give, namely, because of the apostolic authorship of these books.

The profounder question, the religious question, as to the notion and nature of the New Testament, the question as to the meaning of our having any New Testament, was left for the profound and religious soul of Luther to wrestle with as he wrestled with so many questions besides.

After the Council of Florence, Eugene IV, in a bull of the year 1441, had confirmed the Canon of Augustine. But to put an end to the doubts of its own members, and as well to condemn the Protestant movement toward that reopening of the whole question which seemed imminent, the Roman Catholic church in the Council of Trent, in the session of the 8th of April, 1546, officially declared the twenty-seven books canonical. Unfortunately, this Canon of the Council of Trent committed itself also to the reiteration of some traditional opinions, historical and literary, the defence of which, as all men now clearly see, was not at all necessary to the just assertion that these twenty-seven are the canonical books.

Martin Chemnitz, the Reformer, made the luminous remark that the later church could never, by decree, make certain that of which the early church upon historical evidence had remained uncertain.[1] Bellarmine had contended in the Council of Trent that the church could declare canonical and apostolic Scripture concerning which earlier Christians had been in doubt. This it could do out of the

[1] Chemnitz, *Examen Concil. Trid.* 1565. See Holtzmann, *Einleitung*, p. 158 f.

common consent and judgment of Christian people. Not in the sense of the continued iteration of a fixed tradition within an interested institution, but in the large sense of that free spiritual recognition, on the part of the community, of which we spoke above, what Cardinal Bellarmine has here alleged is true. But it is not true in the sense against which Chemnitz strove, as if men's votes could make certain that Paul wrote a book which we have no literary evidence that he wrote. The contention of Bellarmine is true in the sense that the hearts of men may be quite sure that the creative spirit of the Christian origins is in a book whose authorship we very possibly shall never know. This decree of the Council of Trent, by the way, was reiterated by the Vatican Council in the session of the 24th of April, 1870. The Vatican decree was also hardly more than the canonization of tradition in face of the modern movement for Biblical research which in the years from 1835 to 1870 had agitated all the world. It has not been claimed that either the decree of Trent or that of the Vatican was in any great degree the result of fresh and thoroughgoing study of the historical and critical material involved.

But in truth, if we look closely into it, we shall see that the Reformers themselves, despite such soul-stirrings on the part of Luther and Calvin as have been alluded to, did not separate themselves from the Roman church in respect of the idea of the Canon, whatever comments they may have made upon the compass of it. They, too, in the earlier stages of their investigation, revived mainly the ancient doubts as to the area of the Canon. And when these doubts as to the authorship of certain books, and the recovery of the true sense for the historical process by which the Canon had come into being, began to have their logical effect upon the notion and authority of the Canon itself, the Protestants drew back. The idea of the Canon remained the traditional and Catholic one, with the Protestants as well, until the beginning of the nineteenth century. And it must be owned that this idea was the only one which was coherent with the thought of a revelation suspending the faculties of men, and of the might of inspiration as residing in the words themselves. Only the ancient idea of revelation as external and purely miraculous, could have made possible the scholastic Protestant theory of the authority of Scripture which in the seventeenth century prevailed. Men like Luther, Zwingli, and Calvin had, from the side of pure religious intuition, made astonishing fetches into the opposite theory of revelation, which has come now largely to obtain. That theory makes revelation psychologically normal, perfectly human, without being less divine. That idea makes inspiration the influence of God who is Spirit upon man who is spirit too. Such influence leaves the freedom, the initiative, the consciousness of the man receiving the revelation, as natural, as much unimpaired, as is his attitude in the utterance of any other thought which ever came forth from his own soul. In fact, it is in man's own freedom and in the glorifying of his human qualities that the divine is evidenced. This theory accounts perfectly for all the individuality and concrete traits of the particular books. It makes of revelation simply the religious experience in unique depth and significance, together, if you choose, with the power of utterance, for the sake of others, of the thing which a man in his own uplifted spirit has experienced. The Reformers made astonishing fetches into this truth. But they never worked these ideas into the clear, and subsequent generations lost them altogether.

To this we must add that the criticism of the Reformers, and especially that of Luther, was far too subjective and dogmatic to achieve secure results. Personal religious experience had brought to Luther the certainty of his faith. That faith he was ready to prove out of Scripture against all comers. But in so doing he elevated his own understanding, especially of words of Paul, into a standard of judgment of everything else. To him John's writings and Paul's, and of Paul, especially the Epistles to the Romans and to the Galatians, are the core of the Canon, "the right certain and main books." And this in its own sense is entirely true. The rest of the books he deemed to be lower in their intensity of inspiration, and of some of them he speaks almost contemptuously. James is a mere epistle of straw, because it tells of works only instead of speaking of our salvation by faith alone. James has, moreover, nothing concerning the suffering and atonement of Christ. Hebrews is wrong in denying for any man the possibility of repentance. James, Jude, and the Apocalypse are also wrong in their teachings concerning penitence. Apollos must have written Hebrews. Jude and Second Peter are unnecessary letters. Concerning the Apocalypse he is unable to see that it can have been put forth by the Holy Ghost.[1] One sees Luther's point of view. His procedure is subjective and partial in high degree. And yet Luther's thought is entirely sound in one main particular. It is entirely sound in its reassertion of the truth which the Middle Age had almost wholly lost, and which classical Protestantism again forgot, the truth, namely, that some books are inspired in higher degree than are others. Astonishing is the accuracy with which, although Luther's criticism sets out from an entirely different point of view from that of the ancients, he yet fixes upon the same books to which the ancient church had raised objection in its time.

Zwingli says much the same thing concerning the Apocalypse.[2] It is not Biblical; there is no edification in it; he did not understand it. He noted the wildness of the faith and life of those

[1] Luther, *Schluss der Vorrede zur Übersetzung d. N. T.'s von 1522.* This conclusion to the preface was suppressed in later editions. See *Luther's Werke*, ed. Erlangen, Bd. lxiii. pp. 154–170.

[2] Zwingli's *Werke*, ed. Schuler u. Schultheiss, ii. 1. p. 169, *Religionsgespräch zu Bern*, 1528.

THE RENAISSANCE AND THE REFORMATION 199

who gave themselves up too much to the effort to understand it. Calvin, also, though moved less by feeling and more by a sense for history, deemed Second and Third John and the Apocalypse of doubtful authenticity.[1] Second Peter, he says, is unquestionably not by Peter. And Hebrews is not by Paul, although for its religious worth it is a thousand times worthy of its place in the Canon. Even Carlstadt, who had begun the scholastic development of the high Protestant theory of inspiration, yet in a book written in 1520 distinguishes three classes of New Testament writings: first, those of greatest dignity and worth, like the four Gospels; then those of a secondary character, like the Acts and the thirteen Pauline Epistles; and thirdly, those of least authority and significance, like Hebrews and the Apocalypse and the five minor catholic Epistles.[2] The purpose of this discrimination was to minimize the effect of critical assertions which could not be disputed, concerning these books, by declaring that the books were, in any case, of minor consequence. And yet the very doctrine of mechanical and oracular inspiration for which Carlstadt was so zealous surely admits of no such division and gradation of inspired writings as he has here announced. Beza, who died in 1605, seems to have been the last man of that age in the Calvinistic churches who,

[1] On Calvin, see Credner, *Zur Gesch. d. Kanons*, 333 f.; Berger, *La bible au seizième siècle*, 1879, p. 115 f.

[2] Carlstadt, *Libellus de Can. Script.*, *1520*, in Credner, p. 291.

as a devout and thoroughgoing Protestant, permitted himself to doubt the authenticity of certain New Testament books. In the Lutheran church, because, no doubt, of the extravagant veneration for Luther himself, and in the recollection of some of his vigorous utterances, the spirit which allowed itself criticism from the religious point of view lived on a little longer. At least men allowed themselves to make the same criticisms which Luther had made. Their confidence that everything that Luther had said must have been true, blinded them to the fact that such discriminations as those which Luther had made were impossible under their own theory of inspiration. What should have been proved to them was that Luther held no such theory of inspiration. But still, in the end, even these reminiscences failed. Under the dogma men could draw no inferences from them.

The Protestant confessions, as, for example, the Thirty-nine Articles of the Church of England, the Gallican Articles, the Belgic Confession, and the Westminster Confession, were content simply to enumerate the traditional series of books. The Lutheran Confessions referred to them without enumerating them. The authors of these confessions avoided in the main the expression of critical opinions current in their times, and interposed therefore no obstacles of this sort to the advance of investigation in the several communions. On the other hand, the ban of a fixed theory of inspiration was not felt in the Roman Catholic church in the same degree as among the Protestants. Men like Richard Simon, who died in 1712, and Ellies du Pin, who died in 1719, kept alive in France the sense for certain great distinctions. In the Lutheran church J. D. Michaelis, in Göttingen, and Semler in Halle, who died in 1791, were the real beginners of the modern movement. The great contribution has been made since 1835. But, for a reason which we shall presently state, the discussion of this modern movement does not fall within the plan which we have set ourselves.

The reopening of the whole question of the Canon in our day, the thoroughgoing revision of all materials which are involved, cannot have for its issue the alteration of the outline of the New Testament or the denial of its significance as an historic or again as a religious magnitude. For us the New Testament Canon is just that. It is an historic magnitude with a specific relation to the Christian church and of the Christian church to it. It is a body of literature of incomparable worth to the religious life of the world and to our own religious life. And one thing has grown entirely clear to the men of our generation which was not clear to the ancients, nor even to all of the Reformers. The right of a given book to a place in the collection, its spiritual authority, and the significance of that book for the life of the world, are not necessarily involved with the question of the validity of opinions which have been expressed concerning its authorship, its time and circumstance. Concerning these points it is the function of criticism to inquire. The ancients often asserted, and modern men may have repeated, that a given book obtained its place and exerts its power because it was of such and such authorship. Our study in these lectures has put us in sure possession of the fact that the case was often just the reverse. The men asserted the apostolic authorship of a book because they felt its power. We may acknowledge in reference to our collection of New Testament books, that not all of the later and minor decisions concerning it were equally fortunate with the earlier ones. The decisions reached after the movement had attained the period of self-consciousness are the questionable ones. But in the origin of the New Testament the real case was this. In the large, the books took their place in the Christian movement on the basis of recognition of their unique religious worth. They ministered beyond all other writings to the spiritual life. In Coleridge's phrase they "found" men. They brought to men something at least of that incomparable spirit of truth and grace which had been in Jesus Christ. They partook of his revelation. They were steeped in his inspiration. This was the power which men felt. This was the authority which they conceded. Explanations of that power and theories of that authority they offered later.

It has been so ever since. The book has proved its religious worth and exerted its spiritual power in all ages, and under apprehensions which have differed widely from our own. It proves that worth to-day among men who would dissent most gravely in their theory of Scripture from ourselves. But the time is past when men would deem that any critical conclusion whatsoever could alter by so much as one book the compass of the collection. No modern inquirer imagines that the results of any investigation whatsoever could change the relation of the Christian church to this collection or impair the debt to it of religious men. The New Testament is what it is. It is a fixed magnitude. And only the mistaken assertion that those parts of it in which the inspiration is feeble and almost vanishes are of equal ethical and religious moment with those in which it is most sublime, could tempt any man to wish those weaker parts removed. Only the fatal inversion of ideas which leads men to rest the faith of Scripture upon critical hypotheses, rather than to add their hypotheses to their faith, can jeopardize the matter. It is indeed of supreme importance that we should investigate the history of the Canon, in order that, knowing how our New Testament grew up, we may know how we are to understand its real nature and authority. But it is exactly this investigation which reveals to us that, as we above implied, the history of the New Testament Canon is closed. The contribution of the nineteenth century in this department, and that of any criticism which is conceivable in the future, must, henceforth, be a contribution only to the history of opinion concerning the Canon.

Wonderful is the degree in which even private devotional use of the New Testament literature sustains that thought concerning its inspiration and authority which we have here put forth, and illuminates the history which in these lectures we have been following. An actual setting of all New Testament books on the same level of importance has never been achieved. The Apocalypse never signified so much to the church as did the Romans. And this was not at all because of the critical objections to the Apocalypse. Men concurred in that judgment who knew nothing about the critical objections. It was because, with the exception of a few glorious Christian passages, the content and quality of the Apocalypse, its spirit, made no appeal to them. In their devotional reading of the book they read mainly, or only, those passages. Not all the critical difficulties touching the Fourth Gospel have impaired the fact that, of all the Gospels, this is the one which, to this day, most appeals to the religious life of men. Of all the Gospels it is the one whose loss for the spiritual life would be most keenly felt. The catholic Epistles never meant so much as the Pauline. And of the Pauline Epistles, the ones for certain parts of which, critically, the weakest case can be made out, namely the Pastorals, in certain other parts hold the deepest love of Christians, since they seem to reveal most of the saintly and heroic spirit of that man who won the Gentile world. Upon whatever form of evidence you choose to think, citation of proof texts, the choice for reading in public worship or again in private devotion, the difference in the actual use of New Testament books is enormous. The Gospels, which were the earliest part of the Canon, are read probably a hundred times as much as any of the letters. Least read are those very books, with the exception perhaps only of the Hebrews, which were latest added to the Canon. No theory of inspiration has even been able to do away with the fact that men have found some books more edifying than others. The normal inference is that those books which are the most inspiring are the most inspired.

In closing now our study of this part of the wonderful movement which ended in giving to the world our sacred Book, one thing should be said. We have dealt with those facts only which pertain to the human origin and history of the Book. The facts pertaining to the divine side of the Book, in the very nature of the case, have no history which admits of presentation like that which we have here essayed. It is with the Book which is born of the Spirit as it is with the man who is born of the Spirit. "Thou hearest the sound, . . . but canst not tell whence it cometh nor whither it goeth." But a moment's reflection will show that, in our whole study, we have never penetrated the mystery of that which must yet be postulated to account for the holy and wonderful influence which the Book has always exerted, and does now exert, upon the mind and life of the race. On the contrary, the more we have succeeded in penetrating the veil of false mystery which historic remoteness in part, and in part dogmatic misconception, have thrown about the origin of the Book, the more we have succeeded in bringing the facts, in all of their amazing simplicity, into the clear light of day, just so much the more impressive and mysterious does the influence which we have spoken of appear. Just so much the more impossible does it become for us to feel that that influence can be accounted for in any other way than by our owning that there is here something more than that which is merely human.

But many men and women have lost their faith in the inspiration and authority of the Book because they construe differently that inspiration, and have penetrated some of the assumptions upon which that authority has been supposed to rest. Here, as so often in the history of religion, men have felt, by a certain primitive instinct and with irrefragable force, a given truth. But then they have proceeded to offer the most far-fetched and external, the least cogent and defensible, of reasons for their conviction of that truth. Or they offer to a new age reasons which are germane only to the thinking of an age which has gone by. In their own devout imagination, they put these arguments as basis under the great truth. And all the while, it is not the argument which accounts for their impression, but the invincible impression which accounts for all the argument. It is not, as they fondly imagine, by these arguments that they can convey their impression to new minds and other ages. The impression conveys itself. God's truth demonstrates itself ever afresh, and moves new men and brings forth new argumentation as the ages change.

But when the arguments which have passed current and done service crumble, it is pathetic to see men's bewilderment and pain. Then comes the perception that the truth has not crumbled. It has not lost its power and adaptation. It may be in the very act of asserting a new power and assuming a new adaptation. It is then most glorious when the supports by which devoted men sought to prop it are all fallen away. New men will love it and new might will go forth from it. Always in deep religious things this process must repeat itself. Always this lesson must be learned afresh. And always it is as hard as if it had never been learned before. Always in deep religious matters we have to go down beneath what we rashly call the foundations of the truth, and there discover that the truth is the foundation. The thing we built upon it was but superstructure for our own abiding. It is but bare scaffold, and perhaps not even that, for men who will come after us and in whom God's truth will still abide.

But, as we were saying, men have found certain assumptions which have long been made touching the Book to be false, or at least inadequate, and so they have lost faith in the Book. They have lost the influence of the Book out of their lives. This is very illogical, no doubt. But it is very natural. It is to those who in the educated life of our time are bound to feel the stress, that these lectures are addressed. No men are so much interested in knowing the truth about the Scripture as those of us who believe in it. Nothing goes so far to rehabilitate the Book in the reverence and love of thoughtful people as the fearless study of it and of all that pertains to it, by those same methods which in other sciences have proved successful.

We mourn sometimes the loss of the hold of Scripture upon the mind and life of our generation. It would be idle to allege that the sole cause of that loss is that the change of men's thoughts concerning the Scripture has lagged behind the reconstruction of men's ideas on all other subjects through which our generation has passed. It is a fact that the reconstruction of the thought of many men concerning Scripture has thus lagged behind. But it would be idle to allege this as the sole cause of the diminished power of Scripture in men's lives of which we spoke. There are many other causes. But not all of the devout among us realize, and not all of the bewildered will believe, how far the chaos of notions has taken shape and order, how certain much is where some have felt that everything was uncertain.

Of no department of learning is this remark more true than of that of the study of the Scripture. It is a great gain that we have been led on to a theory of Scripture which is in absolutely harmonious adjustment with the theories which modern men must hold concerning all things besides. It is not that, in the blinding light of scientific certainty upon some of these things, that sense of mystery has vanished wherein, after all, religion has her home. It is only that the lines which lead off into the depths of that unfathomed light are the sure straight lines of that which is absolutely rational and natural, so far as the vision which we now have can follow up those lines. It is but the inference from history, as well as the experience of religion, that the Book has within it the power to meet the highest wants of the highest life of our generation. It has been so in all generations. It will be so until by faithful use of this light which God has given us we come to God's better and greater light.

P

LECTURE VI

THE CANONIZATION AND THE ORIGIN OF CHURCH GOVERNMENT

LECTURE VI

THE CANONIZATION AND THE ORIGIN OF CHURCH GOVERNMENT

WE have spoken thus far in these lectures of the origin and growth of that collection of the literature of early Christianity which we know under the name of the New Testament. We need now to stand apart a little from this movement, to set it in what appears to be its true light. The remarkable development which we have endeavored to trace, the evolution of a simple literature into an authoritative Canon, is then first really understood when it is seen in the light of parallel developments which took place in the same age. It has been said that all the great intellectual and spiritual phenomena of a given era may safely be assumed to be but the manifestations of a common impulse, which pervades and possesses the minds of the men of that era. But there are two main comparisons which in this and in the following lecture we shall need to institute. We shall discern that that movement with which we have thus far been dealing is only a part of a far greater movement. Not less illuminating than the discovery that the New Testament has a history such as that which we have tried to sketch, is the recognition that even that history is but the evidence of tendencies and the product of causes which had at least two other issues that are hardly less wonderful than the one which we have named. Nothing in the life of the race is isolated, just as nothing in our own personal experience stands apart and out of relation to all other things. The causes at work in any significant transition often work more broadly than we had at first supposed. They have other consequences, which we presently discover to be closely allied to those upon which we have dwelt. The discovery of these relationships in other quarters often throws a flood of light upon the facts before us in our own.

In this way, therefore, of pendant and illustration we shall endeavor, with all possible compression, to allude to two things which are in their growth most striking counterparts of the New Testament. These are, namely, the beginnings of church government and the earliest stages of the development of Christian doctrine. Were the materials for investigation less scant than they are, and were the study of such materials as we have in more forward state than it is, we should probably discover that the parallel holds in reference to the forms of Christian ritual as well. The epoch in which the spontaneous outpouring of men's praise and their petitions first gave place to forms of worship, established for the aid and training of the multitude, would probably be found to correspond in striking fashion with that of the first crystallizing into confessional forms of the free doctrinal thinking of the earlier age, with that of the consolidation in the episcopal government of the simpler order of the early churches, and with that of the differentiation of the New Testament from the remainder of the early literature. But that is a problem which has not yet been sufficiently worked out.

We cannot heartily adhere to the historic evolution of Scripture, without holding to the evolution of church government, and of doctrine and ritual as well. Or, rather, inasmuch as we, in common with most men since the Reformation, do hold to the evolution of church government, from the simplest and most natural beginnings in the time of the Apostles to the great structure and colossal organization which in the Middle Ages overshadowed all the world; and since, if we ever thought of it, we do hold to the growth of the great historic forms of worship, we cannot therefore consistently do otherwise than hold to the historic development of Scripture and of dogma as well. We do but bring to bear to-day upon the Scripture the same criticism which the Reformers employed so justly and effectively upon the tradition of the church four hundred years ago. We do but vindicate ourselves the children of their spirit. And surely a far nobler and more vital conception of the church has come through the criticism which in the Reformation was applied to the traditional theory of the church.

This is true as to dogma. The confessions, whatever be their names, to which men give their assent, have tended to become to the Protestant church exactly what the tradition is to the Roman church. It has been made in the Protestant polemic a standing reproach to the Roman Catholic church that it rests upon the Scripture and upon the tradition. It has been deemed the fame of the Protestant churches that they rest upon the Scripture alone. But this contention can scarcely be maintained. In the name of creeds and confessions, from the Apostles' Creed down to the confessions of our own time, the attempt has been made to fix an authoritative interpretation of Scripture, and to praise or to blame men as they accord or disagree with that interpretation. But assuredly this is only traditionalism over again. Indeed, one may say that the Roman tradition has this advantage, that it receives its utterance, in the concrete case, from living men. Confessionalism tends to confer the power of the authoritative interpretation of Scripture only upon men who are dead. We have passed through a period of abuse of doctrine, and of the assumption upon the part of some that we can get on without doctrine. But this is merely reaction against an unhistoric notion of the nature of doctrine. Doctrine is nothing but the adjustment of men's thoughts concerning religion to their thoughts concerning all other things. That adjustment is a perennially necessary task. The attempt to hold our thoughts concerning religion out of all relation to our other thoughts is the sure road by which men, according to temperament, arrive at one of two conditions. They end either in having thoughts without any religion or else in having religion without thoughts. Either condition is deplorable. There are signs that we are on the eve of a noble reconstruction of Christian doctrine. That reconstruction is made possible by the clear historic sense which we have gained as to what doctrine is.

So is it also as to Scripture. It was not unnatural that the men of four hundred years ago should set up against the authority of an infallible church an authority of Scripture which they soon came to apprehend in an almost equally external way. Those men could not have done differently. Their theory of Scripture had a certain historic inevitableness and a great historic right. But they did not perceive that the light of history, and that right reasoning upon history which they so successfully applied to the prevailing theory of the authority of the church, would one day have its way with the idea of an external authority of Scripture as well. It ought to be repeated, to the honor of the first generation of the Reformers, that they began thus to reason upon the problem. There is something pathetic in the defection of the later generations of Protestants from this true example of the Reformers. The authority of Scripture, when thought of as something external and not subject to rational review, has come near to being as great a tyranny and source of darkness as was ever the authority of the church. But, as we have seen, the most vital and potent conception of Scripture has been regained for us, the most reverent and worshipful acknowledgment of the authority of Scripture has been again made possible for us, exactly through the historic sense of what the Christian Scripture really is.

So is it also as to the church. It has been the weakness of Protestantism that having, four hundred years ago, abandoned a theory of the church and of ecclesiastical authority which it deemed unhistorical, it had nothing adequate to put in its place. It was well to repeat the maxim of individualism, but we have discovered that individualism is not the whole truth. The social instinct of our time is fundamental. The immeasurable forces of our generation are those of combination, integration, organization. An institution which cannot augment its efficiency by obedience to these principles is doomed. The primary impulse of Protestantism at this moment is to find its way out of that disorganization and rampant individualism of which it was once so proud. There are not wanting those whose trust is that the way out is the way back, the way of recurrence to that ideal of the church and of its authority which ten generations ago was given up. But even those to whom this is not clear well know that principles which have been neglected must be brought again into effective use. And to this revival of the feeling for the Christian church, as church, before which we surely stand, no greater service can be rendered than that which comes through the recovery of the true historic sense of what the principle of organization of the Christian church really is.

It need not be said that it is not the effort of these two lectures, on the origin of church government, and on the beginnings of the history of doctrine, to maintain proportion with that treatment of the Canon which we have thus far attempted. The purpose of these lectures is merely that of illustration. The thing designed is to show yet more fully the significance of the movement which marked the last generation of the second century, and to remind ourselves that we cannot understand the New Testament if we seek to understand the New Testament alone. The New Testament does not stand alone. But for this purpose of illustration only the outline of the discussion is necessary. Details must be gathered from works which make government and dogma their immediate theme.

We assume that Jesus instituted no form of church government whatever. The Apostles instituted only the most rudimentary forms. Their arrangements were not in all cases the same. These arrangements they themselves regarded as subject to amendment, and not binding in the letter, but only in the spirit, upon future time; if indeed their thought in making any such arrangement turned seriously to the future time. Even if Christ and the Apostles had elaborated forms of church government, these would be binding upon us, not in the letter, but only in the spirit of those forms. The very adaptations which then made them efficient would make them inoperative if taken in all literalness now. The permanent element in a religious institution can never be anything but its spirit. The practical adaptations and adjustments, the applications of that spirit, must be mere temporary contrivances. When these forms are perpetuated as if they were the substance of the matter, they become hindrances and not helps. They become the very instruments of bondage and the antithesis of inspiration. The form of church government and of worship given in the Old Testament, which Jesus certainly deemed to have been inspired, he himself criticised from this point of view. Had there been an apostolic form of church government promulgated with authority from the first, we should still have to seek to gather out the divine principles from those old adjustments and to apply them again in our own time. That to which men attribute divineness they have ordinarily conceived as if it had come into existence in its finished, perfect state. They cannot think of its perpetuating itself save as unchanged from age to age. To other minds the divinest of all things is the mystery of growth. To such minds it is not a less divine institution, but it is, if possible, a more divine institution, doctrine, Scripture, which we see working upon the principle of the leaven and growing up like the mustard seed to which our Lord compared his kingdom at the first.

To the men who gathered about Jesus no control was necessary save that of his personality. The authority which the Apostles exerted in the earliest churches, though beyond question very great, was yet assuredly of this same personal sort. It came from their being the witnesses of Jesus and the teachers of a truth till then unknown. When they departed from their little missionary churches they sometimes left friends or pupils to carry on their work. Sometimes they maintained correspondence with those churches. It has been common among scholars of the last few decades to assert that the earliest Christians were guided in the ordering of their simple affairs by the models of institutions about them in the Jewish and in the Gentile world. But we shall see that there was also an inward principle operative in the growing organization, which was original with the Christian body and characteristic in a high degree. We may grant in largest measure the effect of such external influences as those just alluded to. But the growth of the Christian institution is by no means accounted for through the mere imitation of the synagogue, or, again, of the guilds and societies of the Gentile world. Doubtless, to an observer in those earliest generations who viewed the Christian movement from without, it might have seemed as if these nascent Christian societies managed their little interests and framed their organization upon the pattern of other religious societies and of the social bodies which prevailed about them. The names of functionaries, and indeed almost all the terms involved in the discussion of the earliest church government, are unquestionably thus derived from the Jewish religious organizations and from Gentile societies which had only in part religious purposes. In the reaction from the long ages in which men insisted that the origin of church government was all divine, and spoke as if its order had been virtually let down out of heaven, we have passed through a period in which men have seen little but the human element that beyond question entered into it. They reckoned with nothing but the contribution which was made to the evolving organism from its environment. That there was a contribution from the environment all scholars admit. But that there was a vital and intensely characteristic principle operative from within and from the beginning we must confidently assert.

First among the external influences upon the Christian body was undoubtedly that of the Jewish ecclesiastical organization. That the Jerusalem Christian community stood under the very shadow of the synagogal organization need not be said. And, here in this Jerusalem community, all that we can discover beyond the synagogal organization is a certain great personal influence naturally accorded to representatives of the family of Jesus. But everywhere in the Gentile world also there were synagogues, the local communities of the Jews in the dispersion. Out from these synagogues, or from the circle of their proselytes, the earliest Christians often came. Now the distinctive traits of the synagogal government were these. The control was vested in a body of men known as the elders; presbyters is the Greek word. But these elders were originally simply the older men. One recalls the "elders of Israel." They were simply the heads of families. What we here have is the survival of the patriarchal system as this was developed in the Jewish village communities. The elders were equal among themselves, but were presumed to be fitted by experience to advise and rule over others. In their common capacity they constituted a council which was presided over by one of their number. How this presiding officer was chosen, whether he held his office for a fixed term, whether the honor came to him by seniority, or whether it passed in some sort of rotation, these are things which we do not clearly know. Since to the Jewish mind civil and religious matters were not separated, this communal power of the synagogue-council, even in what we should call secular matters, and even after the establishment of the Roman dominion, was great. The supervision of the moral life, and, to a certain extent, the adjustment of relations of property, were among the things which might, at least, be brought before the elders and secured under the sanction of the religious institution rather than laid before the hated foreign tribunal. And, shut in upon themselves as were the Jewish communities in the Diaspora, endowed with extraordinary privileges by the civil authority as in some cases we know them to have been, we may doubt if the synagogue elders in the Diaspora had less power than had those in Palestine.[1] On the other hand, in reference to the assemblies for worship, we must note a democratic trait. It appears to have been the right of every man to read or to speak to edification in the services of the synagogue. There was no distinct class of persons set apart to the privilege and duty touching the word of God. It was not even a function of elders only thus to speak.

But besides the synagogue there were, in the second place, all about the Christians, multitudes of societies of every name and form among the Gentiles. They varied widely, from purely philosophical brotherhoods to associations for the observance of some cult or the performance of some rite, and even to mutual benefit societies, much like our own insurance and burial societies among the poor, the very class among whom the Gospel in the Gentile world at first struck root. These societies seem almost invariably to have had one natural form of organization. There was a council, and then a sort of president for the over-

---

[1] Schürer, *Geschichte des Jüdischen Volkes in Zeitalter Jesu Christi*, 3d ed., 1898, ii. 427 ff., iii. 38 f. (§§ 27, 31). See also Bacher, art. "Synagogue," in *Hastings' Dictionary of the Bible*, and Schürer, *Die Gemeindeverfassung der Juden in Rom in der Kaiserzeit*, 1879.

sight of the society's affairs. He was called episcopus. Of this name our word "bishop" is a mutilation. The title indicated merely the man who had oversight. The root from which it is derived means "to oversee." The council had less power than in the synagogal government, but the head of the council had more. He was truly an officer, and not merely the representative of a class to whom official duties fell. From the literature which refers to these guilds and corporations, and from inscriptions, especially from Asia Minor, which have come to hand, one gets the impression that the episcopus was concerned chiefly with administration, and sometimes almost wholly with finance. There seems to be no doubt that he was generally elected by the whole body whose practical and executive functionary he thus became. It is reasonably certain, also, that in such of these guilds as existed for the observance of the mysteries, for the performance of some one of the many rites which came in from the Orient at the time of which we speak, the episcopus had to do with the observance of the solemn rite. He thus added a religious leadership to the practical function which he performed.[1]

Now from one or the other of these sources, or from both, from the synagogues, that is, and from these pagan associations for charity and worship,

[1] Hatch, *Die Gesellschaftsverfassung der christlichen Kirchen im Alterthum, übersetzt u. mit Excursen versehen, von Harnack*, Giessen, 1883.

students have deemed that the elements were drawn, as the organization of the early Christian church began to shape itself. Sometimes upon the one side, and again, upon the other, the preponderance has been laid. Few scholars now share the opinion that the organization of the Christian church can be explained entirely from the synagogue, and that the Gentile element had no weight.[1] Careful investigation, moreover, of the history of Israel in the time of Jesus has rendered us uncertain of some points touching the organization of the synagogue which were once deemed to be surely known.[2] On the other hand, distinguished scholars, and that only very recently, have been convinced that the relation of the Christian church to these Gentile guilds and corporations explains almost everything.[3] The first discoveries of these relations were so interesting and suggestive that men were somewhat carried away. But it must not be forgotten that exactly the religious ones among these societies were often guilty, under cover of their mysteries, of such abominations, they were often so notoriously immoral, that we can hardly think that the direct comparison with these societies would have brought to the Christians anything but the suspicion of the state and the aversion of the populace.

[1] See, however, Löning, *Die Gemeindeverfassung des Urchristenthums*, Halle, 1889.

[2] See Schürer, as cited above, p. 225, and Sohm, *Kirchenrecht*, 1892, p. 10.

[3] See Hatch-Harnack in the work cited above, p. 225.

CANONIZATION AND CHURCH GOVERNMENT 227

Still, it is generally thought that elements from these two sources were, in one proportion or another, fused together. The usual theory has been that there existed in the church at the beginning two organizations, side by side, and having but little to do the one with the other. The first of these was the growing organization of the teaching function, of which Apostles, prophets, and teachers were the representatives. This was the element derived from the synagogal order. The other organization was that of the administrative function, particularly that of the administering of charity. And of this organization the bishop was the head. It was this which represented the element drawn from the Gentile source. The origin of the episcopate was thus held to be essentially practical.[1] The bishop represented the people and managed funds. It was the apostolic office, the teaching function, which represented God and Christ, and had to do with the word and worship. It was only as Apostles and prophets disappeared, and as the inspiration out of which every member spoke to edification waned, that the teaching function also was transferred to the bishop, and he thus came to be deemed to represent also the Apostles and Christ himself. This general theory prevailed until recently.

[1] See Ritschl, *Entstehung der altkatholischen Kirche*, 2d ed., 1857, p. 350; Holtzmann, *Pastoralbriefe*, 1880, p. 216; Weizsäcker, *Apostolisches Zeitalter*, 1886, p. 630; Hatch, *Gesellschaftsverfassung*, pp. 31 and 34. But against this, see Harnack, *Apost. Kirchenordnung*, p. 286, and *Dogmengeschichte*, Bd. I., 1888, p. 182.

At the present time no one disputes that there are elements of truth in this ingenious construction. No one denies that influences from both sides were felt. But few any longer hold that in these things we have found the secret of the origin of the Christian church. These influences were all merely external ones. They were too little original and characteristic. The early Christian would hardly have called these influences divine. The secret of the organization of the Christian church was certainly a Christian secret and not a Jewish or pagan one. The real sources of this organization were inward and spiritual. The motive force was one which was conceived by the Christians themselves with the highest originality. It was one which fired their imagination and called out their devotion, as nothing which was to their minds only an accommodation from the ancestral synagogue or from the pagan cultus societies ever could have done. That organizing principle was nothing less than the sense of the divine in the midst of the Christian community in this relation also. It was nothing less than the sense of that inspiration which was the universal characteristic of the beginning of the Christian movement. It was nothing less than the belief in the divine gift, the conferment of the grace of Jesus Christ upon some members of the community to do this duty also, just as, through a divine gift and grace, they spoke to their fellows the word of life. It was nothing less than the belief in the divine call of some men to take upon themselves in the name of God the responsibility of practical leadership, to exert influence in truth and love for the ordering of the affairs of the fellowship of believers. It was nothing less than the belief in an enduement of men with spiritual power to do these things, which was exactly parallel to the gift of grace by which men led acceptably the services of worship. And, indeed, this practical service was never separated from the leadership in worship or, at least in the conception of it, from the service of the word. If we should put this theory of the origin of church government in paradoxical form, we should say that an organization for the government of the church, in the sense in which we ordinarily understand those words organization and government, in the sense in which we should naturally attribute rights and powers to the church, — such an organization was a contradiction of the very essence of Christianity and of the nature of the church itself.[1]

There were not those two different tendencies to organization in the Christian church, from the beginning, which we have described above, the one being the organization of the teaching office, which rested solely upon the gift of God, the outward form of which was derived from the synagogue; while the other, the organization for practical administration, represented merely the

[1] See Sohm, *Kirchenrecht*, 1892, pp. 1 ff., and repeatedly. Sohm's contribution to this discussion is epoch-making.

rights and powers of men and took shape from the pagan societies.[1]

The word of God was originally preached, exhortation was given, prophecy was uttered, by any man whom the Spirit of God moved, and according to the measure of grace bestowed upon him. Apostles, prophets, teachers, who exercised this function, might, indeed, themselves be members of the local community. Or they might be messengers from some other community. They might be men who went from one community to another, making such preaching and teaching the occupation of their lives. But the essential thing was the notion of the call of God, of the enduement with power of the Holy Spirit thus to teach. Essential, also, was the recognition on the part of the community that the persons who thus spoke were in reality called of God and were full of a holy spirit for their work. This has been on all hands acknowledged as the basis of the teaching function in the early church.

But we have no cause whatever to assert that the case was different with the executive function. To the minds of those earliest Christians the basis was not different for the duty of the administration of funds, of the care of the poor, of the maintenance of discipline, of the leadership in the assemblies for worship, and, above all, in the celebration of the Eucharist. It is not as if, while the service of the word was rendered at the call of

[1] Sohm, pp. 3, 6, and often.

God and by the endowment of the Spirit, these other services were rendered only upon the appointment of man and with the kind of right which one acquires in secular affairs. On the contrary, it was by the call of God and the gift of grace, it was "in the Spirit," that one performed these duties too. It was the fitness of the service thus rendered which was the direct proof of the divine call. It was the influence of the service thus rendered in the edifying of the body of Christ which was the evidence that the man who volunteered to render it was no mere pretender to the inspiration of the Holy Ghost. It was the answer in the hearts of men and women to the pure spirit of goodness in which these tasks were fulfilled which constituted the basis of obedience of the members of the community to those to whom the honor of fulfilling these tasks fell. Where this goodness and spirit of love were present, obedience was due as to the God from whom the goodness and love came. But where this goodness and spirit of love failed there was no obligation of obedience, but rather the duty of repudiating the leadership of those in whom the cardinal witness to the call of God was lacking. It was therefore not only not a contradiction in terms but it was a perfectly clear idea, when the early Christians said that to those who ruled in righteousness among them they owed allegiance as to Christ and God Himself, and yet were entirely conscious that they were themselves the judges whether these leaders among them did rule in righteousness, and were aware that if these did not rule in righteousness, they owed them no allegiance whatever. It was a perfectly clear idea, and one so simple and so beautiful that we can say only that it is a pity that this idea was so soon obscured. But this also is quite obvious, that a government which can be described in these terms is no government in the human sense. Its rights, laws, and order are not rights and laws in the conventional acceptation of those words.[1]

The church might appear to one outside of it as if made up of little isolated communities, which had no common bond save the bare fact of being committed to one cause. But that was not the semblance which the matter bore to the Christian mind. Underneath the separateness of the individual communities and the apparent existence of church organization only for the local body, underneath this was the great ideal, the universal conception of the church as the people of God under the new covenant. Where Christians assembled, no matter how few of them, there was Christ in their midst. And, conversely, where the Lord was, there was his church. In each one of these little local bodies the spirit of all Christendom was manifest, and all the functions of Christ's institution were performed. Any group of Christians, by the mere fact of assembling together, enters into all the rights and privileges and claims all the

[1] Sohm, p. 16.

promises. It hears the word of the Lord, it receives the revelation of prophets, it baptizes, it observes the Lord's Supper, it ministers to the poor in the Lord's name, it rebukes sin and declares God's forgiveness of sins. It does these things in its capacity as representative, for that time and place, of the whole Christian movement, and as having Christ himself, the head of the church, in its midst. The word of God is not acknowledged to be such because it has been uttered by one who holds an office which in some way commissions him to utter it. The word of God is recognized as such by its own inward power, by its effect on the hearts of men, no matter who utters it. Even a man whose apostolic consciousness is as strong as was that of Paul commends himself, in the last analysis, to every man's conscience in the sight of God. The part played by the wandering prophets in these early generations would be quite unthinkable, did we not assume that when these persons really spoke for truth, love, and goodness, they found acceptance, and when they did not thus speak, they went to another place.

And this, which is true of the preaching, prophecy, teaching, is no less true of the solemn acts of the church in its united capacity, that is, of its charities and philanthropy, of its maintenance of discipline, of its acts of worship, and, above all, of its celebration of the Eucharist. These, too, in the last analysis, are deemed to be done only under the Spirit and guidance of God, and must commend themselves to the consciences of men. In these things, too, the church was but the organ of the authority of God. It is a fundamental fallacy to suppose that the rule of the church could ever be separated from the teaching office, as if this last responsibility were borne by the grace of God, and that other merely by commission of men. The rule of the church could never be separated from the teaching office because it was the word of God and the impulse of His Spirit which was the decisive instance in the whole order and work and discipline of the church.[1] Converts were to be baptized and admitted to the Lord's Supper only upon the ground of the call of God to those converts. Absolution from sin could take place only in the name of God, and so must be a part of the function of him who handles the word of God and knows the will of God. The celebration of the Eucharist could never be a mere executive function. It could never take place without the holy word, the oracles of the prophets, and especially the reminiscence of the Master who suffered for our sakes. Even the administration of charity was only the doing in love, for others, out of the treasure which, through the gift of believers, had become Christ's treasure; as also those to whom the gifts were given were Christ's poor. A man's fitness in character and spirit for the rendering of one or all of these services was the evidence of his call of God, at least for the time

[1] Sohm, pp. 29 f.

being, to render these services. Any man might offer himself for the service, and the church itself was the judge both of the worthiness of him who thus offered, and again of the blessing to all with which the service was attended.

The beginnings of actual organization in fixed forms and with rights and powers, would surely have come with the growing needs and self-consciousness of even single communities worshipping in a given place. Those needs were of various sorts. But the assembly of all Christians of a given place for the celebration of the Lord's Supper was the central point in the life of the Christian community. The Eucharist could indeed be observed at any time, and in any place where two or three were met together. But it was the rule to observe it on the Lord's day, and in an assembly of the whole body of Christians. Here first, probably, made itself felt that necessity of a solemn and representative leadership from within the community itself, which was the beginning of church government. Apostles, prophets, constituted in a way the only functionaries of the universal church. But exactly for that reason it was not from these that the organization of the local community could take its rise. An Apostle, a prophet, as in the earliest days, would lead these services of the assembled Christians on the Lord's day and conduct the observance of the Lord's Supper, if such an one chanced to be present. But some one of blameless life, of power in God's word, whose fitness was also conceded by the multitude, would perform this duty if no apostolic man were present. By the leader in this solemn act of worship was offered the prayer of thanksgiving which gave name to the Eucharist. In connection with the observance of the Lord's Supper were offered the gifts which constituted the church funds for charitable purposes, for the relief of the poor, for the support of widows and of the sick and aged, and of that class, at times not inconsiderable, of those who, after conversion, could not return to their old employments and for whom temporary provision must be made. These funds the leader of the solemn act of worship had the responsibility of administering. If the church had been thought of as a corporation, an association, or society, those funds would have been spoken of as the church funds. They are never in the earliest period thus spoken of. They are always alluded to as Christ's funds, as the Lord's treasures, as belonging to God alone. And he administers them for God who, in prayer, in the leadership of worship, in instruction, interprets to men the word and will of God. Apostles might be prophets. Both were in a sense teachers. But the teacher, in the specific sense, is the settled resident, in contrast to those others, who were more often only visitors. It was the permanent resident in the community, the man who, in the absence of Apostles and in the decline of the prophecy, comforted and admonished his equals and trained up the younger persons — he it was to whom naturally fell the leadership in the service of the Eucharist. The teacher might lack the peculiar prophetic vision; he had not the experience at first hand which was the original endowment of the Apostles, but it was he by whom, in the same gift of the Holy Spirit, the regular edification of the community was carried forward. It was the man with the power of the Holy Ghost in the service of the Gospel, who naturally led also in the Eucharist and administered the sacred fund for charity.

Even the right of the Apostles and of others to be supported out of the fund created by these gifts given at the observance of the Lord's Supper was derived from the Apostles' service to Christ. It was not viewed as compensation for their labors in the particular community, for which they might receive pay out of community funds. The teaching office, in so far as it became an occupation absorbing all the time of men, was sustained always from this point of view. He who teaches, celebrates the Eucharist, administers the charity of the church in Christ's name, may receive for his own support, if he have need, out of the treasure which belongs to the Lord and in order that he may be free from other cares. But no other right of compensation, and no compensation of administrative officers as such, is ever mentioned. In truth, there were no administrative officers as such. Even for the deacons the point of view is always that of the call of God, and not that of the appointment of men, save as men, in appointing, recognized the call of God.

To those only whose word and life awaked response in Christian hearts, to those only whose gifts were verified in the edification of their hearers, was the service in the word of God, the leadership of worship, the power of discipline, and the responsibility of financial administration permanently intrusted. We cannot yet speak of officers. There were no officers, in the sense in which we should understand that word in any other organization. But if the church named such and such an one to be a permanent functionary, its stated leader and teacher and administrator, it was because it believed that God had thus named him. In a very real sense the church chose its officers; yet it did not view itself as choosing them, but merely as recognizing God's choice.

All this language which we have been using has to be divested of some age-long associations before we can realize how simple and beautiful it is. In the associations in which we sometimes meet it, such speech mystifies us and repels. It has been used sometimes as the language of obscurantism and has become the phrase of superstition. Men have sometimes spoken as if the call of God were evidenced by marks which no man could recognize, or at least not recognize by rational process and by moral sense. That has been sometimes put forth as the choice of God which we very well know to have been the choice of men,

CANONIZATION AND CHURCH GOVERNMENT 239

and a very bad choice and from very questionable motives. The result is bewildering. It is worth while to get back to the simple and transparent meaning of these much used phrases, and to realize what was intended by them when they began their life and service in the first pure enthusiasm of the Christian church.

But we must ask ourselves, Who were the presbyters in the organization of the Christian church in the earliest time? The statement made by Jerome, which has been much approved since the time of the Reformation, and which has given no small comfort to the non-episcopal orders, that bishop and presbyter are but different names for the same officer is hardly correct.[1] It would be more true to say that the presbyter of the earliest times was not an officer of the church at all. He belonged to a class which was indeed held in honor, and to which certain natural functions fell. But the presbyterate was not an office. The elders were simply those members of the Christian community who had been some time within its circle, and had given evidence of their Christian character through their deeds of charity and their blameless walk. In the nature of things the official heads of the church would probably be taken from among the elders. And yet not even that was

[1] See Jerome, Ep. 69. 3, and Ep. 146. 1; cf. Lightfoot, *Commentary on Philippians*, p. 97 f., and *Essay on the Christian Ministry*, p. 196; A. V. G. Allen, *Christian Institutions*, p. 79; and Schmiedel, art. "Ministry," in *Encyclopedia Biblica*, iii. 3101.

necessarily the case. The presbyter was not one of the heads of the church in any official sense. There was no appointment to the dignity of a presbyter. No choice placed a man in the class of the elders.[1] But if the presbyter had no office, he had an honored place. When the community had grown too large for all to sit with the bishop at the table in the Eucharist, the presbyters still sat with him there. But they did this exactly in their character as representatives of the people.

There was an ordination to the bishopric. The choice was ordinarily out of the ranks of the elders. And after a presbyter was thus chosen bishop, he was the presbyter by eminence, placed thus, at least for the time being, over the church. The ruling elder was that one of the presbyters who had been chosen bishop. The presbyter, as presbyter, did not rule. The bishop was merely that one of the presbyters who was called upon by the community to take upon him the responsibilities which we have described. The bishop was that one of the presbyters to whom, through the choice of the congregation, testimony was given that he, in the gift of grace, had received the call of God to the service of the word, to lead in the acts of worship, and to administer benevolence. But that a bishop, even after he had thus been chosen, had no legal and exclusive right, is evident from the fact that in the presence of an Apostle he gave

[1] The first trace of the ordination of a presbyter is in the *Shepherd of Hermas*, Vis. iii. 1. 8, 9.

place. It is still further evident from the fact that there were, commonly in these early churches, even in the smallest of them, more bishops than one. The name may have continued to be held by those who formerly exercised the function, or by the whole group of those who exercised it in turn. It is not that they constituted a bishops' college within the local church, as has been often assumed. That would imply organization by right. Their function was by grace. A man's fitness need not have failed when he ceased to do the duty of a bishop. He returned to the rank of the presbyters. But still he was always a presbyter who had been singled out as a bishop. The number of bishops was not a fixed one. We know nothing of an appointed term. The bishop for the time being was merely he who had been called by the congregation to the doing of the appointed task.

And yet, although such was the theory, every circumstance, as the church moved forward in the second century, made for the permanence of one individual in the performance of the bishop's function. Everything tended to transform his task into an office, and to confer upon him ever enlarging powers which corresponded to the responsibility of that office. We said that such was the original theory. But one is fain to ask himself whether it was more than a theory. Was human nature ever such that upon a basis like this it could do work and achieve a purpose in the world? Certain it is that the forces of human nature, and as well the exigencies of the task which the Christian movement set itself, tended ever and inexorably to bring about a change of this ideal and spiritual basis. And this change from the rule of the Spirit to the rule of the bishop is the precise parallel to the transition which we have been studying, from the authority of Christ to that of the written Book. An organization of the church, which was really an organization, became with the enlarging problem and the new time an absolute necessity. Long before the end of the second century the government of the church wore an aspect very different from that of the simple situation which we have described. But elements of this ideal are carried forward and reappear, sometimes in strange shapes, in every organization for government which the church has known. And yet, almost in the purity of its ideal, this simple organization, or rather absence of organization, continued in portions of the world down to the time of the Didachè, at all events, and traces of it may be found even much later. But yet in the Epistle of Clement we may see the beginning of the transformation which is to pass over the whole nature of the thing.

The strife in the Corinthian community was of the nature of a rebellion of the younger element against the elder. It was a strife concerning the bishop's office. It had taken the form of the shutting out of appointed elders from the celebration of the Eucharist.[1] The Roman church felt called

[1] 1 Clement, ii. 3, and cf. xxix. 1. See Sohm, p. 163.

upon to intervene. It sent three of its elders with a letter to allay the strife. The Romans declare that the Corinthian church is acting contrary to the commandment of God. There must be a fixed order in the church. The Apostles had appointed bishops and deacons because they knew beforehand by revelation that just such strife as this in the Corinthian church would certainly arise. It was a sin on the part of the Corinthians to rebel against the representatives of the Apostles, who had not laid themselves open to any reproach in reference to their moral life. One sees here the beginning of the claim of apostolic character for the organization. To these very Corinthians Paul had himself said that God was not the author of confusion.[1] Only when we appreciate that the genius of primitive Christianity was enthusiasm, inspiration, unbounded liberty, and emphasis upon the individual, are we prepared to appreciate why Paul spoke so often and so strongly as he did of order in the Christian churches. The early Christians would have said that the Apostles gave some simple kind of organization to the Christian churches, because order was good. The Romans were prepared to say that the particular form of organization and order was good because the Apostles gave it. We see here the precise parallel to the beginning of the claim of the authority of documents because they were apostolic, and no longer simply because they enshrined the Christ.

[1] 1 Corinthians xiv. 33.

We have here the beginning of the claim that a bishop, once chosen, holds his place and performs his function by right. Ordination is put in the way of gaining a legal quality, instead of having, as before, a character merely of gift and grace. The ideal had been the rule of the word and Spirit of God in the church. But a fixed government of men was becoming a necessity. And the only way in which the rule of the word of God in the church could give place to a fixed government of men, was that that government of men should be proclaimed as provided for in the word of God. It is precisely this which here in the Roman Epistle takes place. Government in the church of the Apostles is proclaimed as provided for in the apostolic writings. What effect this letter may have had upon the Corinthian church we do not know. But the contention which is here put forth had revolutionary effect upon the Roman church itself. It never forgot that for which it had contended. This idea governs, henceforth, the Roman church, that there is a divine order of church government, sacred and inviolable, established at the beginning by the Apostles themselves. We have here the precise parallel to the fact that the church came to deem that it had in the apostolic documents a sacred literature, a Canon, authoritative in this new sense from the first.

The original Christianity was an enthusiasm, an inspiration, an idealism, for which no organization was needed. But after the beginning of the second century the courage of that faith which trusts everything to the word of God and to the spirit in man, steadily sinks. It is this impaired faith, this diminished sense of inspiration, this declining idealism, which demands a church government with formal limitations, with guaranties and rights and powers, for the maintenance of order in Christendom. Just so we have seen that the impaired faith of men in their own inspiration enhanced their sense of the unique inspiration of writings attributed to the Apostles. There was entire justification, there was an historic right, there was a practical necessity, for some such movement. It was inevitable that the kind of organization which we have seen in the Christian church should be transformed into a real government, and that the duty should be laid upon the bishops really to govern. One knows how near lay the abuse of Christian love and trustfulness. We are not left to surmise the absurdities and wickednesses which were perpetrated in the name of the Christian inspiration and enthusiasm, even by Christians themselves. Some even of Paul's Epistles betray that there were things of this sort in the Christian communities, here and there, which occasioned him anxiety. We remember that the Didachè rules that apostles shall not stay more than two days in a place.[1] We recall Lucian's satire on the cynic philosopher, Peregrinus Proteus, and his ridiculous imposition upon the

---

[1] Didachè, xii. 5.

Christian community. There were strong reasons for wishing to get the teaching and worship and administration of charitable funds into the hands of known and trusted men. The exigencies of the period of persecution, the pressure of the doctrinal issue, made it impossible that the church should continue to exist without a real leadership such as had not yet been demanded. That leadership appeared in the emergency. But just so the Canon and the creed were called forth by the same emergency. And in principle all three of these things are apprehended by the Christians as having been present from the beginning in provisions which the Apostles had made.

But if, through the choice to the bishopric, an exclusive right was to be given to the bishop in the celebration of the Eucharist and in the administration of charity, if the initiative was to be taken away from the community and the episcopal authority was to become a fixed order, there must be henceforth only one bishop. And just this, that there shall be but a single bishop in a given community, and that the observance of the Lord's Supper shall not be valid which the bishop does not lead — these are the great contentions of Ignatius. He is never weary of asserting that where the bishop is, there alone is Christ. Significant is the contrast with the text: "Where two or three are gathered together in my name, there am I in the midst of them." For that part of the world for which Ignatius wrote one further point is to be

CANONIZATION AND CHURCH GOVERNMENT 247

noted. Although the single bishop is there, still the definite circle of those who are to attend his communion and to be under his administration has not yet been created. The obligation of the individual to attend communion in a certain place, and under a certain bishop, rather than in another place and in an assembly not presided over by this bishop, has not come to full recognition.[1] But for Justin the bishop of Rome has a definite church community, which from city and country assembles to the Eucharist that he celebrates, and outside of the bishop's assembly, or except by some one whom the bishop deputes, the Eucharist cannot be celebrated.[2] In Rome, therefore, between Clement and Justin, this change has taken place. On the other hand, in Syria, or perhaps Egypt, in the time of the Didachè, about 150 A.D., there were in the single communities more bishops than one; there was no definitive right of any bishop; and, in the Roman sense of that contention, the institution of the bishopric was not carried back to the Apostles. The Eucharist was still celebrated by the wandering apostle when he arrived, and presumably by any Christian of good character.

But it is altogether obvious that the exigencies of the organization, so soon as it grew large and complicated, would involve the placing of some one in charge of the general interests, and the clothing him with an authority which was bound to become

[1] Ignatius, *Ad Magnes.*, 4.   [2] See Sohm, p. 187.

more and more absolute. The disappearance of the class of men known as apostles gave to the presbyters and bishops great power in the name of Christ. The maintenance of discipline among the Christians, as against the low moral standard of the heathen world, gave them yet more. The vast growth of Christian charity in the period of persecution tended in the same direction. In the days of stress the churches of a city or of a province must be able to act in concert and to present a common front. Inevitably the presiding officer of the strongest church, or the strongest man then presiding over any church, would be expected to act in the name of all. The doctrinal emergency was working, as we shall see, for the elevation of the heads of the so-called apostolic churches to a position of unquestioned influence. Some one must be able to define what Christianity was and to defend it before the world. The same causes which we have seen leading the church toward an universally accepted Canon of the New Testament, we now see driving it toward a generally acknowledged and strongly centralized form of government. In the two movements the same conception, namely, that of apostolicity, plays the main part. The matured state of things at the end of the second century is carried back to the middle of the first century; and being attributed, in form and directly, to the Apostles, it gains the weight of their great name. There was no church in all the world for one moment to dispute the natural

CANONIZATION AND CHURCH GOVERNMENT 249

leadership of the church of Rome. And if we add to this that, just at the crucial epoch, for several generations the church of Rome was ruled by a series of very able men, with all the Roman instinct for dominion, we see something of the forces which were working toward the one great result.

Any one can see that the first consequence of the claiming for the church an organization in right was necessarily the externalization of the church. It was the making of the church a power and kingdom in the world, in the sense in which the Roman church has always claimed to be a power and kingdom in the world. This consequence Ignatius did not perceive. But this inference Irenæus and Cyprian drew. To Irenæus, about the year 180, the fact of belonging to the church which is headed by the rightful bishop and the possession of the faith inherited in all the apostolic communities—these are the things which constitute a Christian.[1] These are the means by which his life is brought into touch with the life and spirit of Jesus. For Cyprian, face to face with the Novatian schism, not even the adherence to the orthodox faith was conclusive. The Novatians were not heretical. They were only schismatic. For Cyprian, therefore, it is the holding to the rightful bishop which characterizes the true Christian.[2] Not where the Christian experience is, the gift of a holy spirit in men's lives,

[1] Irenæus, *Adv. Hæres.*, iv. 53. 2.
[2] Cyprian, *Epist.* 69. 3 and 8, and repeatedly.

which had been the bond and condition everywhere at first; not where the Scriptures are; not where the apostolic faith and the rightful bishop are, as with Irenæus; but where the rightful bishop is, there, and there alone, is Christ. Cyprian would not have denied that men may have had the Christian experience in other ways than this which he describes. But the true way is under the allegiance to the rightful bishop. It is through obedience to the bishop that one shows his spirit of obedience to Christ. But for such a zealot's soul as was that of Cyprian, so unmeasured a claim on behalf of the bishopric, and of himself as bishop, could never be made to rest upon the choice and ordination of men, as if such high privilege and inexorable duty could be conferred upon a man by men. Always the consciousness of the original state of things is carried forward, and this enormous power of the bishop is made to rest, not upon any human appointment, but upon inspiration and divine call. The elections of bishops, which, in those sadly troubled times presented often a most painful spectacle, are spoken of always as transactions in which men have no part, save only to concur in that which God has done.

An equally certain consequence of this new order of things since Ignatius, and a consequence which was ever more and more accentuated by Irenæus and by Cyprian, was the attribution to the bishop and to his assistants in the celebration of the Eucharist of a priestly character which gradually and completely took the place of the original Christian priesthood of all believers. The original priestly function in the new covenant had been prayer, and especially the common prayer at the Eucharist. So long as the Eucharist had been celebrated anywhere and at any time when Christians came together, and by any one whom they recognized as having received of God that grace of character which fitted him to celebrate, the Eucharist was a representative act. It was a function of the community. He who administered it was but the agent of the worshippers. But from the moment when it began to be held that the Eucharist could be celebrated, not by any Christian, not even by a presbyter acting for the time as bishop, but only by the one presbyter who had been formally chosen, and only when the bishop chose, and only where he was, the centre of gravity of the whole transaction was changed.[1] The power resided henceforth, not with the community, but with the bishop. The Eucharist became a sacerdotal function, and the long road toward the doctrine of the Mass was entered upon. Even Tertullian calls the bishop "sacerdos." The separation in principle of the clerical body from the mass of believers was begun. And in Cyprian, before the year 250, it was complete.

Moreover, with this right of the bishop to order or to refuse permission for the Eucharist and for the collection of alms which went with the Euchar-

[1] Tertullian, *De Bapt.*, c. 17.

ist, and with his right to control the alms thus collected, went also the duty of deciding who should speak or teach or prophesy in the Christian communities. If the bishop alone could grant that privilege to others, of course he had it for himself. The bishop and those whom he appoints gradually take the place which in the older days Apostles, prophets, teachers had held. The free participation of all Christians in the service of the word of God is at an end. With the growth of the church from without, by conversion of adults from all classes of the heathen; with its growth also from within, through the children born in Christian families; with the necessity of declaring what was authoritative Christian doctrine in face of the heretics and even of answering for it to the powers, came more and more the assumption on the part of the bishop of control over the teaching office as well. This control of the bishop over the teaching office was in complete contradiction to the original state of things, in which every man testified as the grace of God was given unto him. But the original feeling is still shown in this, that this power of the bishop is never viewed as conferred by the congregation in its interests. It is deputed to the bishop by Christ and the Apostles themselves.

The last vestige of the old state of things disappears when Calixtus, who was Bishop of Rome from 217 to 222 A.D., declares that not even for deadly sin may a community seek to remove its bishop. The original state of things had been, as we have seen, that a bishop became such by virtue of the community's recognition of the gifts of God to him which fitted him for his work, and the foremost of all these was a blameless life. In that earlier time if a bishop had been guilty of a serious sin the congregation would not be deemed to have taken away from him the right to officiate. That right would be held to have lapsed of itself. His character constituted the only evidence that he had any such right. It would have been deemed that the grace of God upon which all his service rested was not in him, or had departed from him. Even in Clement of Rome, the reproach against the younger element in the community is explicitly that they had rebelled against appointed bishops concerning whom no sin had been alleged. The implication is that if these had been accused of sin it would have been a different matter. In the century and a quarter since Clement a great change has taken place. So necessary is the bishop, even to the existence of the church; so great is the emphasis upon his outward succession in the line of the Apostles; so impenetrable is the mystery of the divine call; so much is his heavenly enduement made to consist in things other than those simple moral and spiritual qualities of which every man is a judge, that in 220 a bishop of Rome has the hardihood to assert that a bishop's sins are not reviewable by men, and that they do not vitiate his service in the things of God. It is to the honor of Cyprian that he bitterly resented this. But

Stephen, Bishop of Rome from 254 to 257 A.D., maintained the theory in its full practical consequence. The community has no right whatever to seek the removal even of the unworthiest bishop.

Just as in the conflict with Gnosticism and Marcionitism the free teaching which had been characteristic of earliest Christianity was put down by the episcopate, just so in the reaction from Montanism, the last vestige of the original Christian inspiration and of the right to forgive sins through that inspiration, is done away by the episcopate. Zephyrinus and Calixtus both held the claims of the Montanists in this particular as an invasion of the rights of the successors of Peter.[1] The presbyterate remained in some sense, as we have seen, representative of the rights of the congregation. But more and more the presbyters, too, become the aids and functionaries of the bishop. As they sat with the bishop and not with the communicants in the celebration of the Eucharist, they came more and more to be identified with the clergy and separated from the laity. The very word presbyter becomes priest, and loses all sense of its original meaning as elder. Even the deacons are deemed to be in preparation for the priesthood. The order of the clergy arrogates to itself all religious functions in the name of God. The people became passive recipients. The whole institution of the Middle Ages is fully forecast before the third century is

[1] Tertullian, *De Pudicit.*, 1.

CANONIZATION AND CHURCH GOVERNMENT 255

gone. The association of bishops, metropolitans, and patriarchs in the synods remains the characteristic thing in the East, as it is even down to our own day. In the West the power of the Pope overshadows everything. But the theory of the clerical organization is the same in either case.

The monarchical episcopate, culminating logically in the papacy at Rome, came naturally in the development of the church. It was well to say that where two or three were gathered together in Christ's name there was Christ in their midst. It was true that, in that original sense, the church could have no organization. But for the actual state of things, both without the church and within the church as well, for the work which Christianity was destined to accomplish in the world, it must have an organization. That organization did beyond question grow up in experience, and, somewhat, at least, after the manner which we have endeavored to outline. It did absorb large elements from Judaism and from Hellenism, as also, later, it has absorbed large elements from Roman imperialism, from feudalism, and from democracy. That organization was guided by experience. But the church was not conscious of these facts. It would not have admitted them to be facts. It must pay tribute to its original ideal by regarding the organization which through two hundred years had been growing up in most natural fashion among the Christians, as not the outcome of the working of the spirit of the good in leading men, but as the ordinance of the Apostles and as given by the authority of Christ from earliest days. It was a practical necessity that the bishop should rule by right, and, if need be, also by might. But that right and might must not be thought of as if they were derived from men. They must be deemed to have been conferred in the gift and grace of God. Even the most questionable and oppressive phases of this right and might must be thought of as ordained by Christ and the Apostles from the first.

Other institutions beside the church have claimed that their authority was by divine right. We reverently acknowledge the divineness of what is right. But assuredly nothing can have a divine right to be in the wrong. And, least of all, ought we to assert that God confers upon men or institutions the divine right to be in the wrong. We must even assert that when that which claims divine right, though still good, is no longer the best, then the divine right has clearly passed onward to that which is better. In this movement of human institutions and experience lies the advance of men and the progressive revelation of God.

If we ask ourselves who is to be the judge of this good and better and best, even in the case of those institutions which claim to be divine, we must answer, solemnly, humanity, and in the last analysis, the individual man, the soul of the man who seeks the good. If it be answered that the final outcome is, then, the assertion of the right of human reason, we must call it rather the devout assumption of human responsibility, the acknowledgment of a responsibility which we cannot escape if we would, and, trusting ourselves to God, we would not if we could.

But if the Roman church erred in taking the practical issue of several centuries of experience and projecting that against the time of the Apostles, so as to make it appear that the deposit of its own history was an original ordainment of Christ, the Protestants erred on their part in supposing that by the recovery, as nearly as might be, of the simple state of things which obtained in the Apostolic Age we should secure the most perfect adaptation to the complex conditions of the seventeenth or of the twentieth century. Because the mediæval church seemed to have got far away from the conditions of the time of Christ and of the Apostles, men deemed that we should be saved by going back to those conditions. We shall never be saved by going backward. We can never reconstruct conditions. In this sense even the devout cry which we hear so much in our day, "Back to Christ," is misleading. We shall never be saved by going back, even to Christ, save as we mean that we go back to Christ to gather, if we can, something of his perfect spirit out of the manifestation of that spirit in his work, and then go boldly forward with intelligence and courage to do our own work, in our own way, and not in Christ's way and not in the Apostles' way. The rigid adherence to what men take to be gospel simplicity of church organization, in an age like our own whose task is not simple; the insistence upon the old issue of individualism in an age when everything makes for social endeavor and combination, is the path of defeat, despite all the devout intention through which that defeat may come to pass. Painful experience has brought the Protestant bodies, for the most part, to the pass where they admit that they must seek a reconstruction of the church through power of combination and of effective organization for its new life and work. And in that reorganization of the church which we certainly face, there are, in our own age, as there were for the organization of the church in the great creative period which we have been studying, two duties. The one of these duties is that of the rational and fearless appropriation of the materials of the actual world in which we live, as the early church appropriated elements from the synagogue and from the Gentile societies among which it was thrown. The other duty is that of fidelity to the pure and luminous ideal, ethical and not ecclesiastical, the legacy to his institution of Christ's own beautiful and holy spirit, the impulse which in this lecture we have endeavored to describe.

LECTURE VII

THE CANONIZATION AND THE BEGINNINGS OF THE HISTORY OF DOCTRINE

LECTURE VII

THE CANONIZATION AND THE BEGINNINGS OF THE HISTORY OF DOCTRINE

WE have to speak in this lecture of the beginnings of Christian doctrine. In respect of the history of doctrine also we have to note the great transformation through which Christianity passed in the last generation of the second century. From this new side we may throw light upon the process of the canonization. The doctrinal movement also presents a striking and suggestive parallel to the rise of the New Testament. In the evolution of doctrine and in the crystallization of doctrine into authoritative dogma, we shall observe the working of the same forces with which we are familiar in the transformation of the early Christian literature into the Canon of the new dispensation. To the Apostles themselves were attributed propositions whose general sense, indeed, had been inherited in the apostolic churches, but whose form of statement and whose use as a creed reflected the conditions which prevailed in the middle of the second century. In like manner a literature whose relation to the Christian origins and whose spiritual quality had given it a unique place in the Christian communities, came to be viewed almost as if the Apostles themselves had established it as an authoritative canon from the beginning. And as we have seen, the development of church government, pursuing the same general course and having the same historic justification, yet falls in the end under the same explanation.

It seems obvious that Jesus himself taught nothing in the least degree resembling a system of theology. He revealed a religion. Or, more accurately, he made a definite and supreme advance upon all religion which had thus far been revealed. But for the most fundamental propositions in religion he rarely argued. What was newest and most original in his teaching he did not undertake in the conventional sense to demonstrate. He clothed, indeed, a part of his teaching in the forms in which his own nation had cherished its Messianic hope. And in appropriating to his own meaning figures to which his contemporaries attached a different sense, he laid himself open to misunderstanding, even while he sought a clearer understanding on the part of those to whom he spoke. But he never tried to make his sublime moral teaching acceptable to men by setting it in relation to any philosophy then current. His appeal is a clear one to the ethical consciousness and to men's experience. His interest is mainly in the personal and practical, not at all in the metaphysical. His favorite reasoning is, for substance, this: Try what I say and see if it is not true. "If any man will do His will he shall know of the doctrine whether it be of God or whether I speak of myself." No man ever spoke with a more immediate personal authority. But the basis upon which he rests that authority is revealed in that astounding sentence, so little like the words of those who have loudly claimed authority: "If any man believe not my word I judge him not. But the word which I have spoken will judge him at the last day." The authority is simply that of the truth itself, and the final test of that truth is experience. The final proof of the authority of truth to any man is that man's free experience of that truth.

It is almost misleading to call Jesus the founder of a religion. By that phrase it is usually meant to bring him into comparison with those religious founders who have offered to the world a system of thought or an ascetic discipline of life, a ritual practice, or something of that sort. Jesus, strictly speaking, did none of these things. He seems to have aimed to show men how, in love and joy, to live the common life, in full sense of the presence of God and of eternity. His greatest contribution was that in joy and love he lived that life. The contrast between religion and life, fundamental to so many others, was completely alien to him. To him true religion was life, and religion was the true life. The things which men have confounded with religion, thoughts concerning it, discipline of will and feeling in it, certain activities under the impulse of religion, these are not ends in themselves. They are only means to an end, and that end is life. By personal fidelity to his own rule, by being the exalted impersonation of the holiest things which he enjoined, he stamped the beauty and obligation of these things upon the small circle of those who were the witnesses of his career. And these went forth to spread the knowledge of that life and the practice of it among men. This unspeculative character of his teaching is one thing which has given it its permanent hold upon the minds of men, and has fitted it for appropriation to the thought and life of every age.

But in both these particulars, in respect, that is, of the purity of the religious intuition of Jesus, its slight commingling with any philosophical or other elements, and in respect also of the mode of apprehension of his authority, the case was different with some even of the New Testament writers. The Synoptists offer what are, in form, simple statements of fact concerning Jesus' sayings and doings. But, strictly, what we can gather from their narrative is the witness to their understanding of those facts. This is all that in the nature of the case we can ever gather from testimony to facts. And the Evangelists' understanding of these facts took form inevitably from thoughts brought along with them from their own past. It took up into itself elements which had their origin in the type of culture and the prevailing apprehensions of the age. What we are here speaking of may be described as the result of the unconscious reflection of the witnesses. It is the mere consequence of the fact that whatever presents itself to men is taken up into their minds and given off again in the forms natural to the working of those minds.

But the Epistles, without exception, show the beginnings also of a conscious reflection upon Jesus and upon the life of the Christian man. It is this deliberate reflection which makes of Paul the earliest Christian theologian. It was by this reflection that Paul assimilated the revelation to his own intense intellectual life, an intellectual life so much more intense than that of any of the authors of the synoptic tradition. It was through this deliberate reflection that he sought to bring home the meaning and power of the revelation to the thought and life of those to whom he preached. The men could but reflect. The inspiration of Jesus was the most powerful stimulus to the mental nature, as well as to the moral purposes. And beside Paul two, at least, of the authors of the New Testament have recorded their reflections upon the largest scale. These are the author of the Epistle to the Hebrews and the author of the Gospel according to John. It is part of the fulness of the New Testament for which we must give thanks that we have thus the image of Jesus as he is mirrored in at least three distinct types of mind. We have his impulse as it is assimilated to and given off again from at least three defined modes of thought. And we deprive ourselves of the very advantage of this state of things if, while we urge the oneness of the source of the impulse, we fail to reckon with the diversity of these modes of thought and with the inevitable consequence of this diversity for the presentations of the truth concerning Jesus which they severally make.

The background with all of these New Testament authors was, in one way or another, Judaism. With Paul it was actual rabbinism. In all three of the great authors we have named there is a strain besides, which came to them through contact with Hellenism. In Paul this strain is slight. He quotes a Greek poet, but remains a Jew of Jews. His Hellenism was only at second hand. But in both of our other types this strain is Alexandrianism, less or more. In the Epistle to the Hebrews it goes not much deeper than to the allegorizing treatment of narrative, and to things of that sort. But in the Fourth Gospel this element is subtle and pervasive. It reaches to the profoundest depths of speculation as to the nature of God, the person of Christ, the possibility of incarnation, the idea of redemption. The recognition of this progress of doctrine within the New Testament itself is one of the main aids to the understanding of the New Testament. It helps also to the understanding of the inevitableness and the historic right of the progress of doctrine in the Christian church in all ages, to which this progress which we see within the New Testament itself was but the gate.

It is, of course, not our task to attempt to indicate the historical sources or the speculative worth of these beginnings, within the covers of the New Testament itself, of the interpretation of the word and work of Jesus. The sole point with which we are here concerned is to make clear that these main documents of the New Testament are interpretations. These representations of Jesus within the New Testament itself are composite, on the one hand of the spiritual impression which the career and teachings of Jesus made upon the writers, and on the other hand, of ideas in the realm of which the authors lived and moved, and in which the original readers also were probably supposed to move. The New Testament writings, in one view of them, thus themselves constituted the earliest stages of the history of Christian doctrine. And these beginnings of orderly reflection upon Jesus, of interpretation of his teaching, of speculation concerning his work and person, which we have thus seen within the covers of the New Testament, could but be followed up. It is true that the stratum of society to which Christianity in the two generations following that of the Apostles mainly appealed, was not much given to speculation. The adherents of Christianity at this time were gathered chiefly from among the simple people, from the poor, and even from the slaves.

The simplicity of Jesus was better adapted to these than was the reasoning of Paul or the mysticism of John. It is well known that it was not until after the time of Marcion that the influence of Paul began to be great. The Judaizing hatred of Paul accounts in some measure for this fact. But the remoteness and the difficulty of some of Paul's ideas accounts for it yet more. It has been doubted whether Paulinism, that extraordinary adjustment of Paul's new revelation to his Judaism, ever fully commanded any mind save that of the creator of the system, and this upon the basis which his own personal history and strong individuality had given. It is well known that the influence of the Fourth Gospel was, until toward the end of the second century, so slight that it was possible for some men seventy years ago to hold that the Fourth Gospel had not come into existence until the end of that century. That notion is now wholly abandoned. But that it ever could have been held is a proof that the influence of this Gospel upon the doctrinal development of that earliest time was slight. But when men of a different stratum of society began to take their place in the Christian community, when Christianity intellectually, as well as practically, began to make itself at home in the world, the change came very rapidly.

There was, on the part of some, a disposition to regard Christianity in the light of a new law. Through all the stages of Ebionism this tendency may be described as a relapse toward Judaism, with no Christian tenet left except the one, that Messiah had come. The Old Testament religion had been prevailingly apprehended as a law. Then there was what we may call a lapse toward popular heathenism. It was the attempt to mingle with Christianity rites and forms gathered out of the religions of the East, and to give the Christian facts a place in the mythology of these religions. To men who were themselves philosophers this sort of thing was empty. But these men had, in their turn, their own way of domesticating Christianity in the intellectual life of the world. Their way was not to make of it a new law, like those first, and not a new mythology, like the second, but a new philosophy. They tended to handle the Gospel as merely a revealed and divinely authoritative philosophy. They were in danger of evaporating the whole thing into metaphysics, and of losing all interest in the ethical significance of Jesus. This last class, although clearly distinguished in principle, was not always sharply marked off in fact from the preceding one. There were not a few of the Gnostics with whom it would have been hard to say where the speculative element left off and the mythological element began. And then, in the fourth place, there were men like the Montanists, who repudiated culture of every sort, who claimed to revive the primitive inspiration and enthusiasm, whose teaching issued, in some cases, in monstrosities and vagaries absurd and iniquitous.

Against these things what could the church do? Men said: We will go back to Jesus and the Apostles. We will ask, What is Christic and apostolic teaching? We will hold ourselves to that. They did go back to Jesus. They did what men since that time have often done when they used that great phrase, "Back to Jesus!" They took everything they had back with them. There can be no manner of doubt that this was that which the church at the end of the second century faithfully tried to do. It sought to go back to the Apostles and to Jesus. We have seen the men of that time making a more and more sharply defined Canon of New Testament Scripture, as part of their effort to find out just what Jesus, and the Apostles under the immediate inspiration of Jesus, had said. We have seen them building up a strong and authoritative organization of the church, one of the foremost uses of which authority was the settlement of questions of interpretation of what Jesus and the Apostles had said. And now, as we shall go into it a little more in detail, we shall see, at this same time, the growth of the idea of a permanent doctrinal tradition in the Christian church, in which that infallible interpretation had been from the first embodied. We shall watch the growth of the assumption that there had always been an apostolic dogma in the church.

It was the same Irenæus who put forth this idea, whom before we saw, as the asserter of the apostolic form of church government, and who had held of the Gospels that they could not be less or more than four. So here, Irenæus held that the churches founded by Apostles had in his time and had always had, a uniform doctrinal tradition.[1] This agreement of the apostolic churches, together with the continuity of their agreement since the apostolic age, gave to these churches an authority in doctrine which was decisive for all the churches. He thought of this sacred deposit of dogma as he had thought of the tradition of church government and of the Canon, as something given of God from the beginning, necessary for men, and part of the constitution of the universal church. Of course, in the sense in which Irenæus conceived this, such an agreement of doctrine in the apostolic churches did not exist. It never had existed. But most wonderful is the degree in which now, swiftly, under the growing authority of the catholic church and under the impulse of other forces with which by this time we are familiar, such a doctrinal agreement came to exist. And it came to be exercised as an instrument of tremendous practical force. It is the basis of the principle of doctrinal tradition in the Roman church. It is that which was later described by Vincent of Lerins in his famous phrase: "Quod ubique, quod semper, quod ab omnibus creditum est — hoc est vere proprieque catholicum."[2]

If we are right in our distinction between doctrine

[1] *Adv. Hæres.*, i. 10. 2, iii. 3. 1, and iii. 4. 1.
[2] Commonitorium, 3.

and dogma, the development of doctrine itself is as natural and as necessary as the rising of each new day's sun. Doctrine is nothing more than the adjustment of a man's religious ideas to all the other ideas which as a child of his time he holds. The evolution of doctrine is simply the thinking over again of the thoughts concerning religion in the light of all the other thoughts which possess a new generation and in the characteristic spirit of the life of that generation. It is the recasting of the content of the religious consciousness so as to bring this into a form which is harmonious with the other elements given in consciousness. In this sense it would appear that a doctrine which had no evolution and made no progress was the opposite of doctrinal truth. Movement and change belong to the conception of the thing. It is only the religion itself, and not the interpretation of it, which can be permanent.

But this amalgamation of pure moral and religious intuition with the speculative or other notions of a given time — and such an amalgam doctrine always is — may be assumed to have been undertaken in the interest of making religious truth more intelligible to the men of that time. At least, it is the form in which the man of the new time makes that religious truth intelligible to himself and holds secure possession of it for himself. Doctrine commands our reverence as the human form in which the divine truth has temporarily done its work. It is one of the series of human forms in which the divine truth must always do its work. It taxes our ingenuity to separate these entirely separable elements. But the comparison of successive stages of doctrine and of long intervals in its history is the very thing which gives us light upon the question as to what the permanent element of the religion is. The study of doctrinal development, in order to the discovery of what is the passing and what the permanent element of religion, is one of the worthiest tasks to which a religious man could set himself. For if the intellectual element in the combination be no longer current but have become obsolete, it hinders rather than helps men in the understanding of the religious truth. It prevents the adjustment of that religious truth to the mental life of a new time. It makes institutions stationary and futile which, when they keep pace with the world, have the highest usefulness. And if insisted upon, it may occasion the rejection of the religious truth altogether.

And this disturbing factor is still further enhanced when that which had a perfectly proper place as a phase of doctrine cognate to the culture of a given time, becomes dogma. Dogma is doctrine which has forgotten that it ever had a history, and ceased to discriminate between its own passing and permanent, its own human and divine, elements. Dogma is doctrine which has been invested by the decree of institutions, or by the overwhelming sense of its adherents, with authority of a kind of which very possibly the authors of the doctrine never dreamed. Dogma is doctrine which, instead of being authoritative because it creates conviction, seeks to create conviction because it claims to be authoritative. Dogma is doctrine made binding, not upon those to whom its truth is obvious, but upon all and always, and simply because the institution or the consensus of its adherents has said that it should be binding. Dogma in the scientific sense is that part of doctrine which has been sanctioned by the constituted authorities of recognized ecclesiastical bodies. And, for practical purposes, we can reckon only with those main bodies which have attained permanence and exerted a large influence. But if, in the strict sense of these definitions, we should ask ourselves concerning the history of dogma, we should have to say that although even dogma has had some history, although adjustments even of authoritative religious statements have from time to time been forced, yet always this history wears the air of being a history which those who cherished the dogma did not intend to have. History is the contradictory of dogma; as conversely, the failure to make history is the denial of the true nature of doctrine.

Such a transformation of the doctrine of their own generation into a dogma for all generations was the work of the men of that critical period at the end of the second century of which we have said so much. We need not suppose that they

CANONIZATION AND HISTORY OF DOCTRINE 275

were conscious of this nature of the work which they did. But in these very years, and in the closest possible connection with that movement which we have seen producing an authoritative Canon of the New Testament and an authoritative form of ecclesiastical organization, we shall see also the crystallization out of the fluid state of doctrine of a uniform and authoritative Rule of Faith, which was at that very time, indeed, for substance and in the shape of the Roman baptismal symbol, attributed to the Apostles, but whose matured statement received later the actual name "The Apostles' Creed." Therewith is not said but that the main points of the Apostles' Creed did reach back in the tradition of the apostolic churches to the Apostles themselves. But the bringing of these tenets to consciousness, the phrasing them in a particular way, the gathering them into a creed, the clothing of that creed with dogmatic authority, the exacting of the confession of it from candidates for baptism — these were the new elements. The attribution of the Rule of Faith, as rule of faith, to the Apostles put these elements in false perspective. These new elements, also, were now assumed to have been present ever since the time of the Apostles, whereas, in truth, they had but just come into existence.

But let us try in brief to outline the thing which has thus come to pass.

When one reflects how manifold were the elements from which converts to the Christian faith were drawn in the century from the death of Paul to the death of Justin, from about the year 65 to the year 165, one realizes how difficult it would be to define, even in a rough way, that type of teaching which was common to all these elements. And yet the vigor with which Gnosticism was ultimately cast out of the church shows that there was a common teaching among Christians throughout the world, which ultimately came to clear consciousness in the Christian body as its inestimably precious inheritance of truth. Regarding the body of writings long in common possession, we have seen the Christians suddenly become aware of them as the documents of their faith and the new Canon of their sacred Scripture. It is not that the documents then first came into the possession, or even into use in the Christian church. But then first the church came to the consciousness of that which these documents signified. It is not that the main doctrinal statements attributed to the Apostles and elevated to the dignity of a rule of faith thus first became the inheritance of Christians. But then first they were asserted as the essential element in that inheritance and the element which, with all else that might change, must abide.

Of this common body of doctrine a few main points may be named.[1] The Gospel rests upon immediate revelation. It is a message from God to man, the acceptance of which in faith assures salva-

[1] See Harnack, *Dogmengeschichte*, i., 1886, pp. 100 ff.

CANONIZATION AND HISTORY OF DOCTRINE 277

tion. Essential elements of this message from God are these: the demand for repentance of past sins and for the struggle after righteousness; the assurance of forgiveness and of the final victory over evil; and the promise of the resurrection and of eternal life. An essential point, also, in this primitive faith is that this Gospel has come to men through Jesus Christ. It is he who has set forth these truths concerning man and made known the favoring will and the redeeming love of God. He is the Saviour whom God has sent into the world. He stands in unique relation to God. In a peculiar sense he is the Son of God. He has true and full knowledge of God. To him, as reconciler with God, as teacher and exemplar and spiritual power for the life of men, they are to commit themselves. In his spirit men are not to seek after the goods of this world. They are to feel themselves lifted above many of the conditions of life in this world, since Christ himself was a citizen of Heaven and only a sojourner upon earth.

This glad message, which Jesus himself received from God, he committed to Apostles to be preached. And beside that, the spirit of God is to rule in the hearts of all Christians. It is this spirit which confers gifts and graces. It is this spirit which still sends forth inspired prophets. The simple rites of Baptism and the Lord's Supper are both reminders of the grace of God which has been given to men and symbols of the grace which is yet to be given. Differences of sex, of age, of rank, of nationality, of education, and even of ancient religious privilege, such as that of the Jews — all differences which built barriers dividing men are to disappear, since the call of God is to all men. The Christian community rests solely upon that call. Through the blamelessness of their walk and in the spirit of brotherhood to all men, the Christians are to prove to the world the truth of Christianity. The hope that Christ is coming soon again to gather under his own rule his people, scattered as they are among all nations, is not the least of the forces which determine the Christian faith and life.

The basis of this simple faith of the earliest communities was, as we have seen, the Old Testament and the tradition concerning the teaching and life of Jesus. The Christian interpretation made out of the Old Testament a Christian book. In fact, the Christians were the only ones who truly interpreted the book. The Christians were the new and true people of God to whom all the promises belonged. The Jews had forfeited these in the rejection of Christ. As to the tradition concerning Jesus, it would seem that, from very early times, along with the citation of the words of Jesus, there went a brief account of his life and deeds as well. These were perhaps first delineated from the point of view of the fulfilment of prophecy. This was, at all events, the point of view of the Gospel according to Matthew, and presumably of the source of Matthew. It was the point of view which would most appeal to those Christians who had themselves been devout Jews. But then again this narrative concerning Jesus was shaped from the point of view of the portrayal of the wonderful works of Jesus as the authentication of his message. This is the point of view of the Gospel according to Mark.

Very early, three phrases stand out as a sort of summary of this primitive faith. There is, first, the declaration of belief in God the Father Almighty. Then also there is the profession of faith in Jesus Christ, the Son of God. And, finally, there is the assertion of belief in that Holy Spirit which had spoken through the Prophets, which had dwelt in all fulness in Jesus, and which dwells now in the hearts of the obedient. It is easy to see that these were the three assertions under which all others could be grouped. These were the logical centres around which almost everything could be arranged which was said in the New Testament interpretations of the Gospel. In the century from about the year 60 to the year 160 this confession passes current in the general sense of it.[1] But it is not reduced to any fixed formula. It admits, rather, of most various formulation. These simple statements stand in manifold relation the one to the other, and to the inferences which are based upon them all. It is first in the

[1] First Clem. lviii. 2, xlii. 3, and xlvi. 6; Didachè, 7; Ignatius, Eph. ix. 1, and Magn. xiii. 1. 2 ; *Martyr. Polyc.* xiv. 1. 2. See Harnack, *Dogmengeschichte*, Bd. i., p. 107.

Roman community and after the middle of the second century, that we find an exact form of words insisted upon among the Christians, and especially the acknowledgment of that form of words exacted in connection with the rite of baptism.[1] It would seem that while men were anxious to secure what they deemed to be the fundamental faith in Jesus Christ the Saviour, yet, in the sense of any more elaborated theory of the facts here presented, we may say that there was as yet no current theology. Or, if you choose, we may say that there were many theologies current, just as we have seen that in this time there were many gospels current besides the four later canonized, and more bishops than one even in the local community, and no theory concerning the original authority of the bishop such as was later proclaimed. The speculations of authors closely related the one to the other differ among themselves in startling fashion, both in point of departure and in their implications. Terrible or comforting pictures of the future, which were mere products of fantasy, were put forth side by side with calm and simple reflection upon the ethical teaching of Jesus, or, again, with attempts to adjust that teaching to one and another aspect of the prevailing philosophy.

We may take the Apologists for examples. They were converted for the most part in their maturity. They represented widely different horizons of cultivation, and they proceeded to adjust, practically

[1] Caspari, *Quellen zur Geschichte des Taufsymbols*, iii. 3 ff.

CANONIZATION AND HISTORY OF DOCTRINE 281

each man as seemed good in his own eyes, his new-found Christianity to his own previous ideas of whatever sort, or to the presumable ideas of those for whom he wrote. The most naïve are those who, like Tatian, operate with a philosophy while meantime they abuse it roundly as something which for them, in the light of Christ, has been done away. But even to such men it seemed eminently desirable, for the sake of others, to present the Gospel in such a manner as to show its points of contact with all the learning which those for whom they wrote possessed. That by this process some adventurous combinations saw the light may be surmised. It would seem that the Apologists argued that if men were but at one in their belief in the revelation of God, and in Jesus Christ who brought us salvation, and in the desire to follow in his steps, there was the widest freedom in reference to other, and, as they fondly supposed, deeper apprehensions of the Gospel. We should put the matter differently. We should say that the men were at one in the deep things of religion, and differed only in the superficial and unnecessary ones, such as the efforts to define the relation of these simple religious truths to theories then current concerning the origin of the universe, and other similar endeavors. But of course this was not the way in which the Apologists looked at the matter. They would have said that it was comparatively easy for men to be at one in matters of such fundamental religious import as those above named. What they sought to do was to deepen and widen Christianity, each one in his own way, and in the direction of those remoter aspects of speculation or of practice which particularly interested him. And we must not forget that many of these individual views were attributed to the direct inspiration of the Holy Spirit. They were therefore beyond criticism of other Christian men, save, of course, in so far as their consequences might be obviously immoral.

The astonishing divergence of incipient theological forms which stood side by side in the second generation of the second century may be illustrated at the very point which is for us of central importance, that, namely, of the person of Christ. The unanimity of the Christians of this period does not go beyond the hearty agreement upon the scriptural phrases. The senses in which these phrases are used, the interpretations which are put upon them, differ widely. Sometimes divergent interpretations lie side by side in the words of the same author, as if the author did not feel the significance of that divergence. Or, rather, it is sometimes as if the author thought that the greater the number of divergent interpretations which he offered the profounder and more suggestive thinker he was, and the more likely was he successfully to appeal to others who thought in many different ways. We may allow that this last supposition was probably true. But the state of things in which men deemed themselves to be not worse, but better Christians because they thus represented at different times, or even at one and the same time, various incompatible theologies, is, to say the least, an interesting one. It is in strong contrast with the state of things which presently prevailed. These interpretations could not all survive. Not all of them were possible of combination with the vital Christian elements. But this, at all events, is obvious; what was then deemed essential for Christians was the religious content of the phrases concerning Christ. This was the divine truth to which they were bound. What was left free to men was the imaginative and poetical interpretation or, again, the speculative construction which was to be put upon those phrases. With all this divergence of interpretation in the creative period of doctrine, the permanence of these deep religious phrases was the healing and uniting element. But the permanence of these deep religious phrases was also, if we may so say, the misleading element. For so soon as it became axiomatic to a given age that its own interpretation was the only true and right one, the fact that the phrases had been immemorial and unchanged made it natural for the men to think that their own interpretation had been immemorial and unchanged as well. Parallel is the fact which one discovers in reading not a few of the Fathers after Cyprian, and we might add, in reading some ecclesiastical writers almost down to our time, that because the word "bishop" occurs so often in Paul, therefore the whole aspect of the bishopric must have been the same to Paul which in these later times it wore.

The Christian communities were, indeed, associations for the practice of the holy life upon the basis of faith in God and Jesus Christ.[1] At the same time, the conviction was present from the beginning that this life in Christ was the key to all knowledge. And though the Hellenic spirit in its strong bias toward intellectualism gave to this conviction a perverse bent, yet fundamentally the conviction is entirely true. Nothing could have been farther from the clear spirit of Jesus than to suppose that the true life of man does not include also his mental life, or that the fullest life of man in God can be lived without the exaltation of the mental life as well. But when once men of cultivation began to be found within the Christian body, and to desire to explain Christianity for the benefit of the cultivated world outside, when once the intellectual interest was set free, and the fusion of the new religious life with the achievements of the Hellenic spirit in all departments was begun, who was to say how far this process might go? Who was to say which of all the various theories which were so earnestly sought for, and so confidently put forth as the deeper meaning of Christianity, would be found really consistent with the genius of Christianity,

[1] Harnack, *Dogmengeschichte*, i. p. 158.

and which of them would be found destructive of all that was characteristic in Christianity? Who was to say which of these combinations would be found capable of transfiguration through the pure religious spirit which had been in Jesus, and which of them, if left in fusion with Christianity, would issue in the elimination of the religious element altogether? Which of the interpretations then current concerning, for example, the person of Christ, would answer to the needs of sinful men and furnish them with the spiritual power for the imitation of the life of Christ, and which of them would empty the Gospel of its spiritual and ethical significance altogether?

The name Gnostic has been applied with some confusion to a great number of schools and undertakings of all sorts, which were but loosely related the one to the other. There were sects like the Encratites who laid all the weight upon a stringent dualistic theory of the universe, and made Jesus the pattern of the ascetic life. There were, furthermore, whole communities who for centuries drew their knowledge of Jesus from books which made him nothing more than a heavenly spirit, who appeared to walk among men, but whose body and outward contacts and alleged deeds had no reality whatever. There were philosophers who adored the bust of their own teacher, Epiphanes, and had a garland for Jesus, just as they had also for Plato and Pythagoras. And, finally, there were swindlers like Alexander of Abonoteichos, fortune-tellers, counterfeiters, jugglers, who, under the guise of being Christian prophets, were given to pompous speech and conducted superstitious ceremonies, but whose real aim was to lead captive silly women and to cheat unwary men. There were all these, besides men like Basilides and Valentinus, whose great systems have to be taken seriously. And again, there were men like Marcion, who, though hardly in any true sense a Gnostic, bore relation to the movement nevertheless. We may be content to let the word stand if what is meant by Gnosticism is the general phenomenon presented when, for the first time, influences of the world streamed in upon the little Christian body and possessed themselves of certain portions of it. Instructive remains the fact that it was in gnostic circles that the first dogmatic and philosophical treatises touching Christianity were brought forth, the first critical and historical investigations set on foot, the first commentaries on New Testament books produced, the first sense shown for an authoritative Canon of the Christian literature as such. When the Christian church proceeded to do these things it was, to some extent, in answer to that which the Gnostics had already done. At least, the moment at which and the form in which the Christians did these things were determined, to some extent, by that which Gnostics had already done. The things themselves the Christians would beyond question have been compelled to do in any case.

Those Christians who, in the middle of the second century, endeavored at one swift stroke to win the whole Hellenic culture for Christianity, or to make Christianity but a phase of the Hellenic culture, were condemned by the very institution which gradually, and perhaps without being aware of it, followed for some distance in their steps.[1] There are elements conspicuous in this wide phenomenon of Gnosticism which are not Hellenic. There are traits, and those some of the most incongruous and bizarre, which are obviously oriental and not Greek at all. Nevertheless, the decisive impulse was that intellectual one which in the decay of Greek civilization had been carried through the world, and grafted, in some way, upon the life of almost every nation. That the Hellenic spirit in Gnosticism sought thus to possess itself of the Christian community is clear proof of the great impression which Christianity had made upon the world. The Hellenic world was familiar with doctrines which had never been able to produce a life which in appreciable degree accorded with those doctrines. But here was a noble form of life which seemed to be waiting for a doctrine to correspond to it.[2] Here was just the task for this eager, acute, and ofttimes unstable Hellenic genius which found so much greater pleasure in thinking cleverly than in being good. What the Christians had to offer to an age in which some one had said that nothing is certain

[1] Harnack, *Dogmengeschichte*, i. p. 162.   [2] *Ibid.*, p. 170.

save that nothing is certain, was the confidence of their faith in God and man. What they had to offer in an age of incredible moral corruption was the purity of their moral ideal and their heroism in the pursuit of that ideal. What Hellenism, on the other hand, had to offer to a community which, just because of its moral greatness, was more and more drawing to itself the cultivated and reflective classes, was the basis of reflection, from which all cultivated life since Plato had proceeded. One may say that the alliance between these two, between the highest intellectual and the highest moral impulse which the human race has ever received, was inevitable. One may say that the first stage of that association was a triumph for Christianity. It brought Hellenism to bow before a morality, before a character and a religious enthusiasm such as it had never produced or even in far-off way approached. But, on the other hand, Christianity did not escape the absorption into itself of certain elements of Hellenism that were not germane to its true end and spirit, and which less or more have prevailed in it to this day.

That pure moral enthusiasm which was the gist of Christianity, in its sublime endeavor to appropriate to itself the world had been appropriated by the world in a far greater degree than it had any idea of. It had aimed to penetrate and permeate the world. It did not realize how far it had been penetrated by the world. It had taken up its glorious mission to change the world. It dreamed that while changing the world it had itself remained unchanged. As a matter of fact the world was changed — the world of life, the world of feeling, and the world of thought. But Christianity was changed, as well. It had conquered the world, but without perceiving that it illustrated the old law that the conquered give laws to the conqueror. It had fused the ancient culture with the flame of its inspiration. It did not know how much the fused elements of that ancient culture now colored its far-shining flame. It had been a maker of history. But in the meantime it had been remade by its own history. It confidently carried back its Canon, its organization, its dogma, its ritual, to Christ and the Apostles. It did not realize that those, one and all, were born out of its fruitful contact with the world during the century after the Apostles. It deemed them the armor of its defence against the world. It little dreamed that they were themselves the monuments of the fact that it had not altogether defended itself against the world. The dogma was the Hellenization of Christian thought, as the monarchical episcopate was the Romanization of its life, and the Canon the externalization of its spirit and enthusiasm.

This matter has been put in such a way as to seem to give ground for deep pessimism. It has been so stated that we might infer that the progress of Christianity had been but a declension, and its history that of one long defection from a pure ideal. Defection there has been. Not all the things which followed upon the adjustment of Christianity to the life of the world were necessary to the doing of the true work of Christianity in the world. But the adjustment was necessary. Not all these things were even possible of combination with the pure spirit of Christianity. And not all those which were impossible of combination with that spirit have been easily removed. But we must not argue as if Christianity had ever existed in the world as pure spirit, unless, indeed, we should say that it thus existed in the personal life of its Founder. But even that personal life was lived in the most definite and constant adjustment to the conditions given in the time and place in which that life was lived. Incarnation is limitation. The spirit did its work through the flesh even in Jesus. We must not argue as if the spirit of Christianity could ever have done its work in the world save as it became a part of the real life of the world, took up elements of the world into itself, and was itself taken up into the elements of the world. It won the Hellenic world by its degree of Hellenization. It did work in the Roman world by its degree of Romanization. We must not argue that the spirit of Christianity ever will do any work save in fearless combination, thorough fusion, actual ingrafting of its life into the life of the new time and of the life of that time into Christianity. Ideals alone do no work. But religions which do no work are farthest from being ideal. What men call the descent from the dream

CANONIZATION AND HISTORY OF DOCTRINE 291

is the ascent to service. The flesh of an incarnation is in its own way only less glorious than the spirit. We seek to recur to the pure ideal, not in order that we may disparage the services which historically have been rendered by forms of that ideal which were not wholly pure. We seek to recur to the pure ideal, not to decry the strangely commingled forms under which in the great human life the divine spirit has seen fit to work. We are what we are and our world is what it is, exactly because of the services thus rendered. But we seek to recur to the pure ideal because it has always been the weakness of humanity to confound the passing with the permanent, the human with the divine, the essential with that which is adventitious. We seek in all reverence to strip off that which is adventitious only in order that we may hold the more firmly to that which is essential, as we face the work which Christianity is yet to do, and prepare the forms of ethical and intellectual, of personal and social life, into which it is yet to enter.

The main points of the gnostic contention have been touched upon as, from time to time, we have had occasion to allude to the influence of these sects. We need not repeat what has been already said. To the Gnostics Christianity is, indeed, the one true and absolute religion. It includes a system of doctrine revealed by Christ himself. But Christ has revealed this not in the documents which we know, and not through his spirit in the hearts of all men, but in a secret tradition of further mysterious truths handed down as esoteric wisdom in the sects. The Creator of the world is not the God of our redemption. Evil is inherent in matter and inseparable from every contact with it. There are many powers and heavenly persons in whom the absolute God has made Himself known. Jesus is but the last and greatest of these heavenly powers. His earthly life was a mere phantasm, and all that is related as his earthly career is mythology for the uneducated man.

In strict sense Marcion was not a Gnostic.[1] He was led not by a speculative interest, but by a deep moral one. He never acknowledged the difference between the secret and the open type of tradition. He desired to reform the church in his own sense, and only when he failed set up a school for himself. The utter denial of the God of wrath of whom the Old Testament spoke, Paulinism in all its bitterness against things Jewish and none of that affection for Judaism which yet animated Paul, Paulinism with none of the breadth and mysticism of Paul, stringent asceticism, the repudiation of all rites and ceremonies — these were some of the points of Marcion's teaching. Jesus was simply the apparition of the good God who could never have had anything to do with that

[1] Concerning Marcion, see Harnack, pp. 197 ff., Gustav Krüger, art. "Marcion," in Herzog, *R. E.*, 3 Aufl., Bd. xii., 1903, pp. 267–277, and Hilgenfeld, *Ketzergeschichte des Urchristenthums*, pp. 316 f. and 522 f.

which belongs to the senses. The birth of Jesus — not merely the Virgin birth, but any birth whatever — was impossible. His human development was excluded. His bodily life on the earth was a mere semblance. Marcion's scripture shrinks, as we have seen, to the compass of a few letters of Paul, and the Gospel of Luke, much altered to suit his own purposes. Marcion was a zealot and had talent for leadership. But not in the eyes of the sturdiest Puritan could the growing organization and power of the catholic church have found less favor than did these in the eyes of Marcion. The transformation of the teaching function, as it had been in the earliest communities, into the priestly office was offensive to him in high degree. To his strong individualism the tendency to centralization and authority, which possessed the church in his day, was a thing to be resisted. In the sense in which men were beginning to make earnest with that word, Marcion could never have said, "I believe in the holy catholic church." From about the year 160 there seem to have been Marcionite communities, vigorously dissenting from the belief and practice of the main body of the Christian adherents, and refusing to yield to the growing organization of the catholic church. But they were of strict moral life, they had their own confessors and martyrs side by side with those of the regular Christians.

Now it was in antithesis to this general gnostic movement, and more particularly to Marcionitism, that the first form of authoritative statement of Christian doctrine took its shape. It is exactly in Rome, in the field of Marcion's operations, that the first form of confession is discovered which seems to have been used in the preparation of those to be admitted to the membership of the church. It marks a tendency in such instruction as different as possible from that which is still visible in the Didachè and in the Shepherd of Hermas, although the former of these books is put forth explicitly as containing instruction in the spirit and on the authority of the Apostles, and although the latter was also written in Rome and not far from the time of which we speak. The Roman symbol represents the principle of the use in such instruction of a brief compendium or statement of the main points of the faith. Compendia of a sort, forms of confession, seem to have found place even in some of the New Testament Epistles.[1] But until the time of which we are speaking their use was liturgical. The repetition of them was an act of worship. Now, however, we have reached the point where, in connection with the rite of baptism, an exact form of words is insisted upon in confession, as the evidence of good faith upon the part of the candidate, and as a barrier against the intrusion into the Christian body of those holding tenets of the gnostic sects. The significance of this change cannot be exaggerated. From the

---

[1] 1 Corinthians xv. 1 f.; 1 Timothy iii. 16; and see note with references in Harnack, p. 113; Eusebius, *H. E.*, v. 28. 5.

CANONIZATION AND HISTORY OF DOCTRINE 295

time of the introduction of this custom, the solemn profession of adherence to a statement of belief becomes the mark of those who belong to the catholic church, and the very point of their distinction from those who do not. The confession of faith in God the Creator, and in Jesus the Son of God, and in the Holy Ghost, in the simple form in which we have seen it everywhere current, was amplified into a résumé of certain facts of the life of Jesus, and was made to include the mention of certain of the gifts of God unto salvation which are confirmed to us through Jesus. Such gifts are the forgiveness of sins, the resurrection of the body, and the life everlasting. And this confession becomes the bond of union among those within the fold of the church, and as well the summary of the points of distinction between these Christians and those separated from the fold.

Of this Roman Baptismal Symbol the substance is preserved for us by both Irenæus and Tertullian.[1] It would seem to have taken shape not far from the year 160.[2] It is possible that it was phrased under Anicetus, who was bishop of Rome from the year 157 to 168.[3] The form in which we know the

[1] Irenæus, *Adv. Hær.*, i. 10. 1. 2; 9. 1-5; 22. 1; ii. 9. 1; 28. 1; Tertullian, *De Præscript. Hær.*, 13, 14, and especially 21.

[2] Caspari, *Quellen*, iii. pp. 3 ff., Gebhardt, Harnack, u. Zahn, *Patr. Apost. Opp.*, i. 2. pp. 115-142; Kattenbusch, *Das Apost. Symbol*, 1895-1900; McGiffert, *The Apostles' Creed*, New York, 1902.

[3] Harnack, Caspari, Kattenbusch, and McGiffert grant a somewhat wider range.

Roman baptismal symbol is the Apostles' Creed, although the wording of this latter document as we now have it, and as well that particular title for it, are, of course, of considerably later date. And those things which we have just said concerning the origin of the Roman symbol, the determination of the precise period of its origin, the recognition of the tendency which it represents, together with the agreement, almost verbal, of the Apostles' Creed with this Roman baptismal symbol, throw floods of light for us upon the Apostles' Creed. No one conversant with the history of early Christianity can look closely at the Apostles' Creed without a sense of wonder, both at the things which it chooses out for enumeration and as well at the things which were certainly part of the faith of the early Christians which the creed omits to state. Now both the things which the creed says, with the precise turn given in the saying them, and as well the things which the Apostles' Creed does not say, become at once intelligible if one admits that the statement was shaped by the exigencies of the church at the moment when the Roman baptismal symbol was put forth, and, more specifically, that it was guided, in some degree at least, by the antithesis to Marcion and the Marcionites which we have shown.

Irenæus is probably right in affirming that the Roman symbol, which to all intents and purposes is in our hands as the Apostles' Creed, represents a part, though certainly not the whole, of what was generally believed in the apostolic churches in Irenæus' time.[1] Irenæus, of course, does not call the Roman symbol by the name of the Apostles' Creed. But the sense of the formula is carried back in full confidence to the authority of the Apostles. The matter lies in Irenæus' mind in the same manner precisely in which we have observed that the New Testament Canon and the church organization, and the relations of these to the authority of the Apostles, presented themselves to his thought. And of course no long time elapsed until, from this general attribution of the sense of the Roman symbol to the Apostles, even the wording of the creed was ascribed to the Apostles as well. A writing ascribed to Ambrose, and which belongs late in the fourth or early in the fifth century, has a picturesque legend in which the Creed is divided into twelve parts and one of these parts is assigned to each of the Apostles by name. But quite apart from reliance on such a legend as this, for the great body of Christians, and until comparatively recent years, the perspective of the Apostles' Creed has been lost.

Precisely thus, however, through the statement, which in a way is true, that the Apostles ordained bishops, the perspective and the sense of the evolution of the bishopric was lost. There is an obvious sense in which the Apostles' Creed is apostolic, as there is a sense in which no one would dispute that the New Testament is apostolic. But the

[1] Irenæus, *Adv. Hær.*, i. 9. 4.

assumption that the Apostles were the actual authors of the creed, an assumption which in a vague way many generations shared, has had the effect of removing the creed from the historical associations through which alone it can be understood.[1]

This idea of the responsibility of the Apostles for the faith commonly held in the apostolic churches, as it is constantly put forth by the Fathers, rests not so much upon concrete reminiscences of service which the Twelve had rendered in evangelization, and, more particularly, in the establishment of the Gentile churches. It is well known that, apart from the cases of Peter and John, there is very little concrete tradition concerning the activity of the Twelve in the spreading of the Gospel. And even in the cases of Peter and John the certain facts are very few. But the narrative of the Book of the Acts, and, still more, of course, the Epistles of Paul, make the impression that in large part that work among the Gentiles was done by Paul and by men under Pauline influence. The relations of the Twelve to Paul and the Gentile mission were not a little strained. But this fact the tradition of the end of the second century has forgotten. The faith current in the Gentile world is not carried back to Paul alone. In fact, in that faith as by this time it began to be formulated in those apostolic churches, much that is very different from Paulinism is found. The tradition, as it is in the second century, has

[1] Harnack, p. 263.

CANONIZATION AND HISTORY OF DOCTRINE 299

its own ideal construction of the whole matter.[1] It goes back and takes hold of the fact that the testimony concerning Jesus was, by the Master himself, committed to this sacred number of the twelve eye-witnesses who were to go into all the world and preach the Gospel to every creature. The tradition builds upon the fact that the Apostles were thus divinely commissioned to go and teach, rather than upon definite knowledge as to whither they did go or what they taught. The Twelve are thought of as a sort of sacred college, responsible for the work of evangelization and for the substance of preaching. The unanimity of this college of Apostles within itself is given as the very reason why dissent from the faith which the Apostles have everywhere transmitted is not to be allowed. In truth, in the properly organized apostolic churches there is no such dissent. The deposit of faith is thus held to have been given by Christ himself into the hands of the Apostles, and by these to Apostles' pupils. These in turn handed it on to their disciples. And this unbroken chain of witnesses guarantees that from the beginning to the present moment nothing essential had been changed.

No one can doubt that to this formulation of some part of the common faith, as it was then current in important churches, and to the placing of this formula under the authority of the Apostles themselves, is due, in no small degree, the preser-

[1] First Clement, xlii ; Barnabas, v. 9 ; Hermas, *Sim.*, ix. 16, and see Clement of Alexandria, *Alex. Strom.*, vi. 6. 48.

vation of the early Christian doctrinal tradition. There is as little doubt of this as of the parallel fact that to the rise of the Canon we owe the careful preservation and the enhanced influence of the body of the apostolic literature. Some part of the original doctrinal tradition is thus rescued in documentary form. But, on the other hand, we must say that Christianity was thus bound fast to forms which have a definite historical explanation, and which can be rightly understood only in the light of that explanation. The power of expansion of Christianity was hemmed. By the use made of mere assent to propositions, the tendency to emphasis upon the intellectual elements of the Christian faith was unfortunately confirmed.

Quite apart from the specific struggle with Gnosticism, the exigencies of Christian missions would themselves account for the framing of short formulæ touching the most significant points of the Christian belief. These forms were then, upon solemn occasions, repeated; and especially, candidates for baptism uttered them as the confession of their faith. They do not seem to have been made up, to any extent, of the words of Jesus, or even of directions for the moral life. And yet instruction in both of these things unquestionably went hand in hand with the committing of the symbol to memory. A witness to such simple moral instruction is the Didachè. But it was not the points of the Christian morality which appeared to the Greeks foolishness. These were not a stumbling-block to the Jews. These were not the points upon which, in any large way, differences of opinion arose among the Christians themselves. But certain parts of the tradition concerning the revelation of God in Jesus, certain points concerning Jesus' birth, his earthly life, his resurrection, his ascension — these were the points upon which the scorn of the pagans was directed, which the Jews repudiated, and which many of the Christians themselves, like Marcion, interpreted away. It is no wonder that to the men of that time the very existence of the Christian community seemed to depend upon the finding of some authoritative statement of the things which were in dispute. And the emphasis upon just such points would surely grow as the warmth, the originality and enthusiasm, the spiritual consciousness of the life which had been touched by the moral influence of Jesus, waned. Time had been when the majority of Christians knew themselves to be such because, as they would have said, they possessed the Spirit, because they were moved to joy and sacrifice, to the life of love and of obedience, as they saw these illustrated in Jesus and in those who professed faith in him. But now from every quarter, and even in the very name of Christ himself, were being put forth the most various opinions concerning matters of which those simpler Christians of the earlier time had never thought. Upon these, which were often purely matters of opinion, the Christian body itself threatened to be rent in twain, and again, certain parts of it, to be dissolved in the world, nothing characteristically Christian being left. The fixing of a tradition concerning certain facts, and an acknowledged interpretation of those facts, seemed to be a prime necessity. But just as we said in the case of the New Testament Canon, that, quite apart from Gnostics and Montanists, a New Testament would surely have come to pass, so we may say here that, quite apart from Marcionites, we may be certain that a baptismal formula and confession would have taken shape. We may go even farther, and say that when such a confession did come into existence it was certain to be attributed to the Apostles. The men of this time were far enough from the Apostles to make it instinctive with them to desire to fix in writing, in the form also of a rule of faith, what they deemed to have been the Apostles' teaching, and to demand acknowledgment of that rule of faith from all those who sought admission to the Christian institution. Quite apart from Marcionites, a creed called that of the Apostles would certainly have taken shape. But apart from Marcionites it would hardly have taken just this shape which we see.

The baptismal formula is only partially representative of the faith held by the men among whom it arose. The doctrinal antitheses of that time determined less or more the choice of the points which were to be enumerated. A distorted picture is given by a statement of those things concerning which men differ, if meantime the vast mass of those things on which all are agreed, the first principles of the moral life, are not so much as mentioned. A deep misfortune lies in the emphasis which is thus put upon certain merely intellectual elements of the faith, and withdrawn from the ethical and social elements which not only were of more consequence, but which the clearer spirits of that time would have felt to be of more consequence. But they were not the points in dispute. It has been a fatality that this small portion, as assuredly it is, even of the faith then current, should have been given prominence as if it were the whole, or even as if it were the most significant and crucial part of that which Christ and the Apostles taught, the bond of union of those who wished to follow in Christ's steps. The document of a controversy can but be misleading as an historical statement of a case. The difficulty lies in the false perspective of the things which are said, even though all the things which are said should prove to be true. The mistake arises from our not reckoning with the things which are not said.

The force of conviction with which Irenæus puts forth the main points of the Roman baptismal formula — and they are, as we have said, the main points of our Apostles' Creed — as those which had been transmitted from the Apostles' time, and upon which it was now most important that Christians should agree, is epoch-making. Even more definitely is this the point of view of Tertullian. For him it is beyond all dispute that the Rule of Faith is the expression of that to which all apostolic churches hold and have always held, and to which all Christians must hold. In the sharpness of the contention which then prevailed, Tertullian would have had Christians hold no intercourse with those who would not acknowledge this formula. That the confession did thus gradually become the watchword and bond of the Christian brotherhood, there can be no doubt. And yet one learns from Clement of Alexandria and from Origen how long it took, especially in Egypt and the East, to bring this to pass. For in Clement's time in Alexandria, in all his service as the head of the catechetical school, not only is there no evidence of a symbol parallel with the Roman baptismal formula and used for similar purposes, but there is no complex of doctrinal teaching which, after the manner of Irenæus and Tertullian, was carried back directly to the Apostles. As a matter of fact, it was not the Roman Symbol which became the bond of unity of the churches of the East one with another, and of those churches with the churches of the West. That function was reserved for the Nicene Creed, a symbol which took shape five generations later than the Roman Symbol, which is much further advanced theologically, which was of itself of eastern origin, and which had behind it in its mission as an ecumenical creed all the force of the Byzantine Empire and the impulse of the conversion of Constantine. Indeed, the Nicene Creed has

CANONIZATION AND HISTORY OF DOCTRINE 305

always remained the creed of the East. Meantime the Roman Symbol, having been, in the years following the Council of Nicæa, crowded from its position of honor in the West and even in Rome itself, returned after something like two hundred years, with minor changes in the phrasing, and with its direct title as "The Apostles' Creed," and has remained to our day, in the Roman church and in the Protestant bodies which went out from that church far more characteristically the creed of the West than the Nicene Creed ever became.

In this movement for the formulation of the faith in creeds, of which movement we have thus witnessed the first stage, the tendency to exclusive emphasis upon assent and upon the intellectual aspects of Christianity is the most serious thing. It is more serious, even, than that partial and fragmentary character of the creeds which we have observed. We should be greatly mistaken if we supposed that the movement for the formulation of faith rested when, through simple historic statements or religious utterance as in the Roman Symbol, it seemed to itself to have made good its case against the Gnostics and Marcion. On the contrary, with the apologists and still more with the earliest Fathers, it is the instinct to carry the war into Africa, to meet the Gnostic on his own ground, and against the speculations of Marcion and of others to set up a speculative theology of their own, which was to be the approved churchly interpretation of the statements of fact

x

which are gathered in the Rule of Faith and which appear in the Apostles' Creed. The apologetic as it began to take shape, even before the year 160, was the beginning of a process which a hundred years later, in the theology of Origen, reached, for the time, its limit in the complete transformation of the Gospel into a system of theology. What is here put forth by Origen as the meaning of Christianity is really only the religious philosophy of the age of Origen, certified through divine revelation, and in Jesus Christ made accessible to every man.

The difference between the Fathers and the Apologists lies mainly in the fact that the latter in the teaching concerning Jesus have to do only with the Old Testament and with the words of Jesus. They have to do with a New Testament narrative which was not yet fully acknowledged as authoritative by the church. Origen has to do with a literature which has become a Canon, and with a rule of faith which is fast becoming a sole authoritative creed. The Canon and the Rule of Faith are the answers of the church to the question, What is Christianity? And whereas in the Apologists' time all philosophizing of devout men, so only that they did not touch certain very fundamental things, was legitimate, a century later speculation had to hold itself to the documents, and to deal with the facts as these are alleged in the baptismal symbol. Men deemed that in all the speculation which they might indulge, they still only interpreted those facts and documents. And yet this, which Origen and all men like him would have acknowledged to be the true theory of the situation, was soon sadly strained. In the end it was completely reversed. When one views the theological movement which Athanasius led, and which issued in the Nicene Creed, one can no longer say that it was the obvious function of theology to interpret the Rule of Faith. On the contrary, it has become the function of the creed to formulate and sustain theology. These two apprehensions act and react throughout the history of doctrine. The intellectual element more and more preponderates. In the end men actually attempted to place the essential element of Christian faith and the cohesive force of the Christian body in expressions of opinion concerning matters so remote that they may almost be said to have no relation to the Christian life, and if taken seriously, to be necessary causes of division among Christians, rather than of that unity which Christ designed.

And yet so natural were the causes which we have endeavored to indicate, which led up to the making of a theological statement the bond of unity of Christendom, so inevitable were these causes in their working, that we are bound to confess that, save for the exaggerations of which we have just spoken, these causes had, in their own way, a certain great historic right. It is difficult to see how the Christian body, in the time of which we speak, could have escaped entire disintegration without that adherence to some few essentials which was thus in the Rule of Faith provided for. At that time no one seems to have realized this ominous transfer of emphasis from the moral to the intellectual element in Christianity. No one seems to have appreciated the transformation of the Christian society which was taking place. In that society the bond of unity had been the enthusiasm for a person and the joy in imitation of his life. In that community the bond of union came to be the holding of certain tenets which, some of them at all events, belonged in strictness only to the life of that particular time. The interest threatened always to pass to orthodoxy and away from righteousness. The sin lay near of withholding brotherly love from those who could not utter the formula, and even of denying them God's grace. Men did not realize that all this was happening. Men, since that time, have not always been aware of the evils which have ensued. And yet we need only to turn our thought to this matter to perceive how great is the mistake which has been made and to realize that the highest zeal for the honor of Christ does not demand that the mistake shall be continued and confirmed.

LECTURE VIII

THE IDEA OF AUTHORITY IN THE CHRISTIAN CHURCH

LECTURE VIII

THE IDEA OF AUTHORITY IN THE CHRISTIAN CHURCH

WE may begin the discussion of the topic of this lecture by referring to the two passages in the New Testament in which alone, in any sense which illuminates our general theme, the word "authority" is used concerning Jesus Christ himself. The first of these is a passage from the synoptic tradition, which, in the Gospel according to Mark, stands in a reference to Jesus' teaching in the synagogue at Capernaum, at the very beginning of his ministry.[1] In the Gospel according to Matthew the same verse occurs at the end of the record of the Sermon on the Mount.[2] It is related that "When Jesus ended these words, the multitudes were astonished at his teaching; for he taught them as one having authority, and not as their scribes."

The picture of the scribe as he is painted for us in the Gospels, the description of him which we gather from the literature and history of the age, leaves us no question of the meaning of the contrast which is here designed. The scribe taught as one who perpetually referred to his authorities. Jesus taught as one who himself had and exercised authority. He taught as one who himself was the

[1] Mark i. 22.   [2] Matthew vii. 29.

authority. The scribe taught as one who was sure of things only in so far as he ascertained that some one in repute had already said those things. Jesus taught as one to whom the repute of the authorities was a matter which he felt competent to weigh. He taught as one to whose sureness it was not necessary that his utterances should be found in consonance with those of the ancient and the great. There is no trace of anything overweening in his lofty consciousness. But he seems to have felt himself not less original when he chanced to agree with the ancients, and not less confident of his judgments and of himself when he disagreed. To the height of certain of his assurances the greatest of the great had not yet risen. They are such as no man before him ever gave. And no man since he gave them has surpassed the insight which some of these assurances display. The scribe taught as one for whom inspiration was confined to documents, revelation was an ancient history, God's dealing with men was a matter of record, and the past alone the time when men walked with God and when God spoke with men. The scribes still teach in the same way. Jesus taught as one who was himself full of inspiration, who was conscious of himself as revelation, who felt himself to be all taken up into God, and calmly deemed that it was God who, as the force and spirit of his whole life, was manifest in him. There is an immediateness about his spiritual insight and his moral utterance; despite his keen sympathies, there is yet a kind of detachment from his fellows; there is an independence of his judgment concerning men, and an originality of his affirmation touching God, which not even all of our familiarity with it can divest of what is positively startling.

The scribe is the very representative of that use of the letter of which Paul said, that it brings into bondage, killeth.[1] Jesus is the very presence of that spirit which gives freedom, life. The scribes in their influence over others sink to that level of petty tyranny of which those only seem capable who operate with a power which is not their own. Jesus rises to a pitch of self-assertiveness which has never been approached by any human being. And yet that which would be insufferable egotism in another seems fitting in him. It is but the expression of humility in him. After all, it is so transparently evident that it is not himself, but only truth, goodness, God, which in these exalted moments he asserts. He is never more selfless than in these times when he most asserts himself. It is himself only as the exponent of the truth, it is himself only as the revealer of the good, it is himself only as at one with God, that he asserts. "I speak not of myself, but the Father that dwelleth in me, He doeth the works,"[2] — this is his constantly reiterated claim. And the secret of the homage which Jesus has commanded lies in the fact that the conscience of humanity has allowed that claim. If the inhabitants of Capernaum felt

[1] 2 Corinthians iii. 6,   [2] John xiv. 10.

that he spoke as one who had authority, the Fourth Gospel makes Jesus himself say that it was the Father who had given the Son authority.[1]

Devout Jew that he was, the documents and institutions of the ancient faith meant much to Jesus. He attacked the scribes not because these made the sacred authorities to mean too great a thing. He assailed them because they made those documents and institutions to mean merely an outward thing. And yet, over the authority of these documents and sacred institutions, over the laws, customs, and dogmas of the ancient faith, Jesus set himself without a moment's hesitation. "Ye have heard that it hath been said by them of old time: .... but I say unto you."[2] "Moses indeed permitted you these things, but it was for the hardness of your hearts. From the beginning it was not so."[3] The authoritative teachings and organization, the sacred documents — what were these all but just the record and the witness of men's effort to enshrine and to perpetuate that inspiration and authority of Almighty God which, before it was in any institution or in any writing, lightened the minds, controlled the wills, burned in the souls of prophets, of lawgivers and of poets, and which now flamed in Christ's own soul. The Epistle to the Hebrews in its opening verse puts this thought perfectly, apprehending Jesus just as he seems to have apprehended himself, "God having of old time spoken unto the fathers in the prophets, by

[1] John v. 27.   [2] Matthew v. 33.   [3] *Ibid.*, xix. 8.

divers portions, and in divers manners, hath at the end of these days spoken to us in a Son."[1]

And we have lived to see how, in the long course of Christian history, at one time and another, the doctrines, the organization and the documents of the new faith have been operated with in the old way. We have lived to see how these things, which were merely the deposit of some portion of the authority that was in Jesus, have passed under the scribe's own notion of the nature of their authority. We have lived to see each of them in turn so apprehended as if it were possible for them to have immediate authority. In reference to the institutions of that very faith which takes its name from Jesus, that lesson has been again forgotten which Jesus taught with such earnestness concerning the doctrines and the documents of the Jewish faith. He had taught that these have no authority, save as they are the expressions of truth and goodness, embodiments of something of the spirit of the God who is behind them all. If there is one thing that the history which we have been following in these lectures has made plain, it is the thing to which the profoundest philosophy would have led us, even without the aid of the history. We chose the historical rather than the philosophical approach to the whole problem of authority because the historical treatment is one which can be made picturesque and dramatic. It is the one which tingles with human interest and impresses every-

[1] Hebrews i. 1.

body. But if there is one thing which our study in these lectures has brought out with clearness, it is this, that the authority of the things which we have named, that of Christian doctrine, that of institutions and of writings, is but a mediate one. These all have indeed inspiration, but that inspiration is the Christ. Their authority is that of the Christ whom they enshrine. Or, to go still one step farther, it is the authority of the God whom Christ himself incarnated. These things have authority precisely in so far as they embody and perpetuate the personal revelation. The authority is Christ's alone. Or, if Jesus' own mode of speech rings in our ears, and his selflessness rebukes us, we must say again what Jesus said, that the authority of the thing which he spoke lay in its truth; the authority of the goodness he demanded was the eternal authoritativeness of what is good; and his own authority as he sought to show forth God was that of the God whom he showed forth.

We have seen all these things named win in their time their hold upon the world because of that measure of the spirit of Christ which they contained. Gospels came to have their authority because they were the best that men could do to fill the place of Jesus. Books, dogmas, organizations, came to have authority only as they were substitutes for the influence of persons, and especially as they were representative of the influence of the one mighty, quickening personality. Their authoritativeness for a new time depends upon the question whether they are still true and effective representatives. All these, even after they have gained their authority, have continually to be interpreted by personality. It is this personal note which the discussion of the problem of authority in time past has largely lacked. The failure to realize that at bottom authority is only and always of persons has vitiated much of the discussion. Men have spoken of the authority of the church, as if the church could by any possibility have authority, save as it enshrines personality and becomes a sort of sum of the influence of personalities for the guidance of the life of persons in the world. The essence of the authority of the church lies in its representing a corporate experience, which yet was individual experience before it was corporate. We speak of the authority of Scripture. We do not always perceive that we never really get at the authority of Scripture. The question is always, Which is the authoritative interpretation of Scripture? The question is, Who are the interpreters to whom we should defer? They may be the dead, who have formulated for us their interpretation in an honored creed. They may be the living, who represent the tradition of an institution. Or, once more, we ourselves may be the interpreters, if we solemnly take this responsibility upon ourselves. But always the interpreters are persons. The authorities of Scripture, church, and dogma, are operative always and only through persons. This fact, that authority in the last analysis is personal, that it is the authority of God, that it is the authority of Christ and of men only because God indwells in Christ and men, that it belongs to documents, organizations, rites or creeds, only in a sense derived from these, this fact is surely the deepest fact to which our study in these lectures leads.

Even the perverted forms in which the principle of authority sometimes manifests itself, even those strange and humiliating spectacles in which a fanatical, intriguing, or hypocritical personage obtains ascendency over others, cast a curious side-light upon our assertion that all authority is personal. Half crazed themselves, or shrewdly calculating on the weakness of their fellows, these masterful people meet halfway the class of men and women, strangely numerous, who are only too glad to be mastered, and only too willing to lay off their gravest responsibilities upon others if they may. And even the lowest charlatan says, "Come to me," just as Jesus of Nazareth also said, "Come unto me." Documents, institutions, dogmas, can say only, "Go to him." Thus from the opposite extreme of men's experience, from the wastes of human error and the depths of human folly, one gets a singular confirmation of the principle which we discover at the very pinnacle of truth and goodness as these are shown forth in Jesus Christ, the principle that authority is personal. Even the counterfeit has seized upon the true principle. The ultimate authority is that of God.

And the primary witness to God is a man. Authority is, therefore, derivatively, a quality of men in whom the spirit of truth and goodness, the spirit of God, dwells. Only after that can it be said to be a quality of books, of institutions, and of teachings, as these have taken up into themselves and made permanent something of the spirit of these men.

The other passage to which I referred at the beginning of this lecture as using the word "authority" concerning Christ himself, occurs in all three of the synoptic Gospels.[1] It is that passage in which the chief priests and elders of the people are represented coming to Jesus as he taught and saying to him: "By what authority doest thou these things? and who gave thee this authority? And Jesus answered and said unto them, I also will ask you one question, which if ye tell me, I likewise will tell you by what authority I do these things. The baptism of John, whence was it? from Heaven or from men? And they reasoned with themselves, saying, If we shall say, From Heaven; he will say unto us, Why then did ye not believe him? But if we shall say, From men; we fear the multitude, for all hold John as a prophet. And they answered Jesus, and said, We know not. He also said unto them, Neither tell I you by what authority I do these things." Now what is that which Jesus has here said? What is this answer of Jesus, but just the setting forth, in noblest manner, of the effect and working of that true kind of

[1] Mark xi. 28; Matthew xxi. 23; Luke xx. 2 f.

authoritativeness which he claimed? What is this but the confident appeal to the truthfulness of things, to the rightfulness of claims, to the self-evidencing power of that which is divine? This truth of things if a man see, this rightfulness of things if he perceive, this power of what is just and holy if a man feel, no further authority is necessary. And this truth and goodness and the commanding quality of these, if a man does not perceive, if he wills not to obey, no further authority which can be imagined is of the least avail. If these things carry no sanction within themselves, there is no sanction of them. And if they cannot make themselves felt within the man himself, and not merely without him and upon him, then they do but ruin the manhood of him upon whom they make themselves felt. Any other authoritativeness than that of the truth itself, responded to by the nature of the man himself, avails only to dwarf and not to develop the man over whom it prevails. It can but destroy, it can never fulfil, his noblest nature. It crushes down, it never builds up, the manhood wherein his likeness to his God consists.

We often read the passage, as if Jesus had shown merely his acumen in the evading of his questioners. We read as if he had but shrewdly put them into a place from which they could not answer, just as they on their part often tried merely to draw him into difficulty. On the contrary, whatever was the spirit of their questioning, Jesus has here given us the most serious of answers, and

THE IDEA OF AUTHORITY 321

one whose significance we can never overestimate. He calmly puts his own claim on the same basis with the claim of John the Baptist. With a boldness which, if this were not a true reminiscence, a disciple of Jesus might have hesitated to employ, he puts his own divinest teaching, in its first approach to men, on the same level precisely with that on which the teaching of the Baptist stood. It is the level, namely, of that which is obviously true and right, the authoritativeness of which all lies in the fact that it is true and right. He convicts his questioners out of their own mouths of one of two things. Either they have been so perverse as not to see the truth and not to feel the right. And if they have been thus perverse and have not seen the truth of John the Baptist's teaching, why should he deem that the case will be different with his own? Or else they have been disingenuous and have not obeyed the truth which they did see. It is of no use to appeal to any higher authority. There is no higher authority. The very thing which Jesus seems here to be saying is that, in the case of these men the highest authority has been appealed to and, for the time at least, has failed. The relation, as it lies in men's minds, is often the reverse of this. If a man does not see the truth, and, still more, if he will not do it, then one has recourse to his authorities, as if there were some authority above the truth. What Jesus here makes manifest is that the truth is the authority. The authorities have no authority save

Y

because of and exactly in proportion to their truth. Jesus will not appeal save to manhood for the highest things touching the life of man. He will not appeal save to God for the things of God. He will not appeal to the authority of God in such a manner as to suppress men's intelligence and subvert their liberty. He will rather address himself fearlessly to their intelligence, he will quicken in them the sense of inviolable duty. And then he will abide the issue. The issue he seeks is that men shall go forth to their duty with a sense of obligation in which, when it is at its highest, men are most free, and in which yet they are divinely bound. Jesus will put no man under compulsion. Or, rather, he has faced the fact that for man, as God has made him, there is no compulsion. There is no possible compulsion save that which comes with a man's own free recognition of that which, if a man recognize it, must compel him, or else brand him as no true man if he will not be compelled. As the authority of Jesus is that of the God dwelling within himself, so his appeal is to the deepest self, the indwelling God in men. The appeal of Christ to the consciousness of men is so direct and so unerring that any other form of urgency to which through haste or through anxiety men may resort, merely perverts and imperils the whole matter. So truly is this authority of the truth itself the final authority, and so absolutely is the responsibility of a man's attitude toward the truth with the man himself, that nothing that Christ ever sought for mankind is to be gained by an appeal of any other sort. This is the sense of that sublime word of Jesus to which we have referred: "If any man keep not my sayings, I judge him not. . . . The word that I spake, the same will judge him in the last day."[1]

Many of the discussions of the problem of authority are open to this criticism also, that they fail to realize that the sole purpose of a religious authority is the creation of character. And yet the sole possibility of the creation of character is in the free allegiance of a man to that of which he is himself the judge, and which he obeys, not as a mere form of compulsion or of external restraint upon him, but as the authoritative voice within him of that God to whom he cannot be untrue without ceasing to be true to his own self as well. And yet authority, religious authority like every other, is almost always invoked in a sense in which that authority, if yielded to, would itself prove destructive of character. The only purpose which constraint can ever have is this, that it may aid in the highest development of self-restraint. And yet even a just restraint is often applied in such a manner as to array, for the moment, a man's true self against all restraint. Control over men in the mere spirit of authority has usually resulted in the destruction of the men's desire for self-control. It leaves undeveloped the capacity for self-control. It has taken away the

[1] John xii. 47-48.

opportunity and freedom in which alone men could learn self-control. In giving men an outward reliance it takes away all noble self-reliance. The tragedy of the religious education of the race, like the tragedy of the training in many a home, originates in the failure to find the adjustment of these two things. Surely the sole purpose of the authority of the home is the creation and the development of the character of those growing up within that home. And yet the sole possibility of such development of character lies in the free allegiance of those in the home to things which are not true and right because the authorities of the home declare them to be so, but which the authorities of the home enforce because they are true and right. It may be open to the state to say that in its exercise of authority this particular man must be coerced for the sake of the other men. General purposes may supersede individual ones. But exactly in the proportion in which a home admits that principle it ceases to be a home. It has abandoned its purpose for the development of that particular child's character concerning whom it made so disastrous an admission. And in the great house of the world, under the Father who is in Heaven, religion, which is supposed to be the relation of that Father to all his children, can never make that compromise or approach that abandonment of its ideal. Religion is for the sake of the development in character of every man over whom its authority is exercised. It dares not exercise its authority in such a manner as to destroy his character, even though it claim to do so in order to bring about his salvation. His salvation is his character. His character is his salvation.

It will not do to say that there is a religion of authority for the more yielding natures and for the backward portions of the human race, while there is a religion of inspiration for the bolder spirits and the races which are more advanced in ethical development. That is not religion at all which sets before itself a mere outward order in this world, or a mere conferment in the next, and regards the temper of submission as an end in itself. The religion of authority, so called, has no right to exist, save as it leads up to and is dissolved in the religion of inspiration. The discipline of a home has no right to exist save as it leads up to and is eliminated in the self-discipline of those who go forth from that home. The one religion certainly has these two aspects. And it may be that it is as grave a mistake to seek to apply that which we have called the religion of inspiration to a good part of the human race to-day, as it would be to expect those men in their manhood to show self-discipline whose childhood had been set round by no firm and wise discipline. We may be grateful that the so-called religion of authority does for a good part of the human race what the religion of inspiration shows no present capacity to do. But the religion of authority would be a different thing from that which we in history have known under that name, if once it recognized that it has no authority save that of the truth which it expresses and of the goodness which it represents. The parental authority is ennobled in proportion as we realize that in it is nothing arbitrary or mysterious, nothing which exists for the parent's sake alone. The parental authority is a different thing from that which we have sometimes seen, so soon as it is realized that the basis of that authority is only the truth and goodness which the parent himself seeks to obey before he dares seek to exact obedience of others. And the religion of authority would be a different thing from that which we have known under that name, if once it were recognized that it exists, not for its own aggrandizement, not merely as one of the forces of order in this world or for the conferment of benefits in the next; but it exists literally in order that its own methods, and with these its own self, shall be done away. Precisely so the whole need and justification of the home authority arises from the hope and from the struggle and prayer that there will come a time when there shall be no more need of such authority. It is exercised with no other purpose than to bring nearer the time when it will be no longer exercised.

But let us turn for a moment to the concrete sense which the word authority has actually borne in the historic discussions of this subject. We indeed have, over and over again in the progress of these lectures, gained for ourselves a larger sense of that word. Our argument has issued in a conception of authority which makes it essentially inward and spiritual, in the last analysis personal, the authority of truth, of goodness, and of God himself, indeed of God alone. It is this authority of God which has seemed to us to lie behind and to be manifested in the authority of sacred books, of Christian institutions, of doctrines and ritual, and, it is no irreverence to say also, of Christ himself. Christ said of his own authority that it was that of God. We have felt that the divine authority could never have any purpose save that of the development in character of those over whom that authority was exercised. And if ever any of these manifestations of the divine authority have been so apprehended as to impair man's freedom, to diminish his responsibility, to injure his character, in that measure their divineness and the real meaning of their authority has been lost. We have felt this authority as one before which a man may bow in an absoluteness of allegiance which he would yield to nothing outward, and yet it leaves him as free as he was before he bowed. The obedience to this authority makes a man great. The submission of himself to any other is destructive of his greatness. This may be our sense of the word. We may be satisfied in our own minds that this is the deepest sense of that word. We may be convinced that this is the authority which all these others only shadow forth.

But we are well aware that this is not the sense of the word authority which has been common in the discussion of this theme. We must not juggle with words. We must acknowledge in fairness that when men, for the most part at any rate, have talked of the authority of the Scripture, the authority of the church, they have not meant what we have above said. They have thought of this authority as something which, not mediately but immediately, inhered in the Scripture and in the church. They have meant something which was outwardly operative upon men. They have not always thought of the inviolable relation of authority in its working to the highest character of those upon whom it is brought to bear. They have thought of the reward of obedience as something different from the perfected nature of the obedient man himself. They have thought of the authority of church and Scripture not as something which necessarily carried with it the intelligence of men. They have deemed that it commanded men whether it carried their intelligence or not. They have thought of it not as something which informed a man's own free will, but as something which rightfully controlled him even against his will. Indeed, it has often appeared to the devout soul the acme of duty and the substance of its highest privilege thus to be absolutely commanded by the divine. That has appeared the highest joy, the characteristic religious joy, in which a man thus surrenders his intelligence, his will, his whole self to the divine.

Indeed, if we are to speak fairly, we must go still farther. We must own that this religion of an outward authority appeals to that deeper will which is so often, in every one of us, in contradiction with the current will. It allies itself to the sense of mystery in which the wearied understanding often takes its refuge, knowing that God and the things of God are mysterious, after all. One shows himself ignorant of one of the profoundest aspects of all religious history who does not know that the religion of authority, the religion, that is, which apprehends authority in an external sense, addresses itself to some best things in the human soul as well as to some things which are not the best. Whether we find this authority exercised under historic assumptions by the priesthood of an ordered institution, or by some self-constituted leader whose pretensions have obtained among his adherents a credence at which we can never sufficiently be amazed, we should be gravely mistaken if we should ascribe this whole phenomenon to the passion for power, to the desire of one man to control his fellows. A thousand times more it is to be ascribed to the vague and, shall we not frankly say, the true desire of men and women to be controlled. It is to be ascribed to the profound and correct instinct that religion itself is in its essence a control. It is to be ascribed to men's distrust of themselves in face of the things of God; a distrust which sometimes seems to be the only proper attitude of a true man. It is to be credited to men's shrinking from the responsibility which is involved in the guidance and control of their own lives and in the reliance upon nothing except God and themselves. It was not irony, it was mystic passion which made a great soul of a former age to cry: "I believe because the thing is impossible." It has been the very glory of devoted souls to surrender themselves. The harder was the surrender, the deeper was the joy. He who has not found himself at some time in that position has had no deep religious experience as yet. And when one listens to the boasting which is sometimes indulged concerning the sovereignty of every man's intelligence in every matter, even in those of which he has had no experience whatever; and when one hears the assertion of a man's inviolable liberty to follow every whim, as if this word of liberty were the last word of wisest men; one turns to those men whom the Book mastered as it did our Puritan ancestors, whom the church mastered as it did Francis, or whom Christ mastered as he did Paul, and feels as if he had come within the atmosphere of religion once again. He has come into touch again with men who really know what religion is. The acknowledgment of the inadequacy of one's own intelligence, the being emptied of one's own will, the abasement of self, the sacrifice of self, these things, in a degree which the irreligious cannot understand, are among the very objects of the profoundest religious desire. Toward these very things goes out the cry of the deepest religious nature. It requires poise for men to see that while unquestionably this is the true attitude of men toward God, yet that surrender of which we have spoken is too great a surrender for a man to make to any institution, to any dogma, or in this external sense to any book. It is too great a surrender for a man to make to any of his fellows. It is too great a surrender to be made to any save to God alone. But it is through thoughts such as these that one gets the sweep of what men in time past have meant by religious authority. We must reckon candidly with that which they have meant. We must try once more, and from a new side, to see the relation of this thing which men have ordinarily meant by religious authority to that which we ourselves mean.

And the first thing which strikes us when we reflect upon the authorities which have been ascribed to the church and to the Scripture is this, that in these two phrases, the authority of the Scripture and the authority of the church, the word authority is not used in the same sense. It has been one of the unfortunate consequences of the embittered controversy which was once waged that men do not seem to have perceived this fact. Surely herein lies one of the reasons why that controversy, as between the authority of the Scripture and that of the church, never came to any end. Men do not seem generally to have noted that the word authority does not bear in the one of these connections the same meaning which it bears in the other.

By the authority of the church we understand the binding quality which men concede to the deliverances of an institution, which institution they deem to be in some way inspired of God. Those deliverances must, however, be perpetually interpreted into the life of a new time. They are thus interpreted by the tradition, and ultimately by living men, the representatives of the institution and of the tradition. The interpretation is by persons speaking for the church. By the authority of Scripture, on the other hand, has been understood the binding quality which men concede to the statements of a book, which book they deem to be inspired of God. But these statements of the inspired book stand also in need of perpetual interpretation into the life of a new time. The question is always, Whose is the authoritative interpretation?

Men have said that the Scripture interprets itself. This is true. But it does this through the judgment of him who determines what passages are to be understood as interpreting other passages. But the question is, With whom lies the power of that determination? Does a man make it for himself, or shall some other make it for him? And if another makes this determination for us, what is his authority? It is elusive, this impersonal authoritativeness, this external authority of Scripture. We can never get at it. We always seem to be going to come up with it, but we never do. Always there comes between us and this sure authority the veil of the question, Whose is the authoritative interpretation of the Scripture? Even those to whose apprehension the Scripture is a binding letter, an original infallible statement, must admit that they never get beyond the question of the interpretation of that statement. It is too simple to say, The Scripture says thus and thus. What does it mean by that which it thus says? And the moment we have asked that question, What does it mean? we have passed out of the realm of the external, out of the sphere of the letter and of the written oracle, into the realm of the inward and the spiritual. The only question is, Whose inward and spiritual estimate is to prevail?

To this question there are only two possible answers. Either this authoritative interpretation of Scripture is that of an institution, it is that of an historical tradition, it is that of a priesthood, it is that of living persons whose authority is derived from the fact that they represent that institution and tradition. But if this is the case, then we have no authority except that of the church, to which belongs, on this theory, the power to interpret Scripture and to make religious deliverances of any sort. Or else, on the other hand, we must say that the authoritative interpretation of the Scripture is that which vindicates itself as true in the devout and learned thought, it is that which verifies itself in the pure conscience and the humble life of the individual believer. It is that which makes itself known in the reason, feeling, will, of the individual Christian. It is that which commends itself to every man's conscience in the sight of God. There does not seem to be any escape from this dilemma. And this last is the true and invincible position of Protestantism.

But men have not always had the courage of this position. They have sometimes arrayed against this brave interpretation of the individual mind and conscience what they have termed the authority of Scripture. They have not always seen that they therewith only use a phrase. They have not perceived that in refusing at least candidly to weigh a new opinion of the meaning of Scripture which may be offered they do but defer to the opinion of men before them, or of men about them, or merely stand by their own previous opinion as to what the Scripture means. When we say to our fellows, The Scripture says thus and thus, what we mean is, that this is what we think the Scripture says. We think it most honestly. We may long thus have thought. But the man to whom we speak may long and honestly have thought differently. Or in light of new facts he may now have come to think differently. His new facts might well lead us to think differently. It is conceivable that the assertion, The Scripture says this or that, may be merely covering our own refusal to think. We can never escape this personal element. We can never get away from the personal responsibility of our own moral decisions except by having some other persons make those decisions for us. And even then we take the responsibility of deciding to permit these other persons to make our decisions for us. We do not always perceive that this last may be the very gravest possible of responsibilities.

It has been well said that, in giving up to almost any extent the oracular and external theory of the inspiration and authority of the Scripture, the Roman Catholic church gives up very little, so long as it retains the doctrine of its own infallibility and the exclusive right of the interpretation of the Scripture. But the Protestant body in questioning, even ever so little, the verbal infallibility of the Scripture, in making itself in any sense the judge of that before which it yet bows as its own arbiter and judge, renounces, even though it may be all unconsciously, every authority in matters of religion short of God himself, and commits itself by a great act of faith to the divine principle working within humanity, to the religious instinct, to the trained intelligence and the faithful heart of the individual man, as the sole interpreter of Scripture and the only register of the influence of the spirit of God upon the life of man. But between that authority of the church as the official interpreter of the Scripture and this response in our own hearts to the spirit which is in the Scripture there is no real standing ground. The sooner we make this clear to ourselves the sooner we shall be delivered from halfway measures which are worse than no measures at all.

And if now it be said that the issue of all this is to place the authority of reason above the authority of both Scripture and church, we must reply that, in the sense of the responsibility of which we have just spoken, this is unquestionably true. It is the collective reason which claims the authoritative interpretation of Scripture and of tradition in the church. It is the individual reason which interprets that Scripture which the man who rejects the authority of the church embraces as his authority. And yet, this statement of the authority of reason is a very misleading one. It is an entirely misleading statement because we have thus introduced the word authority in still a third sense into this unfortunate discussion. The man who coined the phrase, authority of reason, must surely have been too intelligent to imagine that his new phrase had anything more than a rather taking verbal resemblance to the other two phrases, authority of the Scripture and authority of the church. It has a rather captivating sound if what one seeks is an epigrammatic answer, a lucky evasion of the pressure of the other two authorities. It was just the kind of a phrase with which the recalcitrant mood of the end of the eighteenth century could strut and grow witty. But it was not of the sort which was calculated to shed great light in a discussion which already sorely needed light.

For, in the first place, we must note that it is not for the abstract reason alone, it is for the heart and conscience as well, it is for the will and feeling as well as for the intelligence, it is for the whole manhood of man that the claim above was made that man has the responsibility in the sight of God of judging for himself the Christian communion and of interpreting for his own soul the word of revelation, precisely as he has the responsibility for the following out of any other of the moral purposes of existence. It is the whole life of the man, experience, affection, resolution, as well as mere intelligence, which ought to be gathered into the forming of an opinion of that which touches his whole life. It is only for what Kant called the practical reason that one can make so great a claim. And one recalls Kant's own contempt for mere flippant rationalizing upon these high themes.

And furthermore, we must add that it is the mind and life of a man as these are formed upon the principles and practice of religion to which alone can be attributed the competence to judge religion. It is the mind which has been formed through the principles and practice of music, or of any art, to whose judgment weight can be accorded in reference to matters of that art. It is not claimed that the musical or artistic intelligence is of a sort fundamentally different from any other. But it is an intelligence which has been formed upon a specific experience, and which derives sensitiveness and aptitude and specific competence from that experience. It is not claimed that the religious intelligence is miraculously different from any other intelligence. It is not even claimed that the religious experience is a compartment of experience shut up by itself and cut off from any other. What is claimed is that the religious experience is a real and specific experience. What is claimed is that those only who have had some genuine religious experience have religious intelligence or are competent to pass any serious religious judgment. What is claimed is that only as the intelligence is informed by the religious experience are its judgments concerning religion entitled to any consideration. These are minor matters, however, although it is true that they are matters which are not always thought of by those who use the phrase, the authority of reason. The most serious comment is one which is yet to be offered.

It is a misleading use of language to call that the exercise of the authority of reason which is really nothing in the world but the courageous assumption of one of the fundamental and inevitable responsibilities of human life. The authority is not in the reason. The authority is in the truth which it is the responsibility of man's reason to know and to judge. The authority is precisely where we previously found it, namely, in the true, in the good, in Christ and God, in the last analysis, in God alone. But the responsibility is with men to know the truth and to will to do the truth which they know. That responsibility is one which can by no possibility be taken away from any man. He cannot part with it himself, no matter how much he may desire to part with it. The phrase, authority of reason, can have no real meaning save this, that we are certainly commanded, as in the sight of God, to take our own responsibilities in religion, and not to try to lay off these responsibilities upon some great institution or upon some group of our fellows in whose interpretation of the Scripture we concur, or upon some individual in whose leadership for any reason we have acquiesced.

But with these qualifications, and with these attempts to determine the meaning of the phrase, we are forced to say that the responsibility of reason is absolute. It is true that the Bible is what it is, no matter what a man may think of it. But it is also true that the Bible is to that man just what he thinks it to be. It cannot be anything different to him until he conceives it differently. His belief concerning it is the determining condition and the precise limitation of its influence upon him. The same thing is true as regards the church. The same thing is true concerning doctrine. It is true even as toward Christ himself. We can never get away from this fact, either in the religious relation or in any other relation of our lives. The authority of reason, if men mean by that phrase the thing which we have endeavored to describe, — the responsibility of reason we have preferred to call it, — is absolute. No man escapes that responsibility, not even the man who has delivered himself over most absolutely to some other form of authority in order to escape his responsibility. He exercised his reason even in determining that it was reasonable for him to abdicate his reason. He used his judgment even in determining to trust himself henceforth absolutely to the church and to have no more perplexities of private judgment. He employed his reason in determining that he would thereafter not employ it, or at least not in the same way that he employs it in other matters. It is his opinion of Scripture which leads him to feel that what he takes to be its sense ought to supersede all his other opinions. But he used his reason in forming that opinion of Scripture. It is to his reason that constant appeal is made in order to sustain that opinion of Scripture. He did all this because at the time he deemed it a reasonable thing to do. He continues to do it because he still thinks it reasonable, no matter how much he may proclaim that he allows himself no further reasoning about it.

But if these things are true, then it must be evident how strange and futile are the attempts which have from time to time, and at great pains, been made to coördinate these three authorities. The attempt is to show that the Bible, the church, and the reason are authorities in some way concurrent, the one with the other. They are somehow joint authorities in human life. That they cannot thus be joint divine authorities must be quite obvious. They are not even any two of them authorities in the same sense. They are not even any two of them divine in the same sense. Nothing but confusion of ideas can proceed from the attempt to deal with them all upon the same plane, or to make them all sharers, part and part, in the representation of the divine right and might upon the earth. Authority is of God alone. Jesus himself then most commands us when we perceive how he was himself commanded. We are then most conscious of his authority when we realize how he bowed his whole soul to the authority of truth, of goodness, and of God alone. How much more, then, must the company of his followers and the long experience and august tradition of their institution have authority for us because of that measure of the truth which they enshrine, of the goodness which they embody, and of the spirit of God as it dwelt in Jesus which they reproduce. In so far as they do these things they have authority. But even so, it would be more true to say that the authority is not their own. In so far as they do not enshrine the truth, embody goodness, and incarnate the spirit of Jesus, they have no authority whatever. And if even Jesus himself during his lifetime made his last appeal to truth, goodness, and to God, and left men with the responsibility of judging that appeal, how much more must those shadowings in the Gospel of him who shadowed forth to us his Father, God, be limited to the same quiet appeal to the mind and heart of men. How much more must men, each man for himself, be left to the solemn responsibility of that use, in all humility and prayer, of the right reason, which men cannot abdicate if they would, and would not if they could.

Meantime it is interesting to observe that as criticism more and more makes untenable the old external way of conceiving the authority of the Scripture, there is manifest a definite tendency, in Protestant quarters, to the revival, in some form of it, of the authority of the church. This recurrence was indeed the gist of Newman's contention and of a movement inaugurated now fully two generations ago. The reason intimated above is the reason which at the inauguration of that movement was given almost in those very words. This recurrence from the religion of Scripture apprehended as an outward authority, which is now being shaken, to the religion of the outward authority of the church, which was shaken four hundred years ago, shows, it would seem, how minds once really imbued with the religion of authority shrink from the great change which is passing over us. This recurrence shows, at any rate, how much closer is the affinity between those two forms of the religion of outward authority than has commonly been supposed. Despite the long contest between these two forms of the religion of outward authority, despite the fact that they have long been assumed to be the antitheses the one of the other, nevertheless this must be evident, how much closer is their relation the one to the other, than is the affinity of either with that religion of the spirit and of

THE IDEA OF AUTHORITY 343

inwardness, which in humble trust of right reason and enlightened conscience dares to apprehend its authority as primarily that of the God working within men, and deems all outward authorities as but subordinate. This religion of the authority of the Spirit of God within men, when we shall have advanced to it, will be seen to separate us from some forms of popular Protestantism by a wider interval than that which separated Protestantism from Catholicism four hundred years ago. But this religion of the authority of the good and of the God working within men will be seen, in the light of such a study as that which in these lectures we have followed, to be but a recurrence to the simplicity of that religion in which Jesus himself lived, and which the Apostles propounded at the first. One is reminded of that saying of Goethe: "Without authority mankind has not been able to exist, and yet it brings quite as much error as truth with it. It seizes upon and perpetuates in detail that which should have been suffered to lapse. It rejects and permits to pass that which should by all means have been held fast. And it is on the whole the main reason why humanity has not got on faster than it has."[1]

And yet we must never forget that which often in these lectures we have called historic right. We must never overlook the fact that it is by the adjustment of the ideal to the actual that the ideal does its work in the world. It is never

[1] Sprüche in Prosa: *Über Naturwissenschaft*, 2te Abthlg.

as pure spirit but always in some concrete form, in some manifestation, through some incarnation of itself, that the idea and spirit of things sets itself about its achievement in the world. It will be remembered that the main thesis of that outline of the history of doctrine which we offered was that the development of early Christian doctrine was the slow and unconscious fulfilment, in some part, of that same process of the Hellenization of the substance of Christianity of which process the gnostic movement represented the acute stage. The church did not achieve its victory over those who sought at once to naturalize Christianity in the world of ancient culture without making concessions which ultimately brought the church itself far toward the same goal which those others sought. In a sense the progress of doctrine was a defection from the simplicity of the religious message of Jesus. We have seen that some things which have passed for authoritative Christian doctrine are clearly Hellenic in their origin. The pressure upon the merely intellectual elements of the faith, the undue emphasis upon doctrine, the notion of salvation by doctrine was certainly not Christian. And yet we know that the progress of doctrine was inevitable. Even the course which that development took is, to say the least, historically intelligible. It would hardly be too much to say that that course also was inevitable. In their effort to adjust the convictions which they had concerning Jesus and Christianity to the opinions which they held concerning all things besides, the early Christians were not only fully within their rights but they followed an intellectual necessity. And when in our day men contend for what they call undogmatic Christianity, in so far as they use their language accurately, and really mean dogma rather than doctrine, we may rest content. In so far as they would repudiate a Christianity which lays all its emphasis upon authoritative dogma, we may be satisfied. But in so far as they mean a Christianity which does not seek to express itself in doctrine freshly adjusted to the new thoughts of our own time, in so far, that is, as they would make religion a mere matter of feeling and empty it of all intellectual content, in so far as they deem it the part of piety to decline even to endeavor to adjust the convictions which they hold concerning Jesus and Christianity to the convictions which as children of our own age we must hold concerning other matters, — this would seem to be the pathway to the intellectual discrediting of the Christian religion altogether.

And if we turn from doctrine to church government, the same reasoning applies. The Christian church came naturally in the course of its development to the monarchical episcopate which culminated logically in the papacy at Rome. That episcopate and papacy were in their own place a supreme providence of God. With all their defects they did in their own time the grandest work. Without some such strongly centralized government the church could hardly have survived the shock of the overthrow of the Roman Empire or the invasions of the barbarians, it could scarcely have trained the northern races. But to seek to give to that monarchical system a sanction as original with Christ and the Apostles, or as the final intention of God, is quite another matter. It does not need that sanction. Its authoritativeness was in its usefulness. Its sanction was in its expediency, under certain conditions which then prevailed. For that matter, the Protestant appeal to Scripture for the more democratic form of church government rested, to say the least, upon misapprehension. Those simpler forms of church government were also hardly original with Christ and the Apostles in the sense in which that Protestant claim was made. These also have no authority save in the grand sense of their expediency. They also have no sanction save in their usefulness in times and places to which they are adapted, their usefulness in the making of men in the image of Christ, and in the doing of work effectively in Christ's name.

Whether, in the conditions of modern society, a church government more centralized than that which has generally prevailed in the high Protestant bodies might not be in a true way expedient, is a question most gravely to be debated. Assuredly these bodies feel the need of an increase in their efficiency. They need to be brought into line in some way with the great principle of combination which obtains about us in all other departments of life. But this centralization and combination can certainly be brought to pass without finding its sanction in any unhistorical assumption. It would have abundant sanction in its utility, its holy adaptation to the new needs of the new time. That mere sanction of utility would be something far more divine and more authoritative than would apostolicity, even if we could recover the precise order of the churches of the apostolic age, if meantime it should be proved that the apostolic order, when strictly imitated, was inoperative in the real emergencies and inefficient to the real purposes of church life in our day. And such modifications and adjustments of church government can certainly be achieved without the sacrifice of that principle of individual initiative and of universal responsibility which has been the secret of the Protestant type of piety, and indeed of so much of the progress of the modern world.

The thesis which lay at the basis of our discussion of church government is in one sense entirely correct. The nature of the church, apprehended as a spiritual body and exerting only a spiritual force, is in contradiction to the very conception of law and government based upon rights and powers, in the sense in which these words have always been understood among men. And yet, the evolution of church government is not only explicable, it was justifiable. We should hardly go too far if we should say that even the course which that evolution took was inevitable. The only thing which is not justifiable is that under the assertion of its sacred origin that government should refuse to advance to those further steps in its own evolution which the adaptations to the life of a new time suggest. In itself, the contention against any concrete form of church government to which we above alluded is entirely just, and the organizations which the Christian body has inherited are a defection from the simplicity of Christ. But this consideration is put forth as if there were something distinctively Christian in our having no effective organization, and that, in face of a work in the world so vast and complex that it demands the most efficient organization for its accomplishment — a work which we own that we are under sacred obligation to endeavor to accomplish. But is not this, after all, the same question over again which we asked ourselves concerning the Scriptures? Admit that it is only a small part of the greatness of Jesus which has been preserved to us in the Gospels, and that even that part is seen through the mist of the inevitable apprehensions and misapprehensions of the witnesses. Admit that much is here crystallized, set hard and fast, which in Jesus was all fluid and free. Admit that much has here become letter, or at least has been used by men as a binding letter, which was in him pure spirit. Admit that the worship of the letter which has sometimes prevailed, and not least among those most devout, could hardly have found favor with him who said, "The words that I speak unto you, they are spirit and they are life,"[1] or with his Apostle who declared, "The letter killeth, it is the spirit which giveth life."[2] Admit that in this sense the Scripture itself is a descent from Jesus. Yet at this distance should we know with certainty anything concerning Jesus, save for this deposit of something, at least, of his spirit in the Gospels and again in the Epistles, and indeed save also for the unique position and authority which these writings came to hold in the Christian church?

So is it in regard to that other question. We may admit that the Christian church ought never to be moved save by spiritual impulse and should put forth nothing but spiritual influence. We must own the evils, almost beyond belief, which have come with the notion that the church of God was a sort of state among men, operating with all the means of law and force with which other states must operate. But the vagaries of that other theory, the monstrosities which have been perpetrated under the theory that men are always and only under the impulse of the Holy Ghost — these also are painfully evident. The folly and atrocities committed by these men also are so obvious that we are constrained to say that it is of the guidance of God that the impulse which Christ gave has, in this as in all other respects, been taken up into the common forms of human society and shaped these forms of society to itself as best it

[1] John vi. 63.   [2] 2 Corinthians iii. 6.

could. We may concede that that impulse has operated in the full stream of human history, within the limits of human reason and experience, and, inevitably also, within the limits of human error and passion. But we may safely assert that, even under shapes defective, sometimes sadly human, which have themselves been changed from age to age, yet this divine impulse has thus transformed society as it could not have done in any other way.

It was not unnatural that the men of four hundred years ago should have set up against the authority of the church an authority of the Scripture, which they soon came to apprehend in an almost equally external way. They did not perceive that the devout reasoning and the light of history which they so successfully applied to the first would one day have their way also with the second. No one can doubt that it is a nobler and more spiritual conception of the church which has arisen out of that great discussion. In like manner no one need fear but that it is a nobler, a more inward and spiritual view of the authority of Scripture which is emerging out of the discussion which we are now passing through. The disposition to deny the authority of Scripture altogether, in the first rush of the new historic sense concerning the Scripture, is only the parallel of that extreme to which men went after the Reformation, in which all feeling for the communion of the saints, all interest in the fellowship of believers, seemed for the time to be lost. Men seemed to lose all sense of the supreme worth of the common Christian experience and all consciousness of relation to the historic organism of the Christian life. And yet without this relation the individualism for which the Reformers stood has always been a feeble and even a dangerous thing.

The great difference between the two situations lies in this. That old revolt against the external authority of the church was complicated with all sorts of political considerations. The new birth of civil liberty in modern times bears the most intimate relation to that great awakening of conscience which the Reformation was. The triumph of democracy in the state is only one aspect of that emphasis upon the rights and duties of the individual man in the sight of God which Protestantism has always proclaimed. It is no wonder if in the passions of that political revolt the sense of the spiritual communion also was lost. For the authority of the church, as the Middle Age understood it, was a political tyranny of the most mundane sort. It differed from the other mundane tyrannies only in that it claimed supramundane sanctions for its tyranny. It is no wonder if, in the bitterness of that conflict, the sense for the community of the Christian life and of the validity and authority of the universal Christian experience was forfeited. But nothing is more obvious than the endeavor in the whole realm of Protestantism to-day to regain that feeling for the church which was then in large measure scornfully sacrificed.

The issue in the modern struggle concerning the authority of Scripture is quite different. It is not liberty of thought which, for any large number of persons, is involved in the modern struggle touching the authority of Scripture, as in those old days political liberty was involved in the struggle against the authority of the church. That liberty of thought has been already achieved. It was achieved, in a measure, as part and parcel of that other movement in the Renaissance and Reformation. It was in still larger part the work of the much maligned eighteenth century, and is the title of that century to glory. In fact, by the end of that century the rationalist movement had carried liberty of thought as far as the French Revolution endeavored to carry liberty of life. The history of culture of the nineteenth century has, indeed, been one of marvellous advance. But it has been also in no small degree a history of the recovery of much that was then in flippant arrogance, in the name of reason, thrown away.

The question in debate concerning the authority of Scripture is not now whether science shall be free; whether the study of history shall be untrammelled; whether the whole philosophy of the universe shall be readjusted to the facts, innumerable and of immeasurable significance, which, mainly within the last two generations, have come within our ken. That readjustment is going on irresistibly all about us. It is of no use whatever to set up against it the barriers of an external authority, scriptural or of any other sort. That movement is going on, if we may so say, by a sort of authoritativeness of its own. It is going on by the authority of that amount of truth which, despite mistakes and partial apprehensions and imperfect notions, is yet gradually being discovered. It is going on by the authority of that amount of goodness which, despite all admixtures with the evil, does, nevertheless, in individual hearts and in society, get itself done. And with unerring instinct, men feel that the authoritativeness of that truth which is discovered and of that goodness which is achieved is the authority of God Himself.

Men are therefore bewildered if, when they would follow this authority of indubitable scientific truth and obvious social goodness, they feel themselves checked by that which is urged upon them from other quarters under the name of the authority of God in Scripture, church, or dogma. This latter authority seems often to demand an attitude and to enforce a method different from that to which they are used in the search for other truth. It is sometimes alleged in defence of statements which are in plain contravention of scientific judgments which men would otherwise hold, and of facts which they deem themselves to know. The bewilderment is melancholy. The consequences of this seeming opposition are disastrous for religious life and intelligence. And all the while we clearly perceive that the opposition is only seeming, and the conflict is due but to misunderstanding. The misunderstanding is bound to pass away. But one would like to help it to pass more quickly. All truth is one. All goodness is one. God is the authority of both. The question is not of liberty of thought. The liberty of thought is here.

The question is whether within the universe of things, as we now see them, whether within the world of thoughts such as those which the modern man must hold, the Scripture with its inspiration and authority can find a place. The question is whether, momentarily, these inestimably precious influences may not lose their power. We must speak of such loss as but a momentary one. For any one who views the long course of history knows how often the mode of apprehension of the Scripture and of its inspiration and authority has changed already, and still the central thing to be apprehended has remained the same and gone on to do new and larger work. Something which in time past men have described as revelation and inspiration, something which we ourselves acknowledge as authoritative, is felt by all who frankly come under the influence particularly of the New Testament Scripture. The question is whether these words can be divested of associations and assumptions which to-day hinder rather than help the apprehension of the thing which they seek to describe. The question is whether these facts of revelation and inspiration, can be so put before men that they will appear in perfect consonance with all the other facts which the men know and in harmony with all the ideas which they entertain concerning things besides the Scripture. The question is whether men can be made to see that these authorities, that of the Scripture, and in their measure those of doctrine and of church as well, are simply the authority of truth and goodness, are merely the authority of the spirit of Christ and of God which are here enshrined. The question is whether men can be led to see that these all claim the recognition of their free intelligence and the obedience of their hearts with that same imperiousness, and with no other, than that with which truth and duty claim men everywhere.

Because, the moment this takes place, the miserable misunderstanding of which we spoke must vanish. And this is the thing which is taking place all about us. This is the secret of that interest in the Scripture as literature and history, which is now so widely felt among us. It touches, not merely the devoutest circle in our churches, but is taking full possession of the universities. It works such a revolution that it makes some of those who have the thing most at heart to draw back a little. This is the thing which has come to some of the most learned and fearless of investigators in this field. It is the recovery of the sense of the authoritativeness of Scripture, and particularly of that of the New Testament.

It is the reassertion of this authority in their own lives, and the regaining of enthusiasm on their part for the presentation of their thought concerning Scripture in such fashion that the Scripture may gain control of the lives of others. Men are not generally in revolt against the authority of Scripture. It is not that they repudiate the notion of revelation and disbelieve in inspiration. This is not the case even with all of those who say that they do thus disbelieve. But they are under the intellectual necessity of understanding the authority of Scripture in the same way that they understand every other authority. These facts of revelation and of inspiration must needs be brought into harmonious relation with all other facts. A man's view of God's presence and power, of God's working in these things, must needs be coherent with his view of God's presence and power, and of God's working in all things besides. It is only a period of failure of adjustment which we have been passing through. The cause of religion has lagged behind in the process of adjustment.

And if we should ask why just that cause upon which, of all causes, there would seem to devolve a sacred privilege of leadership should so often lag behind, and need to be forced forward almost against its will and by pressure seemingly from without itself, we should have to answer somewhat thus. In the first place we must allow ourselves no narrow definition of religion. The forces of good and of truth are the forces of God, wherever and however they are manifest, and even though they may not call themselves by His name or deem that they have anything to do with His cause. The life of man is one. The inspiration of God is for man's whole life. The revelation comes to men out of every aspect and relation of their lives. The whole of human existence is the scope of God's guidance and the field of man's obedience, even when men have no idea that it is God whom they obey. It is a constant phenomenon in the history of religion that some small function of religion, worship for example, which can surely have no purpose save as a preparation of the hearts of men for the true religion of a noble life, is yet put forward as if it were the whole of religion. It is a constant phenomenon that the truth which is taught in churches is put forth as if it alone were holy and divine truth; that the life which is lived in the name of Christ is assumed to be the only life which is lived in the spirit of Christ; and that the deeds which are done, we will say, under the impulse of charity, are the only deeds which men call good or deem to have been done for God. It is a constant phenomenon in the history of religion that men come to confound the mere deposit of authority — Scripture, doctrine, organization, whatever it may be — with the creative impulse of God, some small part of which impulse is here deposited. They assign to these an authority which belongs to Him alone. They turn that which is the very record of an inspiration given to men in time past into a hindrance and preventive of like inspiration in the time to come. Then, indeed, that cause of which we should expect the greatest breadth and reality becomes the cause of the utmost narrowness and the centre of all that is artificial. Then, indeed, that force of which we should expect leadership becomes the most conservative of all forces, and claims the sanction of its divineness for being so conservative as it is. It is then the work of that God who works outside of the accepted forms, it is then the work of the men who obey God outside of the accepted forms, to furnish from without, that solemn impulse of religion which the current forms seem not prepared to furnish from within.

We may remind ourselves that in the period before the Reformation the current religion seemed to have allied itself with every form of civil tyranny and to have degenerated into a civil tyranny itself. Yet the primitive impulse of that great revolt was the valuation of the individual which the Gospel had taught. When once that revolt was inaugurated, it was the fact that the religious and moral enthusiasm assumed its control which made of the rise of the states of Northern Germany and of the Puritan Commonwealth in England the earnest and beneficent movement that it was. It was the religious and moral enthusiasm in control of that revolt which made of it the permanent and constructive movement which it was. It was the absence of that religious enthusiasm and sense of moral responsibility in the French Revolution which made of it the disappointing and destructive movement that it was.

We may remind ourselves that at the end of the eighteenth century the forms of current religion seemed everywhere arrayed against the cause of freedom of thought; and we have not even yet passed altogether beyond the state of things in which the church and the Scripture are deemed by some to be the enemies of free thought. And yet the religious and moral enthusiasm, the sense of the sacred responsibility of this freedom of life and thought which we have achieved, — this, and this alone apparently, can save us now from social issues as disastrous as was the civil experiment in France one hundred years ago. The overturning of society at the hands of men whose point of view is that of their economic grievances seems sometimes as imminent as did that assault upon privilege in the name of political equality. But there is this difference. The apprehension of social betterment as the field for moral enthusiasm and for religious endeavor, the deepening sense of the sacred responsibility of freedom, of the obligation of rank, of the accountability of wealth, of the privilege of power — these things are visible all about us. These apprehensions unite all parties. They are the working ideas of the generation, the most encouraging signs of the time.

This moral enthusiasm, this religious consecration to a new and great task, draws its inspiration, as such enthusiasms now for two thousand years have done, from the revelation of God and the memorials of Jesus Christ. Nothing is more notable than is the eagerness with which men turn to the New Testament to discover what was the social teaching of Jesus. Nothing is more salient than the reverence of men everywhere in our day for Jesus. Nothing is more marked than is their acknowledgment of his authority. That acknowledgment of his authority rests indeed upon grounds which are widely different from the dogmatic and ecclesiastical ones. It rests upon ethical grounds. It rests upon so simple a foundation as this, that the men recognize in Jesus of Nazareth one who spoke the truth and who in love did that which was good. Many men outside of the church have this sense of the highest authority, the very authority of God Himself, in the man Jesus Christ.

On the other hand there are many of us who are heartily identified with the Christian church and have the deepest reverence for the New Testament Scripture, who also on our part perceive that our real and ultimate authority is God in Jesus Christ. In the faith of the God who reveals Himself within men, and in the work of the new time which is to transform both church and world, we would join hands with the men of whom we spoke. The authority which they gladly acknowledge is the very authority which we claim, — the eternal authority of truth and goodness, of God himself, particularly as these are manifest to us in Jesus Christ.

INDEX

INDEX

Accusations against Christians, 86.
Acts of the Apostles, 73 ff.
Acts, Apocryphal, 75.
Acts of Martyrs of Scili, 97.
Alexandrine Canon of New Testament, 113, 167.
Allegorical interpretation, 116.
Alogoi reject Apocalypse, 58, 142.
Ambrose, 158, 277.
Amphilochius, 183.
Apocalypse of John, 57 ff.; opposition to, 142 ff.; in Dionysius of Alexandria, 187; in Eusebius, 178, 181; final canonization of, 182, 184.
Apocalypse of Peter, 59.
Apocalyptic literature, outside of the Old Testament, 57.
Apocrypha, meaning of word, 70; of Old Testament, 157; of New Testament, 157.
Apocryphal Acts, 75.
Apocryphal Gospels, two classes, 70.
Apollos, 50, 198.
Apologies, character of, 82 f.
Apologists, 36 ff., 81 f.; task of the, 81; arguments of, 84; attitude to philosophy, 83; and the Old Testament, 84; and the New Testament writings, 85, 135.
Apostles, 28 ff.; meaning of word, 44; support of, 237; Protestant appeal to, 257.
Apostles' Creed, 275, 296, 298, 305.
Apostles' "memorials" concerning Jesus, in Justin, 88.
Apostolic authorship of New Testament books, 29 f.; literature as Scripture, 33; tradition of doctrine, 298.
Apostolic Canons, 183.
Apostolic Constitutions, 187.
Apostolic succession, 129.
Apostolicity, in Irenæus, 130; in Eusebius, 179.
Aristides, 95.
Athanasius, life and works, 184 f.; Canon of, 185.
Athenagoras, 96.
Augustine, life and works, 158 f.; Canon of, 160.
Authority, of Jesus, 10, 21, 312, 360; of Apostles, 221; of apostolic writings, 29 f.; canonical, 7, 13; of Scripture, 7, 217, 332, 340 f., 352, 359; of the Church, 217, 332, 340 f., 342, 351; of reason, 336 f.; personal, 317; religion of, 324, 328 f.

Baptismal symbol, Roman, 275, 294, 295, 303.
Barnabas, Epistle of, 53.
Bellarmine, Cardinal, 195.
Beza, 199.
Bishops, 45; in early church, 240; ordained by Apostles, 243; more than one in local community, 241, 246; choice of, 241; and charity, 246; and the Eucharist, 246; power of, 241, 247 f., 252; priestly character of, 251; sins of, 253; and the Canon, 177.
Book of the Sacrament and the Canon, 187.
Book-religion, 19.

363

Book of the Revelation (see Apocalypse), 56.
Buddhism and canonization, 13.
Byzantium, 173.

Caius, Roman presbyter, 143.
Cajetan, Cardinal, 192.
Calvin, 199.
Canon, definition of, 10.
Canon of New Testament, outline of, 33, 42, 138, 153 f.; authority of, 14; decrees concerning, 26, 33, 160 f.; Alexandrine Canon, 167; Syrian, 189.
Canon of Old Testament, 5; Alexandrine, 157; Palestinian, 157.
Canonization, beginnings of, 15, 25; chronology of, 32 f.; forces and motives of, 124 ff.; a conservative process, 26, 141; in other religions, 11 f.
Carlstadt, 199.
Catholic church, rise of, 35, 169.
Catholic Epistles, 51; final canonization of, 183.
Celsus, 97 f.
Charity, funds for, 236.
Chemnitz, 194 f.
Chiliasm, 143.
Christ, second coming of, 46.
Christian church, and the Old Testament, 5, 19; and Paul's letters, 27; all functions of, deemed inspired, 234; as outward organization, 249.
Christian doctrine, earliest, 277 f.
Christian life, earliest types of, 37.
Christian literature, outside of Canon, classified, 34 ff.
Christianity, literary impulse foreign to, 16; a book-religion, 19; as revealed philosophy, 269; transformation of, at end of second century, 168 ff.; in fourth century, 169 ff.; secularization of, 289 f.
Christians, social status of earliest, 37, 81.

Chrysostom, 184.
Clement of Alexandria, life and works, 113; Canon of, 114 f.
Clement of Rome, First Epistle, 52; allusions to Paul, 25; concerning bishops, 243 f.; his Canon, 53; Second Epistle, 77.
Confession, as bond of union of church, 295.
Confucianism and canonization, 13.
Constantine, conversion of, 168 f.; motives, 171.
Corinthians, Epistles to, of Paul, 49, 75; of Clement, 52.
Councils touching the Canon, Laodicea, 161; Carthage, 160; Florence, 194; Trent, 194; Vatican, 195.
Creed, Apostles', 275, 296, 298, 305.
Creeds, liturgical, 294.
Cyprian, his life and works, 151 f.; church government, 249; his Canon, 152.
Cyril of Jerusalem, 183.

Damasus, 160.
Daniel, Book of, 57.
Deacons, 237.
Decrees concerning Canon, 26, 118; under Augustine, 160; of Gelasius, 162; of Hormisdas, 162; of Laodicea, 161; of Carthage, 160; of Trent, 194; of Vatican Council, 195.
Diaspora, 224.
Diatessaron, 71, 91 ff.
Didachè, 75.
Diocletian, 171 ff.
Dionysius of Alexandria on the Apocalypse, 58, 181.
Doctrine, definition of, 216, 272 f.; types of, in New Testament, 265 f.; apostolic tradition of, 34; in Christian Missions, 300; development of, 307 f.; Hellenic influence upon, 284 f.; 287 f.
Doctrinal forms, variety of, 280 ff.
Documents, authority of, 20.

INDEX

Dogma, definition of, 273 f.; history of, 274.

Ebionism, 269.
Elders in early church, 239.
End of world, expectation of, 16.
Enoch, Book of, 57.
Ephesians, Epistles to, of Paul. 49; of Ignatius, 54.
Epiphanius, 183.
Episcopate, historic right of, 255.
Epistles, in Muratori Fragment, 126 f.
Erasmus, 193.
Eucharist, celebration of, 231, 233, 236, 247, 251.
Eusebius, life and works, 175 f.; Canon of, 177 f.; threefold classification, 178.

Fathers, ecclesiastical, 35.
Fourth Gospel, 63 ff.; influence in second century, 268.

Gelasian decree, 162.
Gentile societies, influence upon organization of church, 221, 224 ff.
Gentiles and the Old Testament, 18.
Gnostics, their secret tradition, 100; their teaching, 284, 291; and the Old Testament, 99; and New Testament writings, 100; and the bishopric, 254.
God, the Father, belief in, 279.
Goethe, 343.
Gospels, the beginning of writing of, 24; read in churches, 24 f.; earliest authority of, 9; the Synoptic, 62; the Fourth Gospel, 63 ff.; local traditions of, 68, 71; according to Egyptians, 68; according to Hebrews, 67; according to Peter, 69, 144; choice of four, 71 f., 117.
Goths, 161.
Greek church, after eighth century, 186.
Gregory of Nazianzus, 183.

Harnack, theory of development of doctrine, 276.
Hebrews, Epistle to, authorship of, 50; dispute concerning, 153; final canonization, 183.
Heretics of second century, 27.
Hippolytus, 150; his Canon, 151.
Holy Spirit, 9; belief in, 279.
Hormisdas, 162.

Ignatius, 54; his epistles, 54.
Influences, unconscious in canonization, 132.
Innocent I, letter of, 160.
Inspiration, rabbinical conception of, 6; Gentile idea of, 6; of all Christians, 55, 104 f., 316; Protestant conception, 196; modern thought of, 355.
Interpretation of Scriptures, 332 ff.
Irenæus, his life, 107 f.; his teaching concerning Apostles, 29, 109; his view of apostolic writings, 130; and the four Gospels, 73, 108; and the Roman Symbol, 295; Canon of, 109.

Jerome, life and works, 155 f.; translation of Scripture, 156; Old Testament Canon of, 157; New Testament Canon of, 156 f.
Jesus, belief in, 279; authority of, 10, 21, 263; and the Old Testament, 17, 21; his religious teaching, 262; apprehension of him in Gospels, 264; in Epistles, 265.
John, Gospel of, 63 ff., 268.
Judaism, influence of in New Testament, 17 ff., 266.
Jülicher, on Pauline Epistles, 50.
Justin Martyr, his life and works, 36, 85 ff.; and the Old Testament, 87; attitude toward prophecy, 89; account of Christian worship, 88; Apostolic "memorials" of Jesus, 88; attitude toward Paul, 89.

Koran, writing of, 4.
Krüger, Christian literature other than canonical, 41.

Laodicea, Council of, 161, 183.
Leaders, Christian, influence of, in canonization, 116, 117.
Literature, ecclesiastical, 35.
Lucifer of Cagliari, 152.
Luther and the Canon, 198.

Marcion, his life, 27, 101 f.; and the Old Testament, 102; his New Testament, 101 ff.; doctrinal teaching of, 292; and the church, 293; his Canon, 102.
Marcionite churches, 293.
Marcus Aurelius, 171 f.
Matthew, "Sayings" of Jesus in Aramaic, 62; Gospel according to, 63.
Maximilla, 105.
Melito of Sardis, apology of, 95 f.
Methodius of Olympus, 145.
Michaelis, J. D., 201.
Mohammed and the Koran, 4.
Montanism and the Bishopric, 254.
Montanus, 105 f.
Motives, doctrinal in canonization, 119, 124 ff.; in Muratori Fragment, 123 ff.; in Irenæus, 129.
Muratori Fragment, 111 f., 123 f.; and the Shepherd of Hermas, 60, 128.

New Testament, description of, 3 f.; authority of, 7, 30; period of production of, 4; first use of the title, 111, 148 f.; devotional use of, 204.
Nicæa, Council of, 175, 184.
Nicene Creed, 305.
Nicholas of Lyre, 192.

Old Testament, period of production of, 4; prophetical character of, 32; Jesus' use of, 17, 21; Paul's use of, 18; among Gentiles, 18; and the Apologists, 84; rejected among Gnostics, 99.
Organization of the church, apostolical, 34, 219 ff.; inspiration of, 228 f.; officers of, 231, 238; influence of the Synagogue, 221 f.; of the Gentile societies, 221, 224 ff.; sanction of, 347.
Origen, life and works, 145 ff.; his Canon, 148 ff.; theology of, 306.

Papacy, the, 345.
Papias, 65.
Paul, his use of the Old Testament, 18; and the Words of the Lord, 22; his epistles, 47 ff.; his doctrinal teaching, 266.
Philadelphians, Epistles to, in Apocalypse, 57; of Ignatius, 54.
Philippians, Epistles to, of Paul, 49; of Polycarp, 56.
Plato, 4.
Polycarp, Epistle to Philippians, 56; Epistle of Ignatius to, 54.
Presbyters, in early church, 239.
Priscilla, Montanist leader, 105.
Priscilla and Epistle to Hebrews, 51.
Prophets, in early church, 44, 235.
Protestantism and the Canon, 191, 200, 216.

Quinisexta, 184.

Reading in churches, the beginning of canonization, 25.
Reason, responsibility of, 338 f., 340.
Reformation, the, and the authority of Scripture, 7; and the Canon, 190.
Renaissance, the, Greek influence in, 190.
Resch, on unwritten sayings of Jesus, 66.
Roman Catholic tradition, 216.
Romans, Epistles to, of Paul, 49; of Ignatius, 54.

INDEX

Ropes, on unwritten sayings of Jesus, 66.
Rufinus, 154.
Rule of Faith, the, 275, 302, 307; attributed to Apostles, 271.

Sayings of Jesus, unwritten, 22, 66.
Scili, Acts of Martyrs of, 97.
Scribes, the, 311 ff.
Scripture, definition of, 10; authoritative interpretation of, 317; Protestants and the, 335; modern study of, 355 f.
Semler, 201.
Septuagint, 157.
Serapion and the Gospel according to Peter, 69, 144.
Services for worship, writings read in the, 136 f.
Seven churches of Asia, letters to, 57.
Shepherd of Hermas, 60.
Simon, Richard, 207.
Smyrneans, Epistles to, in Apocalypse, 57; of Ignatius, 54.
Sohm, on church government, 229.
Song of Solomon, 116.
Synagogue, influence upon organization of church, 221 ff.
Synods, Carthage, 160; Hippo, 160.
Synoptic Gospels, 62.
Syrian church and the Canon, 189.

Tatian, his life and work, 36, 83, 90; the Diatessaron, 71, 91 f.; use of in Syrian churches, 93.
Teachers in early church, 235, 237.
Teaching of the Twelve Apostles, 75 f.; authorities of the Christians in the, 76; (see Didachè).
Teaching, oral, 16.
Tertullian, life, 109 ff.; and the Apostles, 29; and the Roman Symbol, 295.
Theodoret, 116.
Theophilus of Antioch, 96 f.
Tradition, principle of, 281.
Trypho, Justin's dialogue with, 87.
Types, doctrinal in New Testament, 119.

Unwritten sayings of Jesus, 66.

Vulgate, 156, 157.

Words, of Jesus, as authority of Christians, 15, 21, 23, 32; and the Old Testament, 21; citations inaccurate, 23.

Zahn, concerning Tatian, 94; Muratori Canon, 111.
Zoroastrianism and the canonization, 13.
Zwingli, his Canon, 198.

www.ingramcontent.com/pod-product-compliance
Lightning Source LLC
Chambersburg PA
CBHW061422300426
44114CB00014B/1498